W9-AAK-284

Rhetoric and Civic Life

Second Custom Edition for Pennsylvania State University

Taken from:
Ancient Rhetorics for Contemporary Students, Fifth Edition
by Sharon Crowley and Debra Hawhee

Good Reasons: Researching and Writing Effective Arguments, Fifth Edition
by Lester Faigley and Jack Selzer

Compose, Design, Advocate: A Rhetoric for Integrating Written, Oral, and Visual Communication, Second Edition
by Anne Frances Wysocki and Dennis A. Lynch

ISBN 10: 1-269-95848-8
ISBN 13: 978-1-269-95848-6

RHETORIC AND CIVIC LIFE

CONTENTS

CHAPTER 1

How People Learn to Be Civic   1
Michael Schudson

Everyday Life   3
Structures of Attention   5
Shared Enterprise   7
Civic Infrastructure   8
NOTES TO MICHAEL SCHUDSON   11
CONTRIBUTORS   12

CHAPTER 2

The Flight From Conversation   13
Sherry Turkle

CHAPTER 3

Ancient Rhetorics: Their Differences and the Differences They Make   17

Ancient Rhetorics: The Beginnings   22
Comparing Ancient and Contemporary Rhetorics   23
   Extrinsic and Intrinsic Proofs   24
   That's Just Your Opinion   30
On Ideology and the Commonplaces   34
Language as Power; Language as Action   36
Practice, Practice, Practice   39
RHETORICAL ACTIVITIES   41
ENDNOTES   43
WORKS CITED   43

CHAPTER 4

Kairos *and the Rhetorical Situation: Seizing the Moment* 45

Ancient Depictions of *Kairos* 46

Kairos, Change, and Rhetorical Situations 48

    Kairos *as a Means of Invention* 51

    How Urgent or Immediate Is the Issue? 52

    Arguments and Interests 52

    Power Dynamics in a Rhetorical Situation 57

    A Web of Related Issues 59

RHETORICAL ACTIVITIES 59

WORKS CITED 60

CHAPTER 5

Analyzing Written Arguments 61

What is Rhetorical Analysis? 61

Build a Rhetorical Analysis 62

Analyze the Rhetorical Features 62

    Silko's Purpose and Argument 63

    Silko's Use of Logos, Pathos, and Ethos 64

    Silko's Arrangement 66

    Silko's Style 67

Analyze the Rhetorical Context 67

    Communication as Conversation 67

    Silko's Life and Works 68

    The Context of Publication 69

    The Larger Conversation 69

    Silko's Political Goals 70

Write a Rhetorical Analysis 71

Sample Student Rhetorical Analysis 77

CHAPTER 6

About Visual Modes of Communication 82

The Pleasures—and Complexities—of Visual Communication 83

Visible Purposes, Audiences, and Contexts 85

    Visible Purposes 85

Visible Audiences   86

Visible Contexts   87

A Statement of Purpose for a Photo Essay   89

Visible Ethos, Logos, and Pathos   90

Ethos in Photographs   91

What you Already know Because you Look—and a Professional Ethos   92

First, you Make Judgments about the Quality of Different Visual Texts all the Time   92

Second, the Qualities of "Polished and Professional" are Valued in our Day and Place.   93

Pathos in Photographs   95

Obvious Pathos   95

Less Obvious Pathos   95

Pathos and Color   96

Hue   96

Saturation   97

Brightness   97

Analyzing the Rhetorical Effects of Color   97

The Pathos of Type   100

How does Type Evoke Feeling and Emotions?   100

Describing Lettershapes   100

Styles of Type   101

Categories of Type   102

Typefaces for Extended Reading   103

Oldstyle   103

Modern   103

Slab Serif   103

Sans Serif   103

Six-of-One   104

Pictures & Symbols   104

Typefaces for at-a-glance emphasis   104

Novelty   104

Script   105

From Extended-Reading Faces   105

Black Letter   105

Grunge   105

Other   106

The Logos of Arranging Visual Elements   106

The Logos of Arranging Visual Elements How many Elements to Include   107

The Logos of Arranging Visual Elements Creating a Visual
Hierarchy   109

The Logos of Arranging Visual Elements Contrast and Repetition for
Visual Hierarchy   110

The Logos of Arranging Visual Elements Creating Visual Unity
through Repetition   111

   Repeating Alignment   112

The Logos of Type Arrangement   113

   *How the Different **Categories** of Type can Help you Choose Typefaces with
     Strong Contrast   114*

   *Using the **Size** of Typeface to Create Contrast   115*

   *Using the **Shape** of Typefaces to Create Contrast   115*

   *Using the **Position** of Type to Create Contrast   116*

   *Using the **Weights** of Typefaces to Create Contrast   116*

   *Using the **Color** of Typefaces to Create Contrast   117*

   A Note about Building Contrast with Typeface   117

The Logos of Using Words and Pictures Together   119

   Naming the Relationships   120

   Rules for Putting Words and Pictures Together?   120

Analyzing Visual Arguments   121

   Visual Analogies   121

   Visual Symbols   122

   Visual Accumulation   124

A Design Plan for a Photo Essay   126

A Photo Essay   129

Testing and Evaluating Visual Texts   131

   *A Self-test for Visual Texts you Produce—and the Fundamental Questions
     to ask of any Visual Text   131*

   *A **Brochure** Designed for a Nonprofit Organization   131*

   *A Short **Comic** on a Social Issue   132*

   *A **Documentary Photography** Book   132*

   *An Argumentative **Poster**   132*

   *A Short **Video** Public Service Announcement   133*

Designing Slides **to Support** Oral Presentations   134

Thinking Through Production   137

CHAPTER 7

Achieving Stasis by Asking the Right Questions   139

On Inventing: How to Proceed   140

The Importance of Achieving Stasis   141

Theoretical versus Practical Questions   143

The Four Questions   146
  A Simple Example   148

Expanding the Questions   149
  Questions of Quality: Simple or Complex   152
  Questions of Policy   154

Using the Stases   155

ENDNOTES   162

WORKS CITED   162

CHAPTER 8

Conversation and Discussion   163
  John Gastil

Historical Notes on Political Chatter   164

Imagining a Deliberative Conversation   166
  The Ideal Speech Situation   166
  Democratic Conversation   167
  Gricean Maxims   168

Informal Conversation   170
  Drawing on Media and Personal Experience   170
  Community Bonding Through Conversation   172
  Diversity in Conversation   172
  Disagreement and Persuasion   173

Moving from Conversation to Discussion   176
  Cyberchatting   177
  National Issues Forums   178

Dialogue and Deliberation   180
  The Public Conversations Project   181
  Narratives and Storytelling   182

Conclusion   184

ENDNOTES   185

CHAPTER 9

The "Nasty Effect:" Online Incivility and Risk Perceptions of Emerging Technologies 188

Ashley A. Anderson, Dominique Brossard, Dietram A. Scheufele, Michael A. Xenos, Peter Ladwig

Introduction 189

The Formation of Risk Perceptions 190

The Effects of Incivility 191

The Effects of Predispositions 192

Methods 194

Study Context 194

Participants 194

Experimental Design 194

Measurement 195

Analysis 196

Results 197

Discussion 199

Conclusion 201

NOTES 202

REFERENCES 202

ABOUT THE AUTHORS 205

Index 207

Michael Schudson

HOW PEOPLE
LEARN TO BE CIVIC

A SENSE OF citizenship is passed on from one generation to the next, not only in formal education or
through intentional efforts but indirectly or collater-
ally in the small details of everyday life. Lecturing in
London a few years ago, I illustrated this point with
a homely example. I said, "Take, for instance, those
moments in your own family where you assert your
parental authority and declare to your children, 'Eat
your vegetables.'

'No'.

'Eat your vegetables, please.'

'No.'

'Eat your vegetables or there will be no dessert.'

'No.'

'Eat your vegetables or else!'

And one of those little wise guys retorts, 'You
can't make me. It's a free country.'"

In the United States, audiences invariably
acknowledge this illustration with knowing chuck-
les or smiles. In London, I looked out at a roomful
of blank faces—not a soul cracked a smile. They had
politely puzzled expressions. Only then did it dawn
on me. Only then did I realize that no British child in
all of history has ever said, "You can't make me, it's a
free country." And suddenly I knew that democracy is

Reprinted from *United We Serve: National Service and the Future of Citinzenship* (2003), by permission of Brookings Institution.

not just one thing you have more or less of; it comes in an assortment of flavors. Democratic citizenship is not just something one is more or less socialized into; there are different citizenships in different democracies, and each of them is renewed in its own subtle fashion.

What I had taken as an invariant expression of children in any democratic society is, in fact, peculiarly American. It is America, not Britain, that conceives of itself self-importantly and extravagantly and naively and tragically and wonderfully as a "free country." America's children pick that up early on.

But how? How is it American kids learn to say that it's a free country and British kids learn not to? How do people acquire their sense of civic life and how does that sense become second nature? How do we learn the values we are supposed to learn as members of our national culture? I am not asking how to make people better citizens. Instead, I am asking how people learn to be the sort of citizen that society wants them to be. How do they come to know what good citizenship is?

I have no confidence that earnest efforts at teaching U.S. history or turning out the vote or getting more school children to pick up trash on the beach make us good citizens, admirable as these activities may be in their own right. Nor am I convinced that liberal education does the trick either, even though I believe in its values. Political theorist Richard Flathman writes that the greatest contribution liberal education can make to our common political life is to instill a "disposition . . . wary of politics and government."[1] That is not what you normally hear in circles of educators devoted to civics education. But I was reminded of it in the aftermath of September 11. One of the most noteworthy and, to my mind, admirable features of the American response in those first weeks was that many of our leaders, from the president on down, waved the flag proudly but at the same time cautioned citizens about the dangers of flag waving. The only precedent I know for this kind of chastened patriotism in other countries is contemporary Germany, where the Nazi past envelops even the most timid of patriotic demonstrations with a flood of second thoughts.[2] In the United States, I can think of no prior expression of this kind of proud but muted patriotism, a patriotism tempered by its own self-consciousness.

If citizenship is not learned primarily in school or in get-out-the-vote drives, and if college is as likely to induce skepticism about politics as it is fervent devotion to it, where do people learn their sense of civic obligation. This is a question that civic educators themselves need to think about more clearly, deeply, and historically. What I offer here is a briefly sketched framework for doing so.

A citizen is a person who has full membership in a political community, especially a nation-state. In its common legal usage, citizenship means nationality, and its mark would be a passport, a birth certificate, or other citizenship papers. In its political usage, citizenship refers to rights of political participation, and its chief sign is that a person is eligible to vote. In its sociocultural sense, citizenship refers to emotional identification with a nation and its flag, history, and culture. Finally, citizenship has a broad moral meaning, as in the phrase "good citizen." It may refer to a person loyal to the state, and in this sense it is related to patriotism. Even more, it suggests a person who is informed about and takes an active role in civic affairs. Although all of these meanings of "citizen" have some relevance to my inquiry here, the broad moral meaning of civicness is my primary concern.

"How do people become civic?" is in part the question, "How do we come to understand or accept or take for granted what counts as civic?" That is, how do people develop a particular sense of the public good, a willingness to participate in its advancement, and a view of what repertoire of acts will engender a better public life? How do we come to understand or accept or take for granted what counts as civic in our own culture? Four different areas need our attention.

First, we become civic if and when the civic penetrates into everyday life. Second we become civic by what we are called to attend to and what we are called to ignore. Third, we become civic by joining with others in common enterprise. Fourth, we become civic when a civic infrastructure allows, encourages, and supports individual civic engagement. I will say something about each of these points.

EVERYDAY LIFE

First, we become civic when civic activities become a part of everyday life. Think of the recycling bins that, in many communities today, the city or municipality provides so that each household can separate its own recyclables and get them recycled by putting them out at curbside when the city picks up the weekly trash.

Think of the Pledge of Allegiance that children say in school. More is learned in this act by ritual repetition than by the actual words. I would be skeptical that school children understand the Pledge of Allegiance. Take the word "indivisible," for instance. Children learn to pronounce it years before they study John C. Calhoun and the doctrine of nullification, or the Lincoln-Douglas debates, or the Civil War. But the presence of the term "indivisible" in the Pledge is incomprehensible without knowing it to be a reference to the Civil War. In the end, however, that is less the point than that the school day is connected in some vague but unifying way to flag and country.

Think about what kind of education happens in the widespread "red ribbon week" of drug education in our public schools. I remember when my daughter, then in first grade, came home from Drug-Free School Day and told us happily it was Free Drug Day at school. In a personal memoir, essayist Sarah Vowell recalls watching the Mickey Mouse Club on television and singing along with the theme song—but she never quite got the words of it. When the Mouseketeers sang, "forever let us hold our banner high," Sarah thought they were saying, "for every little polar bear to hide."[3] Much more of education is like that than we would ever want to admit. Still, the ritual of something like saying the Pledge, the activity of it, the collective enterprise of it, leaves a residue.

The activity that enters into ordinary life need not be everyday activity. We learn a great deal from ritual moments that come only on rare occasion—like Christmas once a year or voting every year or two. We do not really know how deeply these activities teach us until we imagine how they might be different. Think about what lessons eighteenth-century Virginians learned when they voted or nineteenth-century Americans, in contrast to us. An eighteenth-century Virginian, that is to say a white male who owned property, went to the polling place, spoke his vote out loud in front of the sheriff and in front of the candidates, and then went over to the candidate he had favored with his vote and shook hands. The whole activity was one of ritually reaffirming a hierarchical social order in which each person knew his place. The whole experience reinforced an understanding of citizenship as appropriate deference to community leaders. There was no campaigning, there were no issues, there were no bombastic speeches. The whole point was to invest responsibility for decision-making in trusted senior members of the community.[4]

The nineteenth century experience of voting taught different civic lessons. In the nineteenth century, political parties controlled the elections. On election day, the parties hired tens of thousands of workers to get out the vote and to stand near the polling place to hand out the "tickets" the parties had printed. The voter approached the polling place, took a ticket from one of these "ticket peddlers" from his own party, and went up to the voting station to deposit his ticket in the ballot box. He did not need to look at it. He did not need to mark it in any way. Clearly, he did not have to be literate. He could cast his ballot free of charge, but it would not have been surprising if he received payment for his effort. In New Jersey, as many as one-third of the electorate in the 1880s expected payment for voting on election day, usually in an amount between $1 and $3.[5]

What did a vote express? Not a strong conviction that the party offered better public policies; parties tended to be more devoted to distributing offices than to advocating policies. Party was related more to comradeship than to policy; it was more an attachment than a choice, something like a contemporary loyalty to a high school or college and its teams. Voting was not a matter of assent to ideas but a statement of affiliation with people, and the connection of voter to party ticket peddler underscored that. So did the postelection visit to the party's favorite local tavern. Drink, dollars, and drama brought people to the polls, and other than that social connection, voting was rarely anything more elevated.

Reformers at the end of the nineteenth century saw little in the parties to recommend them. The Mugwumps sought to make elections "educational," and the Progressives tried to insulate the independent, rational citizen from the distorting enthusiasms of party. It is to them that we owe the ideal of the informed citizen, not to the Founding Fathers. In the 1880s, political campaigns began to shift from parades to pamphlets, and so put a premium on literacy. In the 1890s, the Australian ballot swept the nation, and so for the first time in American history, literacy was required to cast a ballot. The novelty of the Australian ballot was that the state took responsibility for printing ballots that listed the candidates from all parties qualifying for the election. This meant that voters received their ballots from state election officials at the polling place, not from party workers en route to the polling place. It meant that the voter had to make a choice of candidates by marking the ballot; and it normally meant that provision was made for the voter to mark the ballot in secret. With this innovation, voting changed from a social and public duty to a private right, from a social obligation to party enforceable by social pressure to a civic obligation or abstract loyalty, enforceable only by private conscience.

In the early 1900s, nonpartisan municipal elections, presidential primaries, and the initiative and referendum imposed more challenging cognitive tasks on prospective voters than ever before. These changes enshrined "the informed citizenry," incidentally provided a new mechanism and a new rationale for dis-enfranchising African Americans and immigrants, and inaugurated an enduring tradition of hand-wringing over popular political ignorance.

Between 1880 and 1910, the most basic understandings of American politics were challenged. Reformers attacked the emotional enthusiasm of political par-ticipation, the corruption in campaign financing and campaign practices, and the role of the parties in usurping the direct connection between citizens and their government. They succeeded in inventing the language by which we still judge our politics: it stresses being informed while it dismisses or demeans parties and partisanship. To put this more pointedly, the political party, the single most important agency ever invented for mass political participation, is the institution that current civics talk and current civics education regularly abhor and that is rendered almost invisible in the way we conduct the actual act of voting. Insofar as the way we *do* vote is a set of enduring instructions to us about the way we *should* vote and the way we should think about voting, the civic lesson of elec-tion day as we have organized it for the past century recommends contempt for parties and partisanship.

We learn a standard of civic practice by practicing civics. We may not live up to it, but we know, at least implicitly and roughly speaking, what it is, what we are supposed to be held accountable for. We learn it in large part by experi-ence—as political theorist Stephen Elkin writes, "Experience . . . must be the teacher of democratic citizens," and this leads him to an interest in the design of local governments, not the design of school curricula.[6] What we do not know or reflect on is that our present standard is only one of a number of possible stand-ards. We learn it so well we do not even recognize what alternatives it excludes.

STRUCTURES OF ATTENTION

The second way we become civic is by what the public is called to attend to and what it is called to ignore. The media and, even more strenuously, political lead-ers, make the decisions about what will be on the public's agenda. In the weeks after September 11, there were many stories in the media about stifling of dissent as the country unified behind the president's war on terrorism. Why were we called to attend to this? How did we know, as we read these stories, that stifling dissent is a bad thing? We assuredly were expected to get that point.

Consider an important recent example of citizenship talk: "What you do is as important as anything government does. I ask you to seek a common good beyond your comfort, to defend needed reforms against easy attacks, to serve your nation, beginning with your neighbor. I ask you to be citizens. Citizens, not spectators. Citizens, not subjects. Responsible citizens, building communities of service and a nation of character."[7]

At first blush, it is hard to object to the concept of citizenship George W. Bush expressed in these words in his inaugural address. Citizenship, he said, is public spirited rather than self-centered, neighborly rather than self-seeking, active and participatory rather than passive and spectator-like. And yet, President Bush advanced a subtext here: do not expect too much from your government. "Americans are generous and strong and decent, not because we believe in ourselves but because we hold beliefs beyond ourselves. When this spirit of citizenship is missing, no government program can replace it. When this spirit is present, no wrong can stand against it." Government should not overreach, government should not overlegislate, government should not overreact. The president favors people who take care of themselves and their neighbors, not those who depend on government for aid and comfort.

Note a second subtext: people are citizens insofar as they do not seek their own comfort, insofar as they serve the nation, and insofar as they hold beliefs beyond themselves. True citizens do not ask, to paraphrase a president from a different party, what the country can do for them, but what they can do for the country. There is no place in this vision of citizenship for individuals to sue for their rights or to invoke the law on behalf of their liberties or to initiate actions for damages against tobacco companies or tire manufacturers. There is no acknowledgment that democracy has been enlarged in our lifetimes when individuals have been driven not by a desire to serve but by an effort to overcome indignities they themselves have suffered. This is important. The most important extension of citizenship in this century was produced by the civil rights movement. Not Thomas Jefferson so much as people like Thurgood Marshall and Martin Luther King Jr. made rights a household term and a household experience. The civil rights movement brought on the extraordinary wave of social movements and rights-centered litigation that has opened doors and windows for African Americans, women, gays and lesbians, people with disabilities, and many others. Why, then, do we cling rhetorically to a vision of civic education and citizenship that excludes the raw power of self-interested action? Why is citizenship reduced to service rather than linked to justice?

There is also an entirely missing text in President Bush's inaugural address: in the idealized world he beckoned his fellow citizens to join, there are citizens, there are neighbors, there are also communities of faith, but there are no parties, and in the good citizen, no partisanship; there are no interest groups, and in the good citizen, no joining with others in organized self-interest; there are no experts, and in the good citizen, no considered judgment about when and how judgment should be delegated. Why are the organizations and individual actors that in fact are the most involved on a day-to-day basis with the operation of government omitted from his account of citizenship?

In times of national crisis, the citizen President Bush envisions is the soldier, who serves country, ignores personal discomfort, and believes in a patriotic ideal. In ordinary times, Bush's ideal is the Rotarian, moved by a sense of neighborliness, Christian charity, and social responsibility but untouched by any sense of having a personal stake in public justice.

Is this the kind of civicness we should be instilling in our children? I don't think so, but that is not my topic here. I am addressing only the question of how people learn to be civic. My point about the president's speech is that it offers one model of civicness, not the only model. It is a powerful model, nonetheless, because the president is the country's best-placed civic pedagogue. As Justice Felix Frankfurter said, "The Presidency is the most important educational system in the country."[8] The president calls us to attention, but in a particular way, not in the only way.

SHARED ENTERPRISE

The third way we become civic is by joining with others in common enterprise, common work, common prayer, or common struggle. I will speak about this only briefly because, in this instance, the same President George W. Bush, whom I have just criticized, has offered a very shrewd analysis. In his press conference a month after September 11, he observed that his administration before September 11 was planning an initiative to be called "Communities of Character." It was, he said, "designed to help parents develop good character in our children and to strengthen the spirit of citizenship and service in our communities." But, he remarked, "the acts of September 11 have prompted that initiative to occur on its own, in ways far greater than I could have ever imagined."[9] He was right. He cited the cases of Christian and Jewish women who went shopping with Muslim neighbors when the Muslim women were afraid to leave their homes alone. There was, indeed, a rekindling of communal feelings, a reaching out to friends, neighbors, and strangers, and a joining in common enterprises of blood drives, fund raising, prayer services, and community memorials all across the country.

People can feel connections with one another and a sense of public purpose at one remove, through the Internet or through a novel, a film, or a news story. I do not know anyone who died at the World Trade Centers, but like almost all Americans, I felt intimately linked to what happened there. That lasted beyond the moment not because citizens feel an intimate acquaintance with Peter Jennings, Tom Brokaw, and Dan Rather (although they may) but because the information and images the media conveyed in this case touched everyone who has ever visited New York or knows someone there, everyone who has ever traveled by air or who has loved ones who travel by air, everyone who has ever been in a high-rise office building. And the horror and anxiety the news evoked in those millions of people were reaffirmed and reinforced in almost every conversation and in almost every glance from person to person, family member to family member, and coworker to coworker in subsequent weeks and months. The experience of September 11 was a national Durkheimian moment, that is, a collective experience where a sense of both power and meaning beyond the personal emerged from face-to-face contact and collective work—collective action embodied, not at a distance.

There is a great deal of attention to that generation, now rapidly aging and dying, that fought World War II, and it has been lionized in the title of Tom

Brokaw's book, as "the greatest generation." Brokaw is not modest about his claims for his parents' generation: "I think this is the greatest generation any society has ever produced."[10] I am not going to quibble over rankings here; surely this generation accomplished a great deal. And, as Robert Putnam has assiduously documented, this same generation continued to be doggedly civic by voting in large numbers, attending community meetings, getting to know neighbors, maintaining church membership and attendance, exceeding the marks of the generation before them and the generations that followed them.[11] All of this I acknowledge. What I do not accept is the implication that this generation was unusually endowed with moral virtue or community fervor. What it was endowed with was the Great Depression and World War II, great collective experiences that forged a generational spirit.

This is not to suggest that the experience of World War II was a spontaneous emotional upheaval undirected by government leadership and institutional transformation. On the contrary, the Roosevelt administration mobilized the power of the state in the national defense to—literally—enlist the nation in the war effort. If September 11 seems to be a fading memory already for many Americans, it may be because the federal government chose in the end not to take advantage of the emotional effervescence of the moment to call on Americans for sacrifice or service. An opportunity was lost to enlarge national service programs like AmeriCorps—or even to call attention to them.

CIVIC INFRASTRUCTURE

Fourth, we cannot become civic if there is no infrastructure of civicness for people to enroll in. Civic life requires maintenance: it requires staff, investment, access. Democracy does not come cheap. Elections cost money, effective service programs cost money, and courts cost money. Justice requires dollars.[12] This is not very dramatic stuff. In fact, it is invisible to most of us most of the time. I saw some of it, however, in the 2000 election, as I watched the mounting of the electoral machinery in my home of San Diego, California. Let me just give you a little sense of it.

On November 7, in one sixteen-hour period, 100 million people broke from their daily routine and voted. It is a mammoth exercise. In California, there were about 100,000 volunteers spending fifteen-hour days manning the polling places. In San Diego County, running the election cost $3.5 million in taxpayer dollars to produce 552 separate ballots and 552 separate voter information guides mailed out to registered voters to prepare them to act as informed citizens. There were 100 training sessions for 6,000 poll workers at 1,500 polling places, 300 of which had special provision for Spanish-speaking voters and all of which were designed to be accessible for the disabled. This is a massive activity, and a great deal of meaning is still to be found in it, what Walt Whitman called this "ballot-shower from East to West, America's choosing day."

There are 552 different ballots because there are 120 political jurisdictions in San Diego County—hospital districts, water districts, community college districts, school districts, congressional districts, assembly and state senate districts, and so on. There were some 800 candidates on the ballot in November. Mikel Haas, then the registrar of voters, told me, "It's like a watch: there are a whole lot of moving parts. Any one of them can trip you up." The registrar's core staff of forty-eight employees was supplemented in the election season by about 300 temporary workers, not to mention the 6,000 poll workers on election day.

Several weeks before the election, I attended what the registrar's office had entitled "Midnight Madness." On the last day to register to vote in San Diego County, the registrar's office stays open till midnight for "drive-through" registration. I came by around 8 p.m. to take a look. In the dark and the drizzle, cars were lined up for most of a long block and then in a single-file line through half the length of the county building. The whole area, though, was lit by a set of four floodlights, illuminating not only the building and the proceedings outside it but also a newly anchored "Uncle Sam" roughly forty feet high—a vast, cheery, red-white-and-blue inflated Uncle Sam. Registrar of Voters Haas had seen it displayed at a Chevrolet dealer. He had driven by and thought, "I have to have that," and he worked out a rental deal to use the inflatable for Midnight Madness.

There must have been between fifteen and twenty registrar personnel in yellow slickers at Midnight Madness. A number of them were directing traffic. In three lines, three people handed registration affidavits on clipboards to the driver-voters in their cars, SUVs, and pick-ups. The drivers were then directed to park while they filled out the form. When completed, they started up their cars again and another yellow-slickered official would come over to the car, take the affidavit, check it to see that it was filled out properly, and then send the new registrant on his or her way.

One senior civil servant I spoke to began her career with court reporting school, then worked in the district attorney's office, then took the test for the position of registrar of voters senior clerk and assumed the job in 1977 at age 26. In 1980 she left and went to work with one of the vendors who mail the sample ballots. "But I missed it . . . I missed the excitement." "Not many people leave here. No one will quit." It is not just this office—from email with her counterparts in other counties, "it sounds the same way." There is a lot of stress in the job, but people love it. She is married to a political consultant who is as interested in politics as she is. "When our child was born," she told me, "our birth announcement said 'height' and 'weight' and 'eligible to vote in 2007.'"

Despite the high morale of workers at the registrar's office, not everyone loves every part of it. One of the least popular sections is candidate services, dealing with candidates and would-be candidates as they learn how to file their papers, as they write up their statements for the voter information guides that in California are sent out to all registered voters, as they submit required campaign finance disclosure forms. "The candidates . . ." my informant began, and then rolled her eyes. She talked about the people who walk in and say, "Here's where I live. What can I run for?" "Who *are* these people?" she asked. When someone wants to file who has no chance at all, who has never even turned up at a meeting of the body they are running for, the personnel in candidate services try to act on behalf of democracy without entering improperly into the process: "We try to politely, well, not talk them out of it, but explain what's involved."

I attended some training sessions for the poll workers, as well as the training session for the trainers. Registrar staff plus a motivational speaker ran this session. There was a strong emphasis on getting people to participate and have a good time in the training. As one of the trainers said, "Adult learning really can be fun, it doesn't have to be toothpicks-in-the-eyelid time."

The training sessions for the poll workers were centered on a "railroad" theme, and the trainers were equipped with train engineers' hats, red bandannas, a loud train whistle, and a small flashing light that mimicked the lights at a railroad crossing. The trainers I observed—two vigorous women in their sixties—blew their train whistles together to start the session, and then they sang a song they themselves had written: "We've been working on the election all the live long day. We've been working on the election, so the voters have their say." Trained to get people talking and involved from the beginning, they asked people to talk among themselves about why they were volunteering their time. After a few minutes, they blew the train whistles again and asked people to tell the whole group what they had found out. Some people talked about the free tacos poll workers would get from a local fast food chain; many others spoke of wanting to do their civic duty. Many volunteered election after election and spoke of it as a kind of addiction—"Once you do it, you're hooked."

Multiply these stories of one registrar's office in one county of one state by the seventy California counties; multiply it again by the fifty states. Multiply it by the journalists who write about politics, the teachers who teach history and civics, the preschool teachers and kindergarten teachers who instruct children about sharing, the counselors, clergy, clerks of court, and others who are all civics teachers on a full-time basis, and you can see that the possibility of civicness for individuals may have less to do with individual virtue than with social investment and collective maintenance.

Civicness requires both volunteers and professionals, both ordinary citizens and experts. The kind of populism one finds in universities that is distrustful of expertise, to the point of self-hatred; that prefers participatory democracy over representation or delegation, to the point of having nothing at all to say about the latter; and that prefers John Dewey to Walter Lippmann or, more generally, romantics to realists, to a degree that refuses engagement with the actual messiness of democratic politics, lies somewhere between dreaminess and irresponsibility.

In thinking through the matter of civic education, I look more to structures, contexts, and institutions within which and through which education happens than to specific psychological processes that succeed or fail to attach individuals to the messages about civic engagement they hear. There are multiple meanings of citizenship afloat in the land, and practices of civic life have changed more rapidly and more radically than our public rhetoric has yet figured out. Many people still learn to participate in politics through community-based, faith-based experience, as was so often the case with the civil rights movement, but many others today come to politics (as is often the case in the environmentalist movement) through what sociologist Paul Lichterman calls "personalist" motivation.[13] Some opportunities for civic engagement fade—like political party rallies—but others arise without social analysts even noticing: if there is a study of the proliferation of charity runs and charity walks, I have not yet seen it. Or consider the enormous changes in women's lives and the movement toward gender equality in the past fifty years, and how the feminization of political and civic life, if you will, has altered civic practices—and should have altered what counts as citizenship and civic engagement. Along with the civil rights movement and the many other rights-oriented struggles that borrowed from it, feminism has extended norms of equality and indignation over injustice into the home, the club, the workplace, and other domains once far removed from political consciousness.

Citizens learn citizenship in everyday life and especially in participating in common civic exercises; in structures of attention shaped by political leaders, the media, the schools, and other voices of authority; in experiences of community solidarity that forge attachments to people beyond us (it is a familiar observation that soldiers fight not so much for their flag as for their comrades); and in structures and institutions that are cultivated and cared for by full-time staff whose work is required to make citizenship possible. Meanwhile, the realm of the civic shifts and expands as the legitimate demands of once-excluded groups enter into play and reshape the basic understandings of civic life.

NOTES TO MICHAEL SCHUDSON

1. Richard Flathman, "Liberal versus Civic, Republican, Democratic, and Other Vocational Educations," *Political Theory*, vol. 24 (February 1996) pp. 4–32 at 26.
2. See, for instance, Frederick Kempe, *Father/Land: A Personal Search for the New Germany* (Putnam, 1999) p. 148.
3. Sarah Vowell, *Take the Cannoli: Stories from the New World* (Simon and Schuster, 2000).
4. On this point and the subsequent paragraphs on American political history, I draw directly on my book *The Good Citizen: A History of American Civic Life* (New York: Free Press, 1998).
5. John F. Reynolds, *Testing Democracy: Electoral Behavior and Progressive Reform in New Jersey, 1880–1910* (University of North Carolina Press, 1988) p. 54. See also Schudson, *The Good Citizen*, pp. 144–187.
6. Stephen Elkin, "Citizen Competence and the Design of Democratic Institutions" in Stephen L. Elkin and Karol Edward Soltan, eds., *Citizen Competence and Democratic Institutions* (Pennsylvania State University Press, 1999) p. 394.
7. George W. Bush, inaugural address, January 2001 (www.whitehouse.gov/news/inaugural-address.html [January 2003]).
8. Cited in Douglas Cater, *The Fourth Branch of Government* (Boston: Houghton Mifflin, 1959) p. 169.
9. George W. Bush, prime time news conference, October 11, 2002 (www. whitehouse.gov/news/releases/2001/10/20011011-7.html#Sacrifices-by-Americans [January 2003]).
10. Tom Brokaw, *The Greatest Generation* (Random House, 1998) p. xxx.

11. Robert D. Putnam, *Bowling Alone* (Simon and Schuster, 2000).
12. See Stephen Holmes and Cass Sunstein, *The Cost of Rights: Why Liberty Depends on Taxes* (W. W. Norton, 1999).
13. Paul Lichterman, *The Search for Political Community* (Cambridge University Press, 1996).

CONTRIBUTORS

Daniel S. Blumenthal is professor and chair of the Department of Community Health and Preventive Medicine, as well as associate dean for community programs at Morehouse School of Medicine. Blumenthal has served with the Medical Committee for Human Rights, the Centers for Disease Control and Prevention in Atlanta, and the World Health Organization. He has been associated with the Emory University School of Medicine, and in 1969 he served as a VISTA (Volunteers in Service to America) volunteer in Lee County, Arkansas.

Harry C. Boyte is both senior fellow and codirector of the Center for Democracy and Citizenship in the Humphrey Institute at the University of Minnesota. Boyte was national coordinator for the New Citizenship, a bipartisan effort to bridge the citizen-government gap. He served as senior adviser to the National Commission for Civic Renewal, headed by former senator Sam Nunn and former education secretary William Bennett. In the 1960s, Boyte worked for Martin Luther King Jr. and the Southern Christian Leadership Conference. He has written seven books on community organizing, citizen action, and citizenship.

Sherry Turkle
Published:
April 21, 2012

THE FLIGHT FROM CONVERSATION

AT HOME, FAMILIES sit together, texting and reading e-mail. At work executives text during board meetings. We text (and shop and go on Facebook) during classes and when we're on dates. My students tell me about an important new skill: it involves maintaining eye contact with someone while you text someone else; it's hard, but it can be done.

Over the past 15 years, I've studied technologies of mobile connection and talked to hundreds of people of all ages and circumstances about their plugged-in lives. I've learned that the little devices most of us carry around are so powerful that they change not only what we do, but also who we are.

We've become accustomed to a new way of being "alone together." Technology-enabled, we are able to be with one another, and also elsewhere, connected to wherever we want to be. We want to customize our lives. We want to move in and out of where we are because the thing we value most is control over where we focus our attention. We have gotten used to the idea of being in a tribe of one, loyal to our own party.

Our colleagues want to go to that board meeting but pay attention only to what interests them. To some this seems like a good idea, but we can end up hiding from one another, even as we are constantly connected to one another.

A businessman laments that he no longer has colleagues at work. He doesn't stop by to talk; he doesn't call. He says that he doesn't want to interrupt them. He says they're "too busy on their e-mail." But then he pauses and corrects himself. "I'm not telling the truth. I'm the one who doesn't want to be interrupted. I think I should. But I'd rather just do things on my BlackBerry."

A 16-year-old boy who relies on texting for almost everything says almost wistfully, "Someday, someday, but certainly not now, I'd like to learn how to have a conversation."

In today's workplace, young people who have grown up fearing conversation show up on the job wearing earphones. Walking through a college library or the campus of a high-tech start-up, one sees the same thing: we are together, but each of us is in our own bubble, furiously connected to keyboards and tiny touch screens. A senior partner at a Boston law firm describes a scene in his office. Young associates lay out their suite of technologies: laptops, iPods and multiple phones. And then they put their earphones on. "Big ones. Like pilots. They turn their desks into cockpits." With the young lawyers in their cockpits, the office is quiet, a quiet that does not ask to be broken.

In the silence of connection, people are comforted by being in touch with a lot of people—carefully kept at bay. We can't get enough of one another if we can use technology to keep one another at distances we can control: not too close, not too far, just right. I think of it as a Goldilocks effect.

Texting and e-mail and posting let us present the self we want to be. This means we can edit. And if we wish to, we can delete. Or retouch: the voice, the flesh, the face, the body. Not too much, not too little—just right.

Human relationships are rich; they're messy and demanding. We have learned the habit of cleaning them up with technology. And the move from conversation to connection is part of this. But it's a process in which we short-change ourselves. Worse, it seems that over time we stop caring, we forget that there is a difference.

We are tempted to think that our little "sips" of online connection add up to a big gulp of real conversation. But they don't. E-mail, Twitter, Facebook, all of these have their places—in politics, commerce, romance and friendship. But no matter how valuable, they do not substitute for conversation.

Connecting in sips may work for gathering discrete bits of information or for saying, "I am thinking about you." Or even for saying, "I love you." But connecting in sips doesn't work as well when it comes to understanding and knowing one another. In conversation we tend to one another. (The word itself is kinetic; it's derived from words that mean to move, together.) We can attend to tone and nuance. In conversation, we are called upon to see things from another's point of view.

FACE-TO-FACE conversation unfolds slowly. It teaches patience. When we communicate on our digital devices, we learn different habits. As we ramp up the volume and velocity of online connections, we start to expect faster answers. To get these, we ask one another simpler questions; we dumb down our communications, even on the most important matters. It is as though we have all put ourselves on cable news. Shakespeare might have said, "We are consum'd with that which we were nourish'd by."

And we use conversation with others to learn to converse with ourselves. So our flight from conversation can mean diminished chances to learn skills of self-reflection. These days, social media continually asks us what's "on our mind," but we have little motivation to say something truly self-reflective. Self-reflection in conversation requires trust. It's hard to do anything with 3,000 Facebook friends except connect.

As we get used to being shortchanged on conversation and to getting by with less, we seem almost willing to dispense with people altogether. Serious people muse about the future of computer programs as psychiatrists. A high school sophomore confides to me that he wishes he could talk to an artificial intelligence program instead of his dad about dating; he says the A.I. would have so much more in its database. Indeed, many people tell me they hope that as Siri, the digital assistant on Apple's iPhone, becomes more advanced, "she" will be more and more like a best friend—one who will listen when others won't.

During the years I have spent researching people and their relationships with technology, I have often heard the sentiment "No one is listening to me." I believe this feeling helps explain why it is so appealing to have a Facebook page or a Twitter feed—each provides so many automatic listeners. And it helps explain why—against all reason—so many of us are willing to talk to machines that seem to care about us. Researchers around the world are busy inventing sociable robots, designed to be companions to the elderly, to children, to all of us.

One of the most haunting experiences during my research came when I brought one of these robots, designed in the shape of a baby seal, to an elder-care facility, and an older woman began to talk to it about the loss of her child. The robot seemed to be looking into her eyes. It seemed to be following the conversation. The woman was comforted.

And so many people found this amazing. Like the sophomore who wants advice about dating from artificial intelligence and those who look forward to computer psychiatry, this enthusiasm speaks to how much we have confused conversation with connection and collectively seem to have embraced a new kind of delusion that accepts the simulation of compassion as sufficient unto the day. And why would we want to talk about love and loss with a machine that has no experience of the arc of human life? Have we so lost confidence that we will be there for one another?

WE expect more from technology and less from one another and seem increasingly drawn to technologies that provide the illusion of companionship without the demands of relationship. Always-on/always-on-you devices provide three powerful fantasies: that we will always be heard; that we can put our attention wherever we want it to be; and that we never have to be alone. Indeed our new devices have turned being alone into a problem that can be solved.

When people are alone, even for a few moments, they fidget and reach for a device. Here connection works like a symptom, not a cure, and our constant, reflexive impulse to connect shapes a new way of being.

Think of it as "I share, therefore I am." We use technology to define ourselves by sharing our thoughts and feelings as we're having them. We used to think, "I have a feeling; I want to make a call." Now our impulse is, "I want to have a feeling; I need to send a text."

So, in order to feel more, and to feel more like ourselves, we connect. But in our rush to connect, we flee from solitude, our ability to be separate and gather ourselves. Lacking the capacity for solitude, we turn to other people but don't experience them as they are. It is as though we use them, need them as spare parts to support our increasingly fragile selves.

We think constant connection will make us feel less lonely. The opposite is true. If we are unable to be alone, we are far more likely to be lonely. If we don't teach our children to be alone, they will know only how to be lonely.

I am a partisan for conversation. To make room for it, I see some first, deliberate steps. At home, we can create sacred spaces: the kitchen, the dining room. We can make our cars "device-free zones." We can demonstrate the value of conversation to our children. And we can do the same thing at work. There we are so busy communicating that we often don't have time to talk to one another about what really matters. Employees asked for casual Fridays; perhaps managers should introduce conversational Thursdays. Most of all, we need to remember—in between texts and e-mails and Facebook posts—to listen to one another, even to the boring bits, because it is often in unedited moments, moments in which we hesitate and stutter and go silent, that we reveal ourselves to one another.

I spend the summers at a cottage on Cape Cod, and for decades I walked the same dunes that Thoreau once walked. Not too long ago, people walked with their heads up, looking at the water, the sky, the sand and at one another, talking. Now they often walk with their heads down, typing. Even when they are with friends, partners, children, everyone is on their own devices.

So I say, look up, look at one another, and let's start the conversation.

Sherry Turkle is a psychologist and <u>professor at M.I.T.</u> and the author, most recently, of "Alone Together: Why We Expect More From Technology and Less From Each Other."

For us moderns, rhetoric means artificiality, insincerity, decadence.

—H. I. Marrou

ANCIENT RHETORICS: THEIR DIFFERENCES AND THE DIFFERENCES THEY MAKE

WHEN AMERICANS HEAR the word **rhetoric,** they tend to think of politicians' attempts to deceive them. Rhetoric is characterized as "empty words" or as fancy language used to distort the truth or to tell lies. Television newspeople often say something like, "There was more rhetoric from the White House today," and editorialists write that politicians need to "stop using rhetoric and do something" as though words had no connection to action. Many people blame rhetoric for our apparent inability to communicate and to get things done.

But that isn't the way **rhetoricians** defined their art in ancient Athens and Rome. In ancient times, people used rhetoric to make decisions, resolve disputes, and deliberate publicly about important issues. Aristotle, an ancient philosopher and teacher of rhetoric, defined rhetoric as the power of finding the available arguments suited to a given situation. For teachers like Aristotle or practitioners like the Roman orator Cicero, rhetoric helped people to choose the best course of action when they disagreed about important political, religious, or social issues. In fact, the study of rhetoric was equivalent to the study of citizenship. Under the best ancient teachers, Greek and Roman students composed discourse about moral and political questions that daily confronted their communities.

Ancient teachers of rhetoric thought that disagreement among human beings was inevitable because individuals perceive the world differently from one another. They also assumed that because people communicate their perceptions through language—which is an entirely different medium than thoughts or perceptions—there was no guarantee that anyone's perceptions would be accurately conveyed to others. Even more important, the ancient teachers knew that people differ in their opinions about how the world works, so it was often hard to tell whose opinion was the best. They invented rhetoric so that they would have means to judge whose opinion was most accurate, useful, or valuable.

If people didn't disagree, rhetoric wouldn't be necessary. But they do, and it is. Two rhetoricians named Chaim Perelman and Lucia Olbrechts-Tyteca remarked that "The use of argumentation implies that one has renounced resorting to force alone" (55). So the fact that rhetoric originates in disagreement is ultimately a good thing because its use allows people to make important choices without resorting to less palatable means of persuasion—coercion or violence. People who have talked their way out of any potentially violent confrontation know how useful rhetoric can be.

On a larger scale, the usefulness of rhetoric is even more apparent. If, for some reason, the people who negotiate international relations were to stop using rhetoric to resolve their disagreements about limits on the use of nuclear weapons, there might not be a future to deliberate about. That's why we should be glad when we read or hear that diplomats are disagreeing about the allowable number of warheads per country or the number of inspections of nuclear stockpiles per year. At least they're talking to each other. As Perelman and Olbrechts-Tyteca observed, wars are the result of a choice to use force instead of rhetoric, an agreement to disagree. But before people of good will agree to disagree, they try out hundreds of ways of reaching agreement. The possibility that one set of participants will resort to coercion or violence is always a threat, of course. But even in the context of impending war, the threat of war can itself operate as a rhetorical strategy that keeps people of good will talking to each other.

Given that argument can deter violence and coercion, the authors of this book are disturbed by the contemporary tendency to see disagreement as somehow impolite or even undesirable. We certainly understand how disagreement has earned its bad name, given the caricature of argument that daily appears on talk television. Thanks to talk shows, argument has become a form of entertainment rather than a means of working through differences or discovering new resolutions. We are apparently not the only ones who feel this way. In October of 2004—three weeks before the 2004 presidential election—Jon Stewart, the host of Comedy Central's *The Daily Show with Jon Stewart*, appeared live on CNN's political show *Crossfire* to register his disappointment with the state of argument in America. In what has now become a famous plea (thanks to viral video on the Internet), Stewart asked then-*Crossfire* hosts Paul Begala and Tucker Carlson to "Stop, stop, stop, stop hurting America." How, exactly, does Stewart think that *Crossfire* is hurting America? The Cable News Network requested an exorbitant sum for us to reprint part of the transcript here, so we urge you to watch the segment on YouTube to see exactly what Stewart, Begala, and Carlson said. In the segment, Stewart disapproves of the hosts' use of the term "debate show" to describe *Crossfire*. In what would become a very heated exchange, Stewart has this to say: "To do a debate would be great. But that's like saying pro wrestling is a show about athletic competition."

Stewart's **analogy,** in which professional wrestling is to athletic competition as *Crossfire* is to debate, is worth dwelling on in part because the move from engaged performance of sports or debate to the sheer entertainment and antics of World Wrestling Entertainment (formerly the World Wrestling Federation) is a move from "real" to "mere." In other words, what could become earnest rhetorical engagement becomes instead a staged spat, "mere" theater. *Theater,* in fact, is the word that Stewart settles on to describe *Crossfire* later in his appearance.

That a current WWE show called *Smackdown* has a title that could well be mistaken for a cable "debate" show helps underscore Stewart's point: like WWE, shows like *Crossfire* seem to exist to dramatize conflict solely for entertainment purposes. In doing so, the so-called debate shows effectively distance argument further from the American public, placing it on the brightly lit set of a television show, making it seem as if "argument" has distinct winners and losers and playing up the embarrassment of "losing." It is interesting to note that after Stewart's appearance on *Crossfire,* CNN canceled the show altogether, but they did not replace it with what Stewart—or we—would consider a debate show.

We wholeheartedly agree with Stewart's criticism. Shows like *Crossfire* perpetuate rhetoric's bad name because the hosts and guests don't actually argue; rather, they shout **commonplaces** at one another. Neither listens to each other or to the guest, who is rarely allowed to speak, and then only intermittently. If you watched the video of the *Crossfire* exchange, you probably noticed how difficult it was for Stewart to maintain a point with the hosts' frequent interruptions. Shouting over one another is an extremely unproductive model of argument because doing so rarely involves listening or responding and seldom stimulates anyone to change his or her mind.

Engaging in productive argument is much different from shouting tired slogans. For one thing, rhetorical engagement is hard intellectual work, and for another, it requires that all parties to an argument listen to positions stated by others. Despite its difficulty, people who live in democracies must undertake productive argument with one another because failure to do so can have serious consequences ranging from inaction on important issues such as global warming, to taking serious actions, such as going to war. Consider this *Fox News* account of an incident that took place during a presidential address to Congress:

CONGRESSMAN YELLS "YOU LIE" AT OBAMA DURING SPEECH

WASHINGTON—In an extraordinary breach of congressional decorum, a Republican lawmaker shouted "You lie" at President Barack Obama during his speech to Congress Wednesday.

    The incident came directly after Obama said, "There are also those who claim that our reform effort will insure illegal immigrants. This, too, is false. The reforms I'm proposing would not apply to those who are here illegally."

"You lie!" Rep. Joe Wilson, R-S.C., shouted from his seat on the Republican side of the chamber.

Wilson's shout drew immediate condemnation from both sides of the aisle, ultimately leading him to apologize. Wilson tried to call Obama to apologize in person, but ended up speaking to White House chief of staff Rahm Emanuel. The contrite congressman "expressed his apologies" to Emanuel, not to the president at whom he had shouted a few hours earlier, Wilson's office said. (FoxNews.com)

Rather than taking the time to listen to the president's argument, Congressman Wilson shouted down a point he disagreed with. In doing so, he took the easier, showier route. But something interesting occurred in the responses to Wilson both in the moment and afterwards in news reports of the incident. Many of the accounts followed the pattern in the news story excerpted here, pointing out the "breach of decorum" and noting that the outburst drew "immediate condemnation from both sides of the aisle." The incident was therefore framed as a rude gesture that violated the unspoken rules of behavior in the halls of Congress. In other words, Congressman Wilson was roundly criticized for exhibiting bad manners rather than for his unwillingness to engage productively with the president's speech—first of all, by listening to it.

In this case, the congressional code of conduct exists to curb behavior such as that displayed by Representative Wilson. But he might not have shouted out of turn at all had not Americans begun to lose sight of the importance of rhetorical engagement in recent years. Joe Wilson was portrayed by the media as a boor because he failed to engage the president's speech rhetorically—first by listening, and then by responding thoughtfully at the appropriate moment in the appropriate setting. Like Jon Stewart, we prefer listening, considering, and responding to shouting, ignoring, or insulting.

The authors of this book are concerned that if Americans continue to ignore the reality that people disagree with one another all the time, or if we pretend to ignore it in the interests of preserving good manners, we risk undermining the principles on which our democratic community is based. People who are afraid of airing their differences tend to keep silent when those with whom they disagree are speaking, or worse, they shout down the speaker without listening. People who are not inclined to air differences tend to associate only with those who agree with them. In such a balkanized public sphere, both our commonalities and our differences go unexamined. In a democracy, people must call into question the opinions of others, must bring them into the light for examination and negotiation, and they must listen to each other. In communities where citizens are not coerced, important decisions must be made by means of public deliberation. When the quality of public deliberation diminishes, so does the quality of democracy.

Ancient teachers called the process of examining positions held by others "**invention**," which Aristotle defined as finding and displaying the available **arguments** on any **issue.** Invention is central to the rhetorical process. What often passes for rhetoric in our own time—repeatedly shouting one's beliefs to browbeat an "opponent" into submission—is not rhetoric. From a rhetorician's point of view, shouts and screams forestall invention. Participation in rhetoric entails that every party to the discussion be aware that beliefs may change during the exchange and discussion of points of view. All parties to a rhetorical transaction must be willing to be persuaded by good arguments. Otherwise, decisions will be made for bad reasons, or for **interested** reasons, or no reason at all.

Sometimes, of course, there are good reasons for remaining silent. Power is distributed unequally in our culture, and power inequities may force wise people to remain silent on some occasions. We believe that in contemporary American culture, people who enjoy high socioeconomic status have more power than those who have fewer resources and less access to others in power. We also hold that men have more power than women and that white people have more power than people of color (and yes, we are aware that there are exceptions to all these generalizations). We do not believe, though, that these inequities are a natural or necessary state of things. We do believe that rhetoric is among the best ways available to us for rectifying power inequities among citizens.

The people who taught and practiced rhetoric in Athens and Rome during ancient times would have found the contemporary unwillingness to engage in public disagreement very strange indeed. Their way of using disagreement to reach solutions was taught to students in Western schools for over two thousand years and is still available to us in translations of their textbooks, speeches, lecture notes, and treatises on rhetoric.

Within limits, the ancients' way of looking at disagreement can still be useful to us. The students who worked with ancient teachers of rhetoric were members of privileged classes for the most part because Athens and Rome both maintained socioeconomic systems that were manifestly unjust to many of the people who lived and worked within them. The same charge can be leveled at our own system, of course. Today the United States is home not only to its native peoples but also to people from all over the world. Its nonnative citizens arrived here under vastly different circumstances, ranging from colonization to immigration to enslavement, and their lives have been shaped by these circumstances, as well as by their genders and class affiliations. Not all—perhaps not even a majority—have enjoyed the equal opportunities that are promised by the Constitution. But unfair social and economic realities only underscore the need for principled public discussion among concerned citizens. Knowledge of rhetoric can help citizens deliberate about these grim realities and determine how to change them for the better.

Knowledge of rhetoric also allows people to discern when **rhetors** are making bad arguments or are asking them to make inappropriate choices. Because rhetoric confers the gift of greater facility with language, it can also teach those who study it to evaluate anyone's rhetoric; thus the critical capacity conferred by rhetoric can make its students more aware of others' manipulative rhetoric. When knowledge about rhetoric is available only to a few people, the power inherent in persuasive discourse is disproportionately shared. Unfortunately, throughout history rhetorical knowledge has usually been shared only among those who can exert economic, social, or political power as well. But ordinary citizens can learn to deploy rhetorical power, and if they have a chance and the courage to deploy it skillfully and often, it's possible that they may change other features of our society as well. In this book, then, we aim to help our readers become more skilled speakers and writers. But we also aim to help them become better citizens.

Sometimes the differences between ancient and contemporary attitudes toward rhetoric and argument are difficult to overcome, but they are crucial to bear in mind as you read this book and learn about the central rhetorical concepts and practices that the ancients espoused. Getting past the widespread negative associations with rhetoric allows us to see that ancient rhetoric is as compatible with prevailing views about language as it is useful for contemporary citizens-in-training. For example, contemporary scholars who think about language now believe that language is a form of action rather than a mere reflection of reality, as had previously been thought. This perspective, that language *does* stuff—that language makes decisions, forms identities, moves people and things around—returns us full circle to the beliefs held by many of the ancients. Before explaining in more detail what we see as the most important differences—and some similarities—between ancient and contemporary beliefs about language and rhetoric, we return briefly to rhetoric's beginnings.

ANCIENT RHETORICS: THE BEGINNINGS

Something quite remarkable happened in the small Greek city of Athens during the sixth, fifth, and fourth centuries BCE. During this period, the citizens of that community evolved a form of government they called *demokratia* (from *demos* [people], and *kratos* [political power]). Any Athenian who was defined as a citizen played a direct role in making important decisions that affected the entire community: whether or not to go to war, to send ambassadors to neighboring countries, to raise or lower taxes, to build bridges or walls, or to convict or acquit people accused of crimes against the state or other citizens.

In the Athenian political system, citizenship was determined by birthright, and thus citizenship was awarded to any adult male who could establish his Athenian heritage, whether he was wealthy or not, aristocratic or not. These were very inclusive requirements for the time, even though they excluded the bulk of the population who were women, foreign-born men, or slaves. Because of this, classical Athens can hardly be said to have been a democracy in our more inclusive terms, although we remind readers that for almost half of its history, the United States limited suffrage to white males. Nor was Athens a representative democracy, as ours is said to be, because the few hundred people who were defined as Athenian citizens participated directly in making political and judicial decisions rather than acting through elected representatives.

The citizens met in the Assembly to make political decisions and acted as jurors at trials. Athenian men apparently took their civic responsibilities seriously. Despite the difficulties entailed in meeting this responsibility—leaving work undone for several days, travel to the city from outlying farms—as many as five hundred or more citizens could be expected to attend and vote in the Assembly when it was in session.

Sometime during the fifth century BCE, all citizens earned the right to speak in the Assembly. This right was called *isegoria* ("equality in the agora" or assembly-place). Most likely, very few citizens exercised their right to speak. When five hundred Athenians met to deliberate on important issues, not everyone could speak at once, nor was everyone sufficiently informed about the issue at hand to speak effectively. The task of filling in the details and of arguing for a course of action fell to people who were trained in speaking, who had sufficient education to understand the issues, and who had the leisure to study the issues at hand. These were the professional *rhetores*. In the fifth century, the term **rhetor** referred to someone who introduced a resolution into the Assembly, but by the fourth century BCE the term meant something like "an expert on politics." Later it came to mean "one skilled in public speaking" as well. In this book, we refer to people who practice rhetoric as rhetors. We refer to people who teach it or theorize about it as rhetoricians.[1]

COMPARING ANCIENT AND CONTEMPORARY RHETORICS

The great age of ancient rhetorics dictates that there will be differences between them and current thinking about rhetoric. Whereas over the past two decades, scholars of language and rhetoric have begun to think about language in similar ways to the ancients, some persistent values and habits in our culture are less hospitable to ancient rhetorics, such as the habit of equating opinion with identity and the resulting view that disagreement is somehow rude.

There were other things that the ancients saw differently as well, like the status of facts. Ancient rhetoricians did not value factual proof as much as other means of argument, whereas **facts** and **testimony** are valued very highly in

U.S. culture (see the chapter on **extrinsic proofs**). Ancient teachers preferred to use arguments that they generated from language itself and from community beliefs during an intellectual process they called **invention.** They invented and named many such arguments, among them **commonplaces, examples, conjectures, maxims,** and **enthymemes** (see the chapters on **stasis, commonplaces,** and on **rhetorical reasoning**). Another difference is that ancient rhetoricians valued opinions as a communal source of knowledge, whereas nowadays opinions are often dismissed as unimportant or held only by individuals. This difference has to do with another assumption that the ancients made, which was that a person's character and her opinions were constituted by the community in which she lived. And because the ancients believed that communities were the source and reason for rhetoric, opinions were for them the very stuff of argument.

Apart from their differing assumptions about facts and opinions, contemporary rhetoricians agree with their ancient counterparts on many points. The first of these is that rhetoric is a situational art. As we will discuss further in the chapter on *kairos* and rhetorical situations, the Sophist Gorgias was most famous for acknowledging the importance of timing and circumstance for creating rhetorical arguments. That is, rhetoric equips people to respond to particular situations in particular places at particular times, and its processes and outcomes depend on these circumstances. This is why our book is full of contemporary examples of issues and arguments. Although each one works to illustrate a rhetorical concept, cumulatively they show how knowledge about rhetoric hinges on careful consideration of **rhetorical situations.** Second, as we noted earlier, contemporary rhetoricians tend to agree with the ancients that language *does stuff.* It makes things happen; it alters the way the world works by affecting belief and effecting change. The sophists were key proponents of this view of language as action. The sophist Gorgias called speech or language "a powerful lord that with the smallest and most invisible body accomplishes the most godlike works" ("Encomium" 8). When you convince a friend to become a registered voter, you have effected a discernible change, and you have done it through language. When your Facebook friend clicks "like" on her favorite TV show and you do the same, the two of you are acknowledging one another—this is doing something (even though critics of Facebook might counter that it's not doing a whole lot). Cicero, who was an extremely skilled and influential speaker in the days of the Roman Republic, asserted that the ends of language use are to teach, to give pleasure, and to move. But the point of instructing or delighting audiences is, finally, to move them to accept or reject some thought or action. Contemporary and ancient rhetoricians are therefore in agreement on these points: rhetoric is situational, and language is action.

Extrinsic and Intrinsic Proofs

From an ancient perspective, one of the most naïve assumptions about the nature of argument goes like this: if the facts are on your side, you can't be wrong, and you can't be refuted. Facts are statements that somebody has substantiated through experience or proven through research. Or they are events that really happened, events that somebody will attest to as factual. In the naïve scenario, facts have a "you were there" quality—if the arguer doesn't have personal knowledge of the facts, she is pretty sure that some expert on the subject does know them, and all she has to do in that case is to look them up in a book. Here are some examples of factual statements:

1. Water freezes at 32 degrees Fahrenheit.
2. The moon orbits the earth.
3. On April 16, 2007, Virginia Tech student Cho Sueng-Hui killed 32 people and himself on his campus in Blacksburg, Virginia.

These are facts because they can be verified through experience or by means of testimony. Individuals can test the accuracy of the first statement for themselves, and all three statements can be confirmed by checking relevant and reliable sources.

But the factual status of facty-sounding statements is not always so straightforward. In contemporary politics, for example, partisans brandish facty-sounding statements as though they are validated or true: "Obama is a socialist" (or a Nazi, or a Muslim, or wasn't born in America). These are beliefs, rather than facts, even though they look like statements of facts. How can an uninformed observer distinguish between facts and what writer Norman Mailer called "factoids"? If a statement of fact seems suspicious, look for verification, either from supporting data or a trustworthy source (see the chapter on extrinsic proofs).

Perceptions, and thus testimony about them, can be influenced by an observer's perspective. Over the years during which we have been writing and revising this book, the National Football League has changed its policy on the use of instant replay several times. In instant replay, the referees watch video recordings of a controversial play taken from several different angles to decide what penalties to assess, if any. Even though professional referees are trained observers of the game, sometimes they simply cannot see whether a player's knee hit the ground before or after he fumbled or whether a receiver managed to keep his feet within bounds while he caught the ball. The problem with instant replay, though, is that sometimes television cameras are not well positioned to see a contested play either. In terms used in this book, the supposedly factual or empirical account yielded by instant replay is often no better at resolving disagreements about violations than is the testimony given by referees. Currently the NFL uses a rather complicated combination of taped replays and referee judgments to make decisions about contested plays. In other words, the NFL has opted to combine facts and testimony as evidence for opinions rendered about close calls. This example interests us because fans seem to trust referees' judgments less than they do that of the television camera operators. Indeed, fans often accuse referees of having an **interest** in one outcome or another, assuming that this interest influences their perception of events. This suggests in turn that football fans may trust machines rather more than they trust human experts, even though the machines are, after all, constructed and operated by human beings. One seldom hears complaints that Fox or CBS placed their cameras in positions that might serve their own interests, at least in the context of football games.

This example highlights the even more interesting observation that the facts of the physical world don't mean much to anybody unless they are involved in some larger **network of interpretation.** In football the relevant network of interpretation is the rules of the game. Without these rules, the exact placement of a player's arm or the exact point at which his feet touched the ground pretty much lose their relevance. (Sometimes football players and fans suddenly switch to a network of interpretation that allows them to read an arm in the face as an act of aggression. If referees think this is the case, they have to assess more penalties until the game's more usual network of interpretation can be restored).

Facts are not very interesting or persuasive unless they are read within a network of interpretation. Consider this advertisement by Cordaid, a Dutch nonprofit organization with a mission of eradicating world poverty:

HANDBAG € 32.-
Food for a week € 4.

Source: Saatchi & Saatchi, Amstelveen, The Netherlands

The facts presented in this advertisement, taken separately, are not all that compelling. It is easy enough to confirm the price of the handbag featured in the image. But when that price is paired with the weekly cost of food for one person in a developing country, the fact begins to take on a whole new set of meanings. What is more, the woman in the advertisement is posed in the attitude of a high fashion magazine advertisement—the pose is one of luxury and privilege. A viewer of this image might expect the woman to be reclined on a velvet couch. Instead, though, she is lying on rough, graveled ground. The photograph adds visual layers to the argument that would not be possible if one only compared the prices. The visual references made in this ad also work as networks of interpretation.

Facts often need to be read within their networks of interpretation, and rhetors ought to consider underlying (and competing) networks of interpretation when offering empirical evidence in an argument. For instance, the factoid that claims President Obama is a socialist emerges from a network of interpretation in which subscription to socialism is held to be little short of treasonous. The belief that the president is not an American may hinge on a perhaps unconscious assumption that Hawaii (where Obama was born) is not a state. In short, rhetors must pay attention to the ideological interests served by statements of facts and testimony before employing them uncritically.

The ancients believed that facts and testimony lay outside the bounds of rhetoric. Aristotle labeled them *atechnoi*—"without art or skill"—and hence **extrinsic** to, or outside, rhetoric. Aristotle defined an extrinsic proof as "those [proofs] that are not provided by 'us' [i.e., the speaker] but are preexisting" (*Rhetoric* I ii 1356a). Such proofs are extrinsic to rhetoric, then, because, as Aristotle figured it, one must *use* rather than *invent* them (1356a). A rhetor needs only choose the relevant facts or testimony and present them to an audience.

Because facts are relatively uninteresting in the absence of a relevant network of interpretation, rhetors seldom argue from a simple list of facts.[2] Today, practicing rhetoricians invent and use a wide variety of nonfactual arguments with great effectiveness. Take a trivial illustration: many video game advertisements are arguments from **example.** Advertisers for a dance-based video game show a group of young adults dancing energetically to a popular song about dancing, while watching images of themselves captured by the game and shown on the television screen. They are having a great time, smiling, laughing, and trying out new dance moves. Advertisers assume that the example will make people reason as follows: "That group of people plays a particular video game, and look at how they move, and how much fun they are having. If I buy that kind of game, I'll be a smiling, dancing, fun-having person too, and all my friends will want to come over to my house for a dance party." The ad writers hope that viewers will generalize from the fictional example to their own lives and draw the conclusion that they should buy the video game. There are no facts in this argument—indeed it is a fiction, a studio set constructed by scriptwriters, graphic designers, directors, and others—and yet it is apparently persuasive.

Rhetors who rely only on facts and testimony, then, place very serious limits on their persuasive potential because many other kinds of rhetorical argument are employed daily in the media and in ordinary conversation. These arguments are invented or discovered by rhetors, using the art of rhetoric. Aristotle described invented arguments as *entechnoi*—"embodied in the art" of rhetoric. This class of proofs is **intrinsic** to rhetoric because they are generated from its principles.

In rhetoric, intrinsic proofs are found or discovered by rhetors. **Invention** is the division of rhetoric that investigates the possible means by which proofs can be discovered; it supplies speakers and writers with sets of instructions that help them to find and compose arguments that are appropriate for a given rhetorical situation. The word *invenire* meant "to find" or "to come upon" in Latin. The Greek equivalent, *heuriskein,* also meant "to find out" or "discover." Variants of both words persist in English. For instance, the exclamation "Eureka!" (derived from *heuriskein*) means "I have found it!" This word was so popular during the nineteenth-century Gold Rush that a town in California was named "Eureka." The Greek word has also given us **heuristic,** which means "an aid to discovery," and we refer to anyone who has new ideas as an "inventor," from the Latin *invenire.*

A **proposition** (Latin *proponere,* "to put forth") is any arguable statement put forward for discussion by a rhetor. A **proof** is any statement or statements used to persuade an audience to accept a proposition. Proofs are bits of language that are supposed to be persuasive. Ancient rhetoricians developed and catalogued a wide range of intrinsic rhetorical proofs, most of which relied on rhetors' knowledge of a community's history and beliefs. The Older Sophists contributed the notions of commonplaces and **probabilities.** Aristotle contributed **enthymemes, examples, signs,** and **maxims,** and Hermagoras of Temnos is credited with the invention of **stasis theory.**

Aristotle discriminated three kinds of intrinsic rhetorical proofs: *ethos, pathos,* and *logos.* These kinds of proofs translate into English as ethical, pathetic and logical proofs. Ethical proofs depend on the rhetor's **character;** pathetic proofs appeal to the emotions of the audience; and logical proofs derive from arguments found in the **issue** itself. Our words *logic* and *logical* are derived from the Greek *logos,* which meant "voice" or "speech," to early Greek rhetoricians. Later, *logos* also became associated with reason.

Here is an example of how the kinds of proofs can help one invent arguments. In late 2009, the mayor of Pittsburgh proposed to make up for the city's budget shortfall by taxing the tuition paid by students attending any of the city's seven colleges and universities. In making his case, the mayor pointed out that the students used the city's services essentially for free and that the city could no longer afford to subsidize college students. The responses to the proposal came quickly and furiously. Given this situation, let's say a University of Pittsburgh student named Julia Jackson wanted to argue against the tax proposal at a city council meeting. She has a number of different arguments available. She might establish a credible *ethos* by pointing out that she is an economics major who has made the dean's list and has lived in Pittsburgh all her life, first as part of a taxpaying family, and now as a student in one of Pitt's high-rise dormitories. She might also note that she has organized volunteer groups to work the city's soup kitchens. Doing so would both establish Julia's ethos as a caring member of the community even as it functions as a **refutation** of the mayor's **premise** that students do not give back to the city. She might also make an emotional appeal by describing her austere life, how even with her low-wage work–study position, she can barely keep up with the rising cost of books and supplies. In addition, there are a good many logical proofs available to Julia in the issue itself. She can reason from **cause to effect:** Pittsburgh already has a problem of losing its young people to places with better economies, Julia might argue; this tax on students will further encourage them to leave as soon as they get their degrees, if not transfer to another, more affordable school. Or she can reason from **parallel case:** "The city of Philadelphia has a large number of universities and colleges, and it has managed to maintain a budget without placing a tax burden on students. Pittsburgh should follow suit." She could also reason from opposing cases: "The city has a steep 'sin' tax; so why would it tax those who are trying to better themselves by getting an education?" Such a logical turn, packed as it is with commonplace values and (in this case) moral arguments, cuts to the heart of the matter and is an example of an **enthymeme.**

As the tax issue escalated to the point of student protest, Rich Lord of the Pittsburgh newspaper, the *Pittsburgh Post-Gazette,* weighed in:

COLLEGE STUDENTS JAM COUNCIL MEETING TO PROTEST TUITION TAX

Some 150 students, bearing petitions that they said bore 10,150 signatures in opposition to the proposed 1 percent tuition tax, filled Pittsburgh Council Chamber this morning, forming a ring around a council that is expected to vote on the levy next month.

Before the council's 10 a.m. public hearing on the tuition tax, students from most of the city's schools of higher education presented petitions and challenged any impression that they contribute little to the city and demand much in services.

"We really, really need to dispel this myth that students are a burden to the city," said Rotimi M. Abimbola, student president at Carnegie Mellon University. Mackenzie Farone, a Point Park University graduate student who also works for that school, said she was "outraged at the light with which college students were portrayed" during the debate on the tuition tax. She said students rent houses for which property taxes are paid, and work, generating wage taxes. "Let's face it, we are the ones that pay the drink tax," she said, to laughs, referring to Allegheny County's 7 percent tax on served alcohol. "Just being honest."

Students "work hard, we learn, and we strive to better ourselves," she said.

The students quoted in this article have located the underlying logic of the proposal to tax students—students are a burden to the city—and have set about refuting that logic. There are a number of ways to respond to such an assumption, and Mackenzie Farone, the student quoted in the article, has chosen to refute it by pointing out that students in fact do pay certain kinds of taxes, especially, she notes with candor, the "sin tax" on alcohol. Such an argument can be found within the rhetorical situation; hence it is an intrinsic proof.

Ancient students of rhetoric practiced inventing a wide variety of intrinsic proofs while they were in school. By the time they finished their education, invention strategies were second nature to them, so that whenever they were called on to compose a speech or piece of written discourse, they could mentally review invention processes. This review helped them to determine which proofs would be useful in arguing about whatever issue confronted them. The means of inventing rhetorical proofs can still provide rhetors with a menu of general arguments they can consult whenever they need to compose. Anyone who becomes familiar with all of them and practices using them in particular situations should never be at a loss for words.

To become adept at invention is not easy, though. Invention requires systematic thought, practice, and, above all, thoroughness. But careful attention to the ancient strategies for discovering arguments will amply repay anyone who undertakes their study and use. Hermogenes of Tarsus wrote that "Nothing good can be produced easily, and I should be surprised if there were anything better for humankind, since we are logical animals, than fine and noble *logoi* and every kind of them" (*On Style* I 214). In other words, to invent arguments is essentially human. But invention also has a less lofty, more practical aim than fulfilling our species' potential: rhetors who practice the ancient means of invention will soon find themselves supplied with more arguments than they can possibly use.

That's Just Your Opinion

There is another category in popular notions about argument that deserves our attention. This is the category called "opinion." People can put a stop to conversation simply by saying: "Well, that's just your opinion." When someone does this, he implies that opinions aren't very important. They aren't facts, after all, and furthermore, opinions belong to individuals whereas facts belong to everybody. Another implication is this: because opinions are intimately tied up with individual identities, there's not much hope of changing them unless the person changes her identity. To put this another way, the implication of "Well, that's your opinion" is that Jane Doe's opinion about, say, sustainable living, is tied up with who she is. If she thinks that driving an SUV while slurping a corn syrup–laden drink from a giant Styrofoam cup is morally wrong, well, that's her opinion, and there's not much we can do about changing her belief or her practice.

The belief that opinions belong to individuals may explain why Americans seem reluctant to challenge one another's opinions. To challenge a person's opinion is to denigrate his character, to imply that if he holds an unexamined or stupid or silly opinion, he is an unthinking or stupid or silly person. This belief may also explain why reporters and other commentators were so shocked by Representative Joe Wilson's shouted comment during the president's State of the Union address; they took it to be a comment on Obama's character, rather than an assessment of his policies.

Wilson seems to buy into this faulty equation because his apology blames his outburst on his out-of-control emotions. This implies that his disagreement with the president was personal rather than what it was: an ideological difference over public policy. This may explain why he shouted, "You lie!" rather than, "I don't agree!" (although that, too, would have constituted a serious breach of congressional decorum). People who misrepresent facts are generally known as liars; people who disagree about policy have an opportunity to engage in rhetoric and perhaps to change one another's minds. When individuals express their emotional responses to the rhetoric of others, however, personal insult and hand-waving dismissal are all that is likely to occur.

Take another example: if someone we know is a devout Catholic, we are often reluctant to share with her any negative views we have about Catholicism, fearing that she might take our views as a personal attack rather than as an invitation to discuss differences. This habit of tying beliefs to an identity also has the unfortunate effect of allowing people who hold a distinctive set of beliefs to belittle or mistreat people who do not share those beliefs. The intellectual habit that assumes religious and political choices are tied up with a person's identity, with her "self," also makes it seem as though people never change their minds about things like religion and politics. But as we all know, people do change their minds about these matters; people convert from one religious faith to another, and they sometimes change their political affiliation from year to year, perhaps voting across party lines in one election and voting a party line in the next.

Ancient teachers of rhetoric would find fault with the equation of opinion and personality on three grounds. First, they would object that there is no such thing as "just your opinion." Second, they would object to the assumption that opinions aren't important. Third, they would argue that opinions can be changed. The point of rhetoric, after all, is to change opinions.

Ancient rhetoricians taught their students that opinions are shared by many members of a community. The Greek word for common or popular opinion was *doxa,* which is the root of English words like *orthodoxy* ("straight opinion") and *paradox* ("opinions alongside one another"). Opinions develop because people live in communities. A person living alone on an island needs a great many skills and physical resources, but she has no need for political, moral, or social opinions until she meets up with another person or an animal because politics, morality, and sociality depend on our relations with beings that think and feel. Let's return to the example of sustainable living to illustrate this point. Here is an excerpt from an article written by *New York Times* reporter Sara Rimer, entitled "How Green Is the College? Time the Showers."

OBERLIN, Ohio—Lucas Brown, a junior at Oberlin College here, was still wet from the shower the other morning as he entered his score on the neon green message board next to the bathroom sink: Three minutes, according to the plastic hourglass timer inside the shower. Two minutes faster than the morning before. One minute faster than two of his housemates.

Mr. Brown, a 21-year-old economics major, recalled the marathon runner who lived in the house last semester, saying: "He came out of the shower one morning and yelled out: 'Two minutes 18 seconds. Beat that, Lucas!' " . . .

So it goes at Oberlin's new sustainability house—SEED, for Student Experiment in Ecological Design—a microcosm of a growing sustainability movement on campuses nationwide, from small liberal arts colleges like Oberlin and Middlebury, in Vermont, to Lansing Community College in Michigan, to Morehouse in Atlanta, to public universities like the University of New Hampshire.

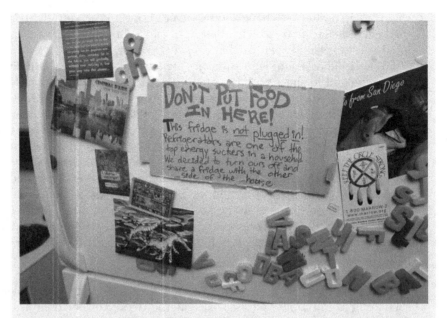

Source: David Maxwell for The New York Times.

While previous generations focused on recycling and cleaning up rivers, these students want to combat global warming by figuring out ways to reduce carbon emissions in their own lives, starting with their own colleges. They also view the environment as broadly connected with social and economic issues, and their concerns include the displacement of low-income families after Hurricane Katrina and the creation of "green collar" jobs in places like the South Bronx.

The mission is serious and yet, like life at the Oberlin house, it blends idealism, hands-on practicality, laid-back community and fun.

"It's not about telling people, 'You have to do this, you have to do that,' " Mr. Brown said. "It's about fitting sustainability into our own lives." And hoping, he added, "that a friend will come over, recognize that it's fun, start doing it, and then a friend of theirs will start doing it."

. . .

"This is a generation that is watching the world come undone," said David Orr, a professor of environmental studies at Oberlin. Projects like the Oberlin house, he said, are "helping them understand how to stitch the world together again."

Dr. Orr's course in ecological design became the incubator for the house when Mr. Brown and the two other founders of SEED, Kathleen Keating and Amanda Medress, enrolled in it last spring. They had done research on sustainability houses at Middlebury, Brown and Tufts, and had persuaded the college to turn over an aging, drafty two-story house. But before they could move in, they needed to make the house energy efficient.

The class studied water and energy use, insulation, heating and cooling, and financing. Nathan Engstrom, Oberlin's sustainability coordinator—an essential position on many campuses these days—gave advice. John Petersen, the college's environmental studies director, checked out the house's wiring.

The college spent $40,000 to renovate the house over the summer, bringing it up to safety code. Mr. Brown used the carpentry skills he had learned from his father to pitch in on weatherizing.

The students moved in last September. . . . All year they studied together in the living room at night so they would not have to turn on lights in the other rooms. They mastered worm composting, lowered the thermostat—keeping it at 60 degrees for most of the winter and piling on blankets—and unplugged appliances. There is no television, but no one seems to consider that a hardship.

"You have the rest of your life to watch TV," Ms. Keating said.

The unplugging of the refrigerator was not so easy. The house is divided in two, and each half has a kitchen. With everyone eating meals at a nearby student-run co-op, a decision was made to save energy by disconnecting the refrigerator and appliances in one kitchen. But which one?

"The fridge was kind of controversial," Ms. Bob-Waksberg said. "We kind of had a little feud going on for a while. We talked it out."

Equipped with the notion of shared opinion, we can see that Lucas Brown's opinion about sustainable living is not "just his." Rather, he shares it with other people like former vice-president Al Gore, a proponent of sustainable living, and Laurie David and Bill McKibben, two well-known environmental activists. He shares it with the other students living in his house, and a host of students on campus, who are part of Oberlin's sustainability efforts, as well. He also shares his opinion with thousands of people whom he has never met—with everyone who believes, as he does, that it is wrong to continue excessive use of resources such as water and energy with little regard for global warming. Oberlin, where Mr. Brown goes to school, is particularly hospitable to environmental concerns and has taken a leadership position among colleges and universities. (It might be easier for Mr. Brown and his housemates to care about global warming in a college town as opposed to, say, in a community in a state such as Texas, where the oil industry has a stronghold.) And if his opinion is not just his, it follows that, should he wish to, Mr. Brown can change his opinion without changing his identity.

This is not to deny that changing one's opinion, particularly about deeply held political or even religious beliefs, is very hard work. But it can be done, and it can be done by means of a systematic examination of the available positions on an issue. Sustainable living is an interesting example in this regard because it was until recently a minority belief and practice. Arguments supporting minority beliefs and practices must actively be sought out; often they are not available in venues that convey more dominant opinions, such as mainstream media. As few as five years ago, it took work to find arguments against the wastefulness of American lifestyles, and proponents of sustainable living could only become so after rejecting a more dominant view. Opinions and practices that are dominant, on the other hand, can be accepted without much thought or investigation. Most Americans born after the Second World War grew up believing in the infinite availability of water, gasoline, and electricity, often driving long distances on vacations and idling at drive-thrus waiting for food that was shipped to the restaurant. That individuals and major corporations have very recently felt the need to examine their "carbon footprints"—and that the phrase "carbon neutral" has entered into the mainstream—indicates that previous practices have met with a rhetorical challenge significant enough to threaten their status as a commonplace, that is, as a dominant, mainstream belief that used to "go without saying" (see the chapter on commonplaces).

If we locate opinions outside individuals and within communities, they assume more importance. If a significant number of individuals within a community share an opinion, it becomes difficult to dismiss that opinion as unimportant, no matter how much we like or detest it. Nor can we continue to see opinions as unchangeable. If Lucas Brown got his opinion about sustainable living from somebody he knows, something he read, or a film he saw, he can modify his opinion when he hears or reads or sees a different opinion from somebody else. For example, perhaps his economics professor may caution that the American economy will take a nosedive if legions of Americans suddenly begin to pay attention to carbon footprints. Communication researchers have discovered that people generally adopt the opinions of people they know and respect. Lucas Brown is aware of this phenomenon, as evidenced when he hopes that "a friend will come over, recognize that it's fun, start doing it, and then a friend of theirs will start doing it." Opinions are likely to change when we lose respect for the people who hold them, or when we meet new people whom we like and respect and who have different opinions. Opinions, that is, can be contagious.

Ancient teachers of rhetoric believed that rhetorical reasoning, which is used in politics, journalism, religious argument, literature, philosophy, history, and law—to name just a few of its arenas—is fully as legitimate as that used in any other field. And even though it uses appeals to community opinion and to emotions, if it is done responsibly, rhetorical reasoning is no more or less valid than the reasoning used in science.

ON IDEOLOGY AND THE COMMONPLACES

We suggested earlier that networks of interpretation—the way people interpret and use facts—have persuasive potential, whereas facts by themselves do not. Contemporary rhetoricians use the term **ideology** to name networks of interpretation, and that is the term we use for it in the rest of this book.

An ideology is a coherent set of beliefs that people use to understand events and the behavior of other people; they are also used to predict events and behaviors. Ideologies exist in language, but they are worked out in practices. They are sets of statements that tell us how to understand ourselves and others, and how to understand nature and our relation to it as well. Furthermore, ideologies help us to decide how to value what we know—they tell us what is thought to be true, or right, or good, or beautiful in a community.

Each of us is immersed in the ideologies that circulate in our communities once we begin to understand and use language. Hence ideologies actually produce "selves"; the picture you have of yourself has been formed by your experiences, to be sure, but it has also been constructed by the beliefs that circulate among your family, friends, the media, and other communities that you inhabit. You may think of yourself as a Christian, or a Jew, or a Muslim, or as secular. In each case, you adopted a set of beliefs about the way the world works from some relevant community (in the last case, you may have reacted against dominant ideologies). Even though identities are shaped by ideologies, they are never stable because we can question or reject ideological belief. As we have suggested, people do this all the time: they undergo religious conversion; they adopt a politics; they decide that UFOs do not exist; they shorten the length of time they spend in the shower; they take up exercise because they have become convinced it is good for them. Often, it is rhetoric that has brought about this ideological change. Ideology is the stuff with which rhetors work.

We mean no disrespect when we say that religious beliefs and political leanings are ideological. Quite the contrary: human beings need ideologies to make sense of their experiences in the world. Powerful ideologies such as religions and political beliefs help people to understand who they are and what their relation is to the world and to other beings.

Sometimes people make small changes because the ideological bias of a customary practice has been called into question by the community with which they identify. For example, the first edition of this book used a BC/AD dating system. This nomenclature is ideological because it is Christian (BC stands for "before Christ," whereas AD abbreviates the Latin *anno Domini*, "in the year of the Lord," and is used to designate the years after the birth of Christ). In the second edition, we adopted a new and increasingly customary dating system **BCE/CE,** which stand for "before the common era" and "common era," respectively. We realize, as one of our critics has pointed out to us, that changing the naming system still does not alter the calendar itself. The year "zero" is still associated with the birth of Christ. But in changing from BC/AD to BCE/CE, we made an ideological choice to use secular terminology. In doing so, we follow our own beliefs as well as scholarly convention—the common practice in a broad community of scholars. (If this were a book about the history of Christianity, we might have made a different choice.)

Ideologies are made up of the statements that ancient rhetoricians called commonplaces. The distinguishing characteristic of a commonplace is that it is commonly believed by members of a community. These beliefs are "common" not because they are cheap or trivial but because they are shared "in common" by many people. Commonplaces need not be true or accurate (although they may be true, and they are certainly thought to be so within the communities that hold them). Some commonplaces are so thoroughly embedded in a community's assumptions about how the world works that they are seldom examined rhetorically. Here are some examples of commonplaces that circulate in American discourse:

> Anyone can become president of the United States.
>
> All men are created equal.
>
> Everyone has a right to express their beliefs because free speech is protected by the Constitution.

Please note that even though these statements are widely accepted in American discourse, they are not necessarily true for all Americans. In other words, outside the communities that subscribe to them, commonplaces may be controversial. If you disagreed with us earlier when we asserted that "men have more power than women," your disagreement should alert you to the presence of a commonplace that is accepted in some community to which we belong but not in the communities with which you identify. In a case like this, the commonplace is contested. Contested commonplaces are called **issues** in rhetoric, and it is the point of rhetoric to help people examine and perhaps to achieve agreement about issues.

Most people probably subscribe to commonplaces drawn from many and diverse ideologies at any given time. Because of this, and because our subscription to many of our beliefs is only partially conscious, our ideological beliefs may contradict one another. For instance, if John believes on religious grounds that people ought to help support the poor, he may find that belief to be in conflict with his conservative politics, which teach that people ought to keep the vast majority of wealth they have earned. Thus John's ideology contains a potential contradiction. This is not unusual because ideology is seldom consistent with itself. In fact, it may be full of contradictions, and it may (and often does) contradict empirical states of affairs as well. For example, the commonplace that affirms that "Anyone can become president of the United States" overlooks the reality that all presidents to date have been men.

Ideology and commonplaces are crucial for rhetoric; they help shape the issues we deliberate. Such issues—matters about which there was some disagreement or dispute—greatly interested ancient rhetoricians. Nothing can become an issue unless someone disagrees with someone else about its truth or falsity or applicability or worth. Furthermore, issues do not exist in isolation from the people who speak or write about them. For the ancients, these issues grew out of life in a community. Young people studied rhetoric precisely because they wanted to be involved in decisions that affected the lives of their family, friends, and neighbors. Students of ancient rhetoric did engage in a good deal of practice with artificial **rhetorical situations** taken from history or literature or law (the rhetorical exercises were called *progymnasmata* and **declamation**). However, this practice was aimed at teaching them something about the community they would later serve, as well as about rhetoric. In other words, they did not study rhetoric only to learn its rules. Instead, their study was preparation for a life of active citizenship.

LANGUAGE AS POWER; LANGUAGE AS ACTION

Ancient rhetoricians were aware that language is a powerful force for moving people to action. They also knew that communicating by means of language or gesture constitutes its own form of action. The Older Sophist Gorgias went so far as to say that language could work on a person's spirit as powerfully as drugs worked on the body. As he said, language can "stop fear and banish grief and create joy and nurture pity" ("Encomium to Helen," 8). Gorgias taught his students that language could bewitch people, could jolt them out of their everyday awareness into a new awareness from which they could see things differently. Hence its persuasive force. If you doubt this, think about the last time you went to a movie that made you cry, or saw a commercial that convinced you to buy something, or heard a sermon or lecture that scared you into changing your behavior.

Isocrates argued that language was the ground of community because it enabled people to live together and to found cultures ("Nicocles" 5–9). Communication was the mutual exchange of convictions, and communities could be defined as groups of human beings who operate with a system of roughly similar convictions. For Isocrates, language was the *hegemoon* (prince, guide) of all thought and action. He pointed out that language makes it possible for people to conceive of differences and to make distinctions like man/woman or good/bad. It also allows them to conceive of abstractions like justice or reality. The contemporary rhetorician Wayne Booth put forward an Isocratean view of rhetoric in his book, *The Rhetoric of Rhetoric,* when he asserted that "the quality of our lives, especially the ethical and communal quality depends to an astonishing degree on the quality of our rhetoric" (xii).

Ancient teachers never assumed that there is only one way to read or interpret a discourse. Audiences inevitably bring their ideologies, their linguistic abilities, and their understandings of local rhetorical **contexts** to any reading or listening they do. Contexts such as readers' or listeners' experiences and education or even time of day inevitably influence their interpretation of any discourse. This is particularly true of written discourse, which, to ancient ways of thinking, was set adrift by authors into the community, where people could and would read it in as many ways as there were readers (Plato, *Phaedrus* 275). Today, however, people sometimes think that the sole purpose of reading is to glean information from a text, and this belief is reinforced in school when students are expected to take tests or answer a set of questions about their reading to prove that they comprehended the assignment.

But people do many things when they read a text for the first time, and determining what it says is only one of these things. When you read any text, especially a difficult one, you simply can't find out what it says once and for all on your first trip through it. You can't consume written words the way you consume a cheeseburger and fries. When written words are banged up against one another, they tend to set off sparks and combinations of meanings that their writers never anticipated. Unfortunately, writers are ordinarily not present to tell readers what they intended to communicate.

Sometimes unintended meanings happen because written letters and punctuation marks are ambiguous. A popular Facebook page called "'Let's Eat Grandma' or 'Let's Eat, Grandma!': Punctuation Saves Lives" comically illustrates the misunderstandings that can result from a simple omitted comma. There are only twenty-six letters in the English alphabet, after all, and just a few marks of punctuation in the writing system. So most of these letters and marks must be able to carry several meanings. For example, quotation marks can signify quoted material:

> "'Get lost,' he said."

But they can also be used for emphasis:

> "We don't 'cash' checks."

Or they can be used to set off a term whose use a writer wants to question:

> "This is not a 'liberal' interpretation."

The last two uses are called "scare quotes." In speaking, the work done by punctuation is conveyed by voice and gesture, but writers do not have the luxury of conveying meaning through their bodies; instead they must rely on stylistic and other indicators to negotiate meaning in their writing (see the chapter on **delivery**).

The meanings of words differ, too, from person to person and from context to context. Indeed, the meanings of words are affected by the **contexts** in which they appear. In current political discourse, for example, words such as *patriotism, freedom,* and *justice* can mean very different things to the people who use them, depending on whether they subscribe to conservative or liberal ideologies. The slogan "support our troops" has been used by those in favor of the military presence in Iraq and Afghanistan as well as those who oppose it. Because people are different from one another, they have different responses to the same discourse.

When we listen to someone speaking, we have several contextual advantages that readers do not have. If we misunderstand a speaker, we can ask her to repeat herself or to slow down. This is why press conferences, lectures, and class presentations often feature a question-and-answer session. Our chances of misunderstanding spoken language are also decreased by the fact that we can see and hear the person who is speaking, and we can interact with her as well. Thus we can support our interpretation of the meanings of her words with our interpretations of her facial and bodily gestures and the loudness and pitch of her voice. Too, we are often acquainted with people who speak to us, whereas often we do not know writers personally. And even if we don't know a speaker well, we do understand our relationship to her. If a speaker is your mother rather than your teacher or boss or fitness instructor, you can rapidly narrow down the range of possible meanings she might convey when she commands you to "Shape up!" All these kinds of contexts—physical and social—help us to interpret a speaker's meaning.

But these contexts are not available in any writing, which is composed for an audience of people who are not known to the writer. So writers have to guess about the contexts that readers will bring to their reading. Usually those contexts will be very different from the writer's, especially in the case of a book like this one that introduces readers to a new field of study. Our experience as teachers has taught us that our familiarity with rhetoric and its terminology often causes us to take some of its fundamental points for granted. When we do this in a classroom students can ask questions until they are satisfied that they understand. But readers cannot do this. So even though we have tried very hard to make the contexts of ancient rhetorics clear in this book, people are bound to understand our text differently from each other and perhaps differently from what we tried to convey. Ancient rhetorics were invented by cultures that have long since disappeared, and that is one potential source of differential understanding in this particular text. But writers always fail to match their contexts with those of readers, and this kind of differential understanding is universal. It arises simply because writers can only imagine readers—who they are, what they know.

To put all of this another way: writers and speakers always fail to put themselves precisely in their readers' and listeners' shoes. This potential for differential understanding is not a curse, but rather it is what allows knowledge to grow and change. The ancients understood this, and that's why they celebrated **copiousness**—many arguments, many understandings.

Because ancient rhetoricians believed that language was a powerful force for persuasion, they urged their students to develop *copia* in all parts of their art. *Copia* can be loosely translated from Latin to mean an abundant and ready supply of language—something appropriate to say or write whenever the occasion arises. Ancient teaching about rhetoric is everywhere infused with the notions of expansiveness, amplification, and abundance. Ancient teachers gave their students more advice about the divisions or **canons** of rhetoric—invention, arrangement, style, memory, and delivery—than they could ever use. They did so because they knew that practice in these rhetorical arts alerted rhetors to the multitude of communicative and persuasive possibilities that exist in language.

This leads us to another important feature of ancient rhetoric: the belief that messing around with language is fun. Composition need not be undertaken with the deadly seriousness that is sometimes brought to it today. Contemporary students often want to "get it right" the first time and forget about it. Ancient peoples, on the other hand, fooled around with language all the time. The Greeks sponsored poetry contests and gave prizes for the most daring or entertaining elaborations on a well-known theme. Romans who lived during the first centuries CE held rhetorical contests called declamations, the object of which was to compose a complicated and innovative discourse about some hackneyed situation involving pirates or angry fathers. The winner was the person who could compose the most unusual arguments or who could devise the most elaborate amplifications and ornamentations of an old theme.

PRACTICE, PRACTICE, PRACTICE

To return to the positive side of Jon Stewart's analogy equating competitive athletics with real debate—or, in this book's terms, with rhetorical engagement—it is interesting to note that many teachers of rhetoric in ancient Athens and Rome found it useful to think of rhetorical training and performance as roughly analogous to athletic competition. As one of us argues in another book, the ancients deemed the struggle of competition (agonism) to be productive and beneficial, and in the context of rhetoric, they believed hard work paid off. Many ancients devoted themselves to devising conceptual tools and training methods that would help their fellow citizens become strong rhetors—active citizens equipped to think about issues of the day. All the ancient rhetors and rhetoricians mentioned in this book believed that rhetoric is a complex and flexible art that can nevertheless be learned and taught. And although there was much disagreement among the ancients about the best way to learn rhetoric, most of them agreed on three points: practice, practice, and practice.

Too often contemporary classrooms treat practice-based activities and exercises as "busywork," something to fill time between "real" assignments. We believe this is because of a heavy emphasis in today's classrooms on writing-as-product. In case it isn't clear by now, the ancients placed less emphasis on the product—the finalized speech or the finished piece of writing—and more emphasis on learning and shaping rhetorical skills through constant activity and practice. The best comparison for the ancient model of rhetorical education is the immersion technique of foreign language learning, wherein students speak only the language being learned. Likewise, these activities and exercises encourage you to see rhetoric all around you, to engage it analytically, and to practice improving your use of rhetoric when you speak and write.

Aelius Theon, one of the early developers of *progymnasmata*, or rhetorical exercises, had strong faith in their effectiveness:

> It is quite evident that these exercises are altogether beneficial to those who take up the art of rhetoric. For those who have recited a **narration** and a **fable** well and with versatility will also compose a history well. . . . Training through the *chreia* not only produces a certain power of discourse but also a good and useful character since we are being trained in the aphorisms of wise persons. Both the so-called **commonplace** and **description** have benefit that is conspicuous since the ancients have used them everywhere.
>
> (Aelius Theon, *Progymnasmata* Preface 1)

Ancient rhetoric teachers believed their students would become competent rhetors if they combined study of rhetorical principles with lots of practice composing. This book is designed to strike that same balance.

The *progymnasmata* brought to the students' attention patterns in language. The regular and varied practice at composing often has the surprising effect of making people enjoy writing and speaking just by making them more familiar as activities. *Progymnasmata*, as the classicist Ruth Webb argued, did not key to the "end result" but rather sought to cultivate rhetorical sensibility through constant—and constantly changing—rhetorical activity (300).

The *progymnasmata* and, later on, the imitation exercises we recommend might feel strange to contemporary students. When asked to imitate a passage written by an author you admire, you might feel as if you are violating some sort of rule about copying. Beliefs about rhetorical style have, in many ways, emulated popular thinking about opinions and argument: style has become an "individual," ineffable thing.

We disagree. And so would the ancients. We would never encourage students to violate copyright laws or university policies concerning plagiarism, but we also believe that imitation has nothing to do with stealing. Imitation exercises, if practiced in the way that the ancients practiced them, can lead you to a more finely tuned rhetorical method of reading and listening. That is, when reading and listening rhetorically, we read and listen as much for *how* a writer or speaker builds an argument with words, sentences, paragraphs, and sections as for *what* the writer or speaker is arguing. And what is more, although plagiarizing (copying work from someone else) is easy (that's why people do it), imitation exercises can be extremely difficult. This is because imitation exercises ask you to try new approaches and to innovate within those approaches. Imitation exercises can be as challenging as they are fun.

Professional rhetors know that much more work is produced during invention than is actually presented to audiences. That is, not everything that is composed actually ends up in a finished piece. Some ancient exercises are for practice, whereas others draw attention to style. Still others increase understanding of rhetorical principles. Practice is never wasted effort, though, because everything a rhetor composes increases copiousness—a handy supply of arguments, available for use on any occasion.

RHETORICAL ACTIVITIES

1. Look around you and listen. Where do you find people practicing rhetoric? Watch television and read popular newspapers or magazines with this question in mind. Jot down one or two of the rhetorical arguments you hear or see people making. Presidents and members of Congress are good sources, but so are journalists and parents and attorneys and clergy and teachers. Do such people try to support these arguments with facts? Or do they use other means of convincing people to accept their arguments?

2. Consider Jon Stewart's point about the state of argument in America today. Have you encountered any examples recently of argument-that's-not-really-argument? How can you tell the theatrical sort of argument from the rhetorically engaged?

3. Think about a time when you tried to convince someone to change his or her mind. How did you go about it? Were you successful? Now think about a time when someone tried to get you to change your mind. What arguments did the person use? Was he or she successful?

4. Try to answer this question: What counts as persuasion in your community? Here are some questions to start from: Think of a time when you changed your mind about something. How did it happen? Did somebody talk you into it, or did events cause you to change the way you think? How do the people you know go about changing their minds? How does religious conversion happen, for example? What convinces people to stop smoking or to go on a diet? How do people get to be racists, or become convinced they ought to stop being racist? How does a president convince a people that they ought to support a war? Make a list of arguments that seem convincing in each of these cases.

5. The Roman teacher Quintilian underscored the importance of rhetorical situations to composing when he suggested that students should consider what there is to say; before whom, in whose defense, against whom, at what time and place, under what circumstances; what is the popular opinion on the subject; and what the prepossessions of the judge are likely to be; and finally of what we should express our deprecation or desire (*Institutes* IV 1 52–53).

   If you are at a loss for something to say or write, you can use Quintilian's list as a heuristic, or means of discovery. Begin by thinking about the communities of which you are a part, and make a list of these: your families, relatives, and friends; your house or dormitory, your street, barrio, town, city, or reservation; your workplace; your school, college, or university; groups you belong to; your state, country or nation, and the world. What positions do you take on issues that are currently contested in your communities? This exercise should help you to articulate what you think about such issues.

   a. Start with this question: what are the hotly contested issues in the communities you live in (the street, the barrio, your hometown, your school, your workplace, the reservation, the state, the nation?) Make a list of these issues. (If you don't know what these issues are, ask someone—a parent, teacher, friend—or read the editorial and front pages of a daily newspaper or watch the local and national news on television or access news sources on the Internet.)

   b. Pick one or two issues and write out your positions on them. Write as fast as you can without stopping or worrying about grammar and spelling. Use a computer or mobile device if you have access to one and are fast on a keyboard, or write by hand if that is more comfortable for you. At this point you are composing for your use only. So don't worry about neatness or completeness or correctness; write to discover what you think about these issues. Write for as long as you want to, but write about each issue for at least fifteen minutes without stopping. Remember that thinking is exercise, just like running or bicycling, so don't be surprised if you tire after a few minutes of doing this work.

   c. These writings should give you a clearer view of what you think about one or two urgent issues. Let them sit for a while—an hour is good but a couple of days is better. Then read them again. Now use Quintilian's questions to find out your positions on community issues. What is the popular opinion on each issue? What is the position taken by people in authority? What is your position on the issue? Are there policies or practices you advocate or reject? With which members of your communities do you agree? Disagree? On what issues? What positions are taken by people who disagree with you? How will the community respond to your propositions?

   d. Now you should have an idea about which issue interests you most. Be sure to select an issue that you can comfortably discuss with other people. Write about it again for a while—say fifteen minutes.

e. Give what you've written to someone you trust; ask him or her to tell you what else they want to know about what you think. Listen carefully, and take notes on the reader's suggestions. Don't talk or ask questions until the reader finishes talking. Then discuss your views on the issue further, if your reader is willing to do so. If your reader said anything that modifies your views, revise your writing to take these changes into account.

f. Keep these compositions as well as your original list of issues. You can repeat this exercise whenever you wish to write about an issue or when you are asked to write for a class.

6. Begin recording in a journal or notebook the arguments that you commonly hear or read.

ENDNOTES

1. We encourage readers who are interested in the history of ancient rhetorics to consult the appendix to this book. You might also want to consult some of the histories cited in the bibliography. The bibliography also lists modern editions of the major works of the most influential ancient rhetors and rhetoricians. If you are interested in reading the works of the ancient rhetors and rhetoricians themselves, cheap editions of many of these can be found in the classics or literature sections of many bookstores, and they are available in libraries, too.

2. Recital of the facts connected with an argument does reinforce a rhetor's **ethos,** or persuasive character (see the chapter on ethos). If a writer or speaker demonstrates that she knows the facts of a case, her listeners or readers will increase their respect for her and her argument.

WORKS CITED

Booth, Wayne. *The Rhetoric of Rhetoric: The Quest for Effective Communication.* Oxford: Blackwell, 2004. Print.

Desmet, Christy. "*Progymnasmata.*" In *Classical Rhetorics and Rhetoricians: Critical Studies and Source*s. Ed. Michelle Ballif and Michael G. Moran. Westport, CT: Praeger, 2005. 296–304. Print.

Fleming, David. "The Very Idea of a *Progymnasmata.*" *Rhetoric Review,* 22.2 (2003): 105–120. Print.

Foxnews.com. "Congressman Yells 'You Lie' at Obama During Speech." (September 10, 2009) <http://www.foxnews.com/politics/2009/09/10/congressman-yells-lie-obama-speech/>). Online.

Groopman, Jerome. *How Doctors Think.* New York: Houghton Mifflin, 2007. Print.

"Jon Stewart's America." *Crossfire.* CNN, Atlanta. Original Airdate: 15 October 2004. Transcript: <http://transcripts.cnn.com/TRANSCRIPTS/0410/15/cf.01.html.> Online.

Kennedy, George. *Progymnasmata: Greek Textbooks of Prose Composition and Rhetoric.* Leiden: Brill. 2003. Print.

Lord, Rich. "College Students Jam Council Meeting to Protest Tuition Tax." *The Pittsburgh Post Gazette* November 30, 2009. <http://www.post-gazette.com/pg/09334/1017398-100.stm>. Online.

Perelman, Chaim, and Lucia Olbrechts-Tyteca. *The New Rhetoric: A Treatise on Argumentation.* Trans. John Wilkinson and Purcell Weaver. Notre Dame: The University of Notre Dame Press, 1969. Print.

Rimer, Sara. "How Green Is the College? Time the Showers." *The New York Times* May 26, 2008. <http://www.nytimes.com/2008/05/26/education/26green.html>. Online.

Sprague, Rosamond Kent. *The Older Sophists.* Columbia: South Carolina University Press, 1972. Print.

Webb, Ruth. "The *Progymnasmata* as Practice." in *Education in Greek and Roman Antiquity.* Ed. Y. L. Too. Leiden: Brill, 2001, 289–316. Print.

Woods, Marjorie Curry. "Weeping for Dido: Epilogue on a Premodern Rhetorical Exercise in the Postmodern Classroom." *Latin Grammar and Rhetoric: From Classical Theory to Medieval Practice.* Ed. Carol Dana Lanham. London: Continuum Books, 2002. 284–294. Print.

If the whole of rhetoric could be thus embodied in one compact code, it would be an easy task of little compass: but most rules are liable to be altered by the nature of the case, circumstances of time and place, and by hard necessity itself.

—Quintilian, *Institutes*
II xi

KAIROS AND THE RHETORICAL SITUATION: SEIZING THE MOMENT

ANCIENT RHETORICIANS RECOGNIZED the complexity of rhetoric, and therefore they realized that teaching such a flexible art was a difficult task. Rhetoric cannot be reduced to a handy list of rules on writing or speaking because each **rhetorical situation** presents its own unique set of challenges. A rhetorical situation is made up of several elements: the issue for discussion, the audience for the discussion and their relationship to the issue, as well as the rhetor, her reputation, and her relation to the issue. Rhetors must also consider the time and the place in which the issue merits attention.

Because each rhetorical situation is unique, each occurs in a time and place that can't be wholly anticipated or replicated. The proverb that tells us to "strike while the iron is hot" is certainly applicable to rhetoric: issues sometimes seem to appear (or reappear) overnight; others, such as capital punishment and abortion, seem remarkably enduring in American discourse. Sometimes issues are available for discussion, but audiences who are ready to hear about them cannot be found; at other times an audience for a given issue seems to coalesce overnight. A few years ago, for example, almost no one in the corridors of power

45

was interested in issues of privacy online. As we write, however, Americans in general are becoming more aware of the issue, thanks in large part to Facebook's initial disregard for its users' privacy. Magazines and newspapers have begun to feature articles on privacy and social networks, and television news makes frequent reference to it. And now it seems that public officials are beginning to pay attention, too. In rhetorical terms, the issue of online privacy has finally found a national audience.

Rhetors must always be prepared, then, to meet the moment and find the place where the sometimes-sudden conjunction of issues with their appropriate audiences appears. The ancients knew this, and they had a name for the right rhetorical moment: they called it *"kairos."* A multidimensional and flexible term, *kairos* suggests a special notion of space and/or time. Because American English does not have a term quite like *kairos,* a bit of explanation is in order.

ANCIENT DEPICTIONS OF *KAIROS*

The Greeks had two concepts of time. They used the term *chronos* to refer to linear, measurable time, the kind with which we are more familiar, that we track with clocks and calendars. But the ancients used a second term—*kairos*—to suggest a more situational kind of time, something close to what we call "opportunity." In this sense, *kairos* suggests an advantageous time, or, as lexicographers put it, "exact or critical time, season, opportunity" (Liddell and Scott 859). The temporal dimension of *kairos* can indicate anything from a lengthy time to a brief, fleeting moment. *Kairos* is not about duration, but rather about a certain kind or quality of time, a period during which opportunities appear to those who are prepared to take advantage of them. In Roman rhetoric, the Latin word *opportunitas* was used in a similar manner; its root *port-* means an opening, and from it we get English verbs such as *import* and *export* as well as an old-fashioned word for a door or window, *portal. Kairos* is thus a "window" of time during which action is most advantageous. On Wall Street there are *kairotic* moments to buy, sell, and trade stock to maximize gains. Victorious sprinters often accelerate at just the right time to pass their opponents. The success of a joke or funny quip depends on its timing, or the *kairos* of its delivery.

Kairos was so important for ancient thinkers that it became a mythical figure. Lysippos, the famous ancient sculptor of athletes, chose to "enroll Kairos among the gods" (Himerius, *Eclogae* XVI i). It is little wonder that someone knowledgeable about competitive athletics—where timing and an awareness of the situation are critical—would render *kairos* into human form.

The picture of Kairos in Figure 4.1 provides a good way to think about the rhetorical situation. Indeed, the rhetor is much like Kairos, bearing many different tools. Not just anybody can balance precariously on a stick while displaying a set of scales on a razorblade in one hand and depressing the pan with another; such feats require practice. As you can see in Figure 4.1, Kairos is concerned about balancing the particulars of the situation, just as he perches tenuously on the blade's edge. His winged back and feet suggest the fleeting nature of time and situations. Perhaps the most remarkable and well known characteristic of Kairos, however, is his hairstyle.

FIGURE 4.1

Kairos, from a bas-relief in Turin. Reprinted from Zeus: A Study in Ancient Religion *by Arthur Bernard Cook.*

Kairos was said to have hair only in the front, suggesting that one must keep an eye out for the opportune moment and seize it by grasping the forelock before it passes.

Figure 4.2 shows another depiction of Kairos, still with wings, this time holding a wheel, again suggesting movement. In this depiction Kairos is flying on the back of another mythical figure: Pronoia, the figure of foresight. Sitting dejected in the background is her counterpart, Metanoia, who is the figure of afterthought or hindsight. This scene, like the forelock in Figure 4.1, suggests the importance of anticipating opportunities and seizing them before they pass by. These figures underscore the many dimensions of *kairos*.

The ancients were certainly aware of the relevance of *kairos* to the art of rhetoric. Indeed, the Older Sophist named Gorgias was famous for having based his theory of rhetoric on it. Philostratus, an ancient historian, tells us that Gorgias may have invented extemporaneous speaking:

> For coming into the theater of the Athenians, he had the boldness to say "suggest a subject," and he was the first to proclaim himself willing to take this chance, showing apparently that he knew everything and would trust to the moment (*toi kairoi*) to speak on any subject. (Sprague 1972, 30)

By acknowledging the importance of *kairos*, Gorgias's rhetorical theory accounted for the contingencies of rhetorical situations, for the timely conjunction of issues and audiences. Gorgias studied the particularities of each situation as a means of invention; that is, his awareness of the right time and place helped him to discover compelling things to say.

FIGURE 4.2
Kairos, from a bas-relief in Thebes. Reprinted from Zeus: A Study
in Ancient Religion *by Arthur Bernard Cook.*

Isocrates, too, emphasized the importance of *kairos*, claiming that people
need to discuss prevailing issues before their currency dissipates:

> the moment for action has not yet gone by, [thereby making it] futile to bring up this
> question; for then, and only then, should we cease to speak, when the conditions
> have come to an end and there is no longer any need to deliberate about them.
> ("Panegyricus" 5, 2)

For Isocrates, the urgency and currency of a situation demand action, which
calls for lively rhetorical exchanges about an issue. But if an issue has lost its
immediacy, then the rhetor must not only deliberate about the issue; she also
needs to make a case for its relevance to a given time and place.

KAIROS, CHANGE, AND RHETORICAL SITUATIONS

Alongside the Older Sophists, we believe that the world is always changing
and that knowledge itself is full of contraries; that is, knowledge is never certain. *Kairos* draws attention to the mutability of rhetoric, to the ever-changing

arguments that can be found in connection with a particular issue. The available arguments on a given issue change over time because the people who are interested in the issue also change—their minds, their beliefs, their ages, their locations, their communities, and myriad other things. Individuals can become deeply interested in issues, and then they grow disinterested; people change their tastes in music and food and clothing over time, and they change their beliefs and interests as well. An individual may be religiously observant as a child and grow utterly indifferent to religion as an adult (or vice versa). A second individual may have no interest whatever in politics until she joins a community—friends, neighbors, or roommates—that is passionately engaged in political activity. Shared or communal belief changes as well, although this apparently happens more slowly. Americans have been arguing about gun control off and on for over two hundred years, but national interest in the issue waxes and wanes. Interest usually grows when some event, such as a campus shooting, turns the nation's attention to the issue. That is to say, a campus shooting can open a *kairotic* moment in which discussion of gun control seems more urgent than it does at other times.

Kairos also points to the situatedness of arguments in time and place, and an argument's suitability depends on the particulars of a given rhetorical situation. The particulars of a rhetorical situation include the rhetor, of course: her opinions and beliefs, her past experiences, as well as her position on an issue at the time she composes a discourse about it. But the rhetorical situation also includes the opinions and beliefs of her audience at that time and in that place, as well as the history of the issue within the communities with which they identify.

Aristotle claimed that rhetoric seeks the available proofs, and these proofs are made available by the interactions of human beings who find themselves in particular sets of circumstances. That is, rhetorical situations create the available arguments. No one would care about gun control if people were not killed and injured by guns; no one would argue about online privacy if it did not affect our daily lives, and no one would try to convince others to adopt sustainable living practices if the stakes for the future were not so big.

A *kairos*-based rhetoric cannot seek or offer certainty prior to composing, then. Rather, *kairos* requires that rhetors view writing and speaking as opportunities for exploring issues and making knowledge. A rhetoric that privileges *kairos* as a principle of invention cannot present a list of rules for finding arguments, but rather it can encourage a kind of ready stance, one in which rhetors are not only attuned to the history of an issue (*chronos*), but are also aware of the more precise turns taken by arguments about it and when they took these turns. One way to consider the *kairos* of an issue, then, is to explore the history of the issue; another is to pay careful attention to the arguments made by other parties to the issue to cultivate a better understanding of why people are disagreeing at a particular time and in a particular place. In short, the rhetor must be aware of the issue's relevance to the time, the place, and the community in which it arises. Rhetors who understand all the contexts in which issues arise will be well equipped to find convincing arguments in any given situation. Let's say a blogger wants to compose a post about the phenomenon of pinkwashing, a new word that combines pink (the color of the ribbons designed to raise awareness of breast cancer) and the word "*whitewashing.*" It is a pejorative term responding to the use of breast cancer awareness as a marketing tool to sell products, many of which are manufactured by processes that create carcinogens. (Another, related, term is greenwashing—we bet you can figure out what that means.)

Pinkwashing is also more generally used to apply to instances of Facebook memes in which Facebook users alter their status updates in ways that are supposed to raise awareness of breast cancer. The blogger who is agitated by this issue and wants to challenge her reader's enthusiastic embrace of what some people call "slacktivism" (a slacker's version of activism) can begin by looking around for recent and recognizable instances of pinkwashing that help her make an opening for her argument. Or, even more likely, some instance of pinkwashing will leap out at her, motivating her to write in the first place. That particular instance might well open the rhetor's eyes to other issues embedded within the situation.

This description may make it sound like the rhetor need only lie in wait, and issues will come to him. Nothing could be further from the truth. A rhetor inventing by means of *kairos* needs to pay attention to the world around him. Such a rhetor will want to read, watch, and listen to the news. He will want to pay particular attention to things that agitate him. Given that opinions take shape in a community, chances are the rhetor is not alone in his agitation. Here is an excerpt from an article that was apparently sparked by a certain agitation about a Facebook meme ostensibly promoting breast cancer awareness. The piece was published in the online magazine *Salon* and written by Tracy Clark-Fory.

THE FLIRTY FIGHT AGAINST BREAST CANCER

In yet another tiresome viral campaign, women update their Facebook status with where they "like it"

I was already experiencing serious ocular strain from all the eye-rolling induced by breast cancer awareness month when I came across the "I like it" campaign. It's yet another attempt at viral breast cancer activism via awkwardly sexual Facebook status updates. Last time around, women impishly posted the color of their bras with no explanation. This time, ladies are telling us how and where they "like it." For example, "I like it on the bed." A sampling of recent "I likes" include: the kitchen table, the back seat of a car, my nightstand, the floor, in the closet, on the stairs, on a bar stool and on the washing machine. This is meant to raise awareness—not about kinky female fantasies, but, inexplicably, breast cancer. . . .

Here's my question, though: Now that you have our attention, what do you have to *say?* As I wrote about the bra color campaign, "It essentially trumpets: *Hey, breast cancer exists and I'm wearing a bra!* Or, seeing as the status updates mention nothing about disease, perhaps it translates to the more succinct: *Breasts exist!* Either which way, it isn't news to the vast majority of us." It's troublesome enough—not to mention sadly cynical—when breast cancer is sexualized in the service of delivering an actual message. Without an actual message, it just seems plain dumb.

It may seem like something as trivial as a viral Facebook campaign can't possibly spark a serious argument. But it can, and it has. In this short article, the writer offers a catalogue of issues raised by the campaign: the sexualization of a deadly disease, the purpose or effectiveness of awareness campaigns, the use of social networking tools to stand in for activism. Indeed, what begins as a series of eye rolls could lead to serious argument, and Clark-Fory's piece only scratches the surface.

Paradoxically, rhetors can step into a *kairotic* moment when it appears only if they are well prepared to do so. Rhetorical preparedness includes an awareness of the communities who are interested in an issue, as well as awareness of their positions on it. Many communities have a stake in the issue of using social network programs to raise breast cancer awareness. Those groups of people include, for example, Facebook users who were perplexed by the mysterious meme and those who know about it and chose to participate. Other communities might include feminists; Facebook's board of directors; women with breast cancer; families of women with breast cancer; or various nonprofit groups such as National Breast Cancer Awareness Month, an organization responsible for having the month of October devoted to raise awareness about the disease; founders and leaders of and contributors to the Susan G. Komen Breast Cancer Foundation, where the pink ribbon campaign got its beginning; and members of smaller, more local communities who have worked together to organize races or events to benefit breast cancer. This is a long list of relevant communities, but it indicates the sort of initial homework that must be done by a rhetor who wants to understand the *kairos* of an issue.

A list of interested communities can serve as a **heuristic** because it can be used to ascertain the available arguments that circulate among interested parties. For example, Facebook users who changed their status updates to indicate where they "like it" might argue that such a campaign is effective because it causes people to think about breast cancer for a moment. Members of Facebook's board of directors might argue that the networking site helps to spread awareness faster than any other kind of campaign. Still other communities, such as women with breast cancer, might think this particular way of raising awareness is ineffectual, distracting, and insensitive to the pain of others. And feminists might remind people that because breasts are constructed as sexual objects in our culture, such an approach harms women in general.

Preparedness also includes some knowledge of the history of the issue. In her short argument, Clark-Fory connects this particular meme to a previous one about bra color and digs up the originating logic of that campaign. Other rhetors who wish to explore this issue might want to learn about the history of public advocacy for breast cancer awareness and find out about various awareness and fundraising campaigns.

Kairos as a Means of Invention

As the preceding paragraphs make clear, *kairos* can serve as a means of **invention**. Invention, remember, is the art of discovering all the arguments made available by a given rhetorical situation. *Kairos* is but one of several means of invention we explore in this book—others are the **stases**, the **commonplaces**, and the **topics.** All these means of invention can generate heuristics, which are usually lists of questions that help rhetors to investigate issues systematically.

Because *kairos* is not only temporal but also spatial, its exploration can generate questions such as these:

1. Have recent events made the issue urgent right now, or do I need to show its urgency or make it relevant to the present? Will a history of the issue help in this regard?

2. What arguments seem to be favored by what groups at this time? That is, which communities are making which arguments? How are their interests served by these arguments?

3. What venues give voices to which sides of the issues? Does one group or another seem to be in a better position—a better place—from which to argue? In other words, what are the power dynamics at work in an issue? Who has power? Who doesn't? Why?

4. What lines of argument would be appropriate or inappropriate, considering the prevailing needs and values of the audience?

5. What other issues are bound up with discourse about this issue right now, in this place, and in this community? Why?

How Urgent or Immediate Is the Issue?

Usually, urgency depends on the audience as well as the existing situation; that is, it depends on recent activity around an issue. Some issues have a relatively short shelf life. *Kairos* is fickle, and as is suggested by his winged shoes, he is also fleeting. The first edition of this book was written in 1990, and we have now revised it several times. Each time we revise, we update the issues we use to illustrate our points so that they will be familiar to our current readers. Most of the issues we dealt with in earlier editions no longer seem urgent. And yet one or two—such as abortion and gun control—appear to have real staying power within American discourse. So in this edition we continue to use both as examples of highly contested contemporary issues. We do this despite feedback from teachers at southern colleges and universities suggesting that many of their students have already made up their minds about abortion and hence do not wish to consider it in the detail required by rhetorical invention. This is an example of how *kairos* can be place based as well.

If you become interested in an issue that does not seem urgent at the moment, it might help to remember that *kairos* is akin to the Latin term *opportunitas*, an opening. Is there an opening for you to begin making new arguments on a particular issue? If not, can you create such an opening?

Arguments and Interests

The specific arguments that are currently circulating about a particular issue play an important role in creating *kairos*. Who makes what arguments and why? What **interest** might motivate someone to object to pinkwashing? In the short editorial we quoted earlier, Tracy Clark-Fory suggests that one campaign is questionable at best, because it doesn't send a clear and unified message. A number of other rhetors writing about the broader issue of pinkwashing link it to different issues. Peggy Orenstein picks up on the sexualization angle that Clark-Fory complains about and notes that it ignores people with cancer: "Rather than being playful, which is what these campaigns are after, sexy cancer suppresses discussion of real cancer, rendering its sufferers—the ones whom all this is supposed to be for—invisible." Investigative writer Barbara Ehrenreich considers the pinkwashing part of a strategy to keep a happy face on what is otherwise a very grim disease, as part of what she called in a speech to the Breast Cancer Action group the "perkiness and relentless cheerfulness of the breast cancer culture."

More often than not, investigation of a single issue can lead to a host of other, related issues. Sometimes there are as many issues packed together as there are communities interested in what at first glance seemed like a singular issue. An analysis guided by *kairos* will help sort through the various interested communities and their motivations.

We have already suggested that financial considerations often motivate arguments. Groups like Breast Cancer Action and the Susan G. Komen Foundation (a private foundation that supports breast cancer research) have taken opposite stances on corporate partnerships. What motives or values might have fueled the interests of those, like the Breast Cancer Action group, who want to put a stop to pinkwashing? What groups would accept or reject their position? Why?

Considering the interests at stake in an issue can help a rhetor decide the most advantageous way to frame an argument for a particular audience at a particular time. Most issues that capture our attention are highly complex, and they resonate differently among groups with differing political and social agendas. Before launching an argument about a hot social issue, then, a rhetor who wishes to argue persuasively would do well to tune in to arguments already in circulation. Furthermore, he should examine the values and assumptions that drive those arguments. Rhetors who do this can maintain a *kairotic* stance that readies them to speak to various sides of the issue, supporting those that he finds convincing and refuting those with which he disagrees.

To show how consideration of the values and interests in circulation around an issue can help rhetors generate arguments, we now turn to a frightening event: a shooting at Virginia Tech University. Early on the morning of April 16, 2007, police were called to a dorm room on that campus, where they found two people dead from gunshot wounds. Two hours later, a gunman opened fire in a classroom building, killing 30 more people before killing himself. It did not take long for this event to trigger arguments about gun control. Here is one such argument, published in the magazine *The Economist* days after the shooting took place.

AMERICA'S TRAGEDY

In the aftermath of the massacre at Virginia Tech University on April 16th, as the nation mourned a fresh springtime crop of young lives cut short by a psychopath's bullets, President George Bush and those vying for his job offered their prayers and condolences. They spoke eloquently of their shock and sadness and horror at the tragedy. The Democratic speaker of the House of Representatives called for a "moment of silence." Only two candidates said anything about guns, and that was to support the right to have them.

Cho Seung-hui does not stand for America's students, any more than Dylan Klebold and Eric Harris did when they slaughtered 13 of their fellow high-school students at Columbine in 1999. Such disturbed people exist in every society. The difference, as everyone knows but no one in authority was saying this week, is that in America such individuals have easy access to weapons of terrible destructive power. Cho killed his victims with two guns, one of them a Glock 9 mm semi-automatic pistol, a rapid-fire weapon that is available only to police in virtually every other country, but which can legally be bought over the counter in thousands of gun-shops in America. There are estimated to be some 240 m guns in America, considerably more than there are adults, and around a third of them are handguns, easy to conceal and use. Had powerful guns not been available to him, the deranged Cho would have killed fewer people, and perhaps none at all.

But the tragedies of Virginia Tech—and Columbine, and Nickel Mines, Pennsylvania, where five girls were shot at an Amish school last year—are not the full measure of the curse of guns. More bleakly terrible is America's annual harvest of gun deaths that are not mass murders: some 14,000 routine killings committed in 2005 with guns, to which must be added 16,000 suicides by firearm and 650 fatal accidents (2004 figures). Many of these, especially the suicides, would have happened anyway: but guns make them much easier. Since the killing of John Kennedy in 1963, more Americans have died by American gunfire than perished on foreign battlefields in the whole of the 20th century. In 2005 more than 400 children were murdered with guns.

The Trigger and the Damage Done

The news is not uniformly bad: gun crime fell steadily throughout the 1990s and early 2000s. But it is still at dreadful levels, and it rose sharply again in 2005. Police report that in many cities it rose even faster in 2006. William Bratton, the police chief of Los Angeles (and formerly of New York), speaks of a "gathering storm of crime." Politicians on both sides, he says, have been "captured" by the vocal National Rifle Association (NRA). The silence over Virginia Tech shows he has a point.

The Democrats have been the most disappointing, because until recently they had been the party of gun control. In 1994 President Bill Clinton approved a bill banning assault weapons (covering semi-automatic rifles plus high-capacity magazines for handguns) and the year before that a bill imposing a requirement for background checks. But Democrats believe they paid a high price for their courage: losing the House of Representatives in 1994 shortly after the assault-weapons ban, and then losing the presidency in 2000. Had Al Gore held Arkansas or West Virginia or his own Tennessee, all strongly pro-gun, he would have won the election. These days, with hopes for a victory in 2008 dependent on the South and the mountain West, it is a brave Democrat who will talk about gun control. Some of them dismiss the very idea as "insensitive."

Mr. Bush however, has done active damage. On his watch the assault-weapons ban was allowed to lapse in 2004. New laws make it much harder to trace illegal weapons and require the destruction after 24 hours of information gathered during checks of would-be gun-buyers. The administration has also reopened debate on the Second Amendment, which enshrines the right to bear arms. Last month an appeals court in Washington, DC, overturned the capital's prohibition on handguns, declaring that it violates the Second Amendment. The case will probably go to the newly conservative Supreme Court, which might end most state and local efforts at gun control.

Freedom Yes, but Which One?

No phrase is bandied around more in the gun debate than "freedom of the individual." When it comes to most dangerous products—be they drugs, cigarettes or fast cars—this newspaper advocates a more liberal approach than the American government does. But when it comes to handguns, automatic weapons and other things specifically designed to kill people, we believe control is necessary, not least because the failure to deal with such violent devices often means that other freedoms must be curtailed. Instead of a debate about guns, America is now having a debate about campus security.

Americans are in fact queasier about guns than the national debate might suggest. Only a third of households now have guns, down from 54% in 1977. In poll after poll a clear majority has supported tightening controls. Very few Americans support a complete ban, even of handguns—there are too many out there already, and many people reasonably feel that they need to be able to protect themselves. But much could still be done without really infringing that right.

The assault-weapons ban should be renewed, with its egregious loopholes removed. No civilian needs an AK-47 for a legitimate purpose, but you can buy one online for $379.99. Guns could be made much safer, with the mandatory fitting of child-proof locks. A system of registration for guns and gun-owners, as exists in all other rich countries, threatens no one but the criminal. Cooling-off periods, a much more open flow of intelligence, tighter rules on the trading of guns and a wider blacklist of those ineligible to buy them would all help.

Many of these things are being done by cities or states, and have worked fairly well. But jurisdictions with tough rules are undermined by neighbours with weak ones. Only an effort at the federal level will work. Michael Bloomberg, the mayor of New York, has put together a coalition of no fewer than 180 mayors to fight for just that. Good luck to him.

This piece answers our first question, about urgency: when it was published on the heels of the shootings, recent events had indeed made the issue of gun control urgent once again according to these *Economist* writers. The writers begin, interestingly, by twice broadening the issue beyond the individual Virginia Tech shooter, linking him to the Columbine killers and then to their easy access to destructive weapons. The implication here is that this is a problem unique to the United States—and here it is worth noting that the *Economist* is published in England. The *Economist* writers therefore offer the perspective of concerned outsiders, but outsiders who know a good deal about U.S. politics. The writers also address the power dynamics in the situation, noting that government leaders had yet to tie the event to the need for gun control, and suggesting that public figures often ignore *kairotic* moments because they would rather not have thorny issues brought front and center when they are not ready to discuss them. Federal legislators' relative silence on the matter stands in contrast to the local officials and the citizens discussed in this essay. The writers tie the Virginia Tech massacre to other school shootings, which did little to change gun laws at the federal level. They also point suggestively to the more diffuse, less head-turning cumulative numbers on gun murders in the United States. In this way, they use the Virginia Tech murders as an occasion to address the problem of gun-related murders in the United States more generally.

The *Economist* piece ends by discussing the groups that have been working for stricter gun control. In the process they begin to answer our second question: which arguments seem to be favored by which groups at this time?

The shootings at Virginia Tech were so devastating that they still persist in cultural memory and retain *kairos*. Each spring, the anniversary of the shootings presents a renewed occasion to discuss issues related to the shootings. Three and a half years later, the Virginia Tech tragedy was invoked in a Texas debate about guns on campus. Here is a blog entry describing the debate, written by Titania Kumeh and published online at *Mother Jones*:

DO GUNS AND COLLEGE MIX?

Should students be allowed to carry concealed weapons on college campuses? Yesterday, the question entered the national limelight after a 19-year-old University of Texas student fired four rounds through the campus with an AK-47 before killing himself. No one else was hurt, the Associated Press reports. But the incident has Texas Gov. Rick Perry—a dude who goes jogging with a loaded pistol—calling for a relaxation of the state's gun-free college laws. He told the AP:

> There are already guns on campus. All too often they are illegal. I want there to be legal guns on campus. I think it makes sense—and all of the data supports— that if law abiding, well-trained, backgrounded individuals have a weapon, then there will be less crime.

It's a stock argument for pro-gun partisans: Students and faculty with concealed carry permits need the ammo to shoot back if a crazed gunmen enters their school. But a 2002 Violence Policy Center study found that sometimes, *just* sometimes, even the people permitted to carry concealed weapons can become the crazed gunmen. From 1996 to 2001, 41 concealed-handgun license holders in Texas were arrested for murder and attempted murder. And permit holders were arrested for weapons offenses 81 percent more often than the state's general 21-and-over population. Just a decade ago, after launching a year-long investigation into the Lone Star State's licensing laws, the *Los Angeles Times* reported that 400 criminals with prior convictions had been issued concealed-carry permits despite background checks. And more than 3,000 licensees had since been arrested, including a computer analyst who shot a bus driver in the chest because he'd nearly missed the bus.

But there's another group on Perry's side: Students for Concealed Carry on Campus. At the annual Gun Rights Policy Conference last weekend in San Francisco, SCCC president David Burnett cited the 2007 Virginia Tech shooting—in which "a young and mentally deranged individual took a firearm," killed 32 people, wounded 17 others, then killed himself—as an example of why licensed gun holders should be allowed to carry them on campus. "The only alternative that we have is to duck and cover," Burnett said. "A lot of these college campuses like to pretend that they are exempt from the freedoms that we have to carry a concealed weapon." In protest, 130 campuses have participated in "Empty Holster Contests," according to Burnett, where they wear their holsters to school sans guns as a symbol that they are disarmed and vulnerable.

Currently, Colorado and Utah allow concealed weapons on campuses. But gun advocates have vowed to press the state on the side of public armament. A Texas state representative, Republican Joe Driver, plans to file legislation (again) that would invite gun-toters back to school, cocked and locked. Criminals "would not go to a place where they don't know who has a gun," Driver says. "I think it's an absolute deterrent."

Kumeh begins her argument with a simple question—"Should students be allowed to carry concealed weapons on college campuses?"—and then describes the question's newfound urgency or *kairos* in the wake of the incident at the University of Texas. After characterizing the case in favor of guns on campus, Kumeh dismantles it. Using statistics and an example, she fashions an argument by means of a suppressed premise: even well-trained, properly licensed individuals can lose their temper and use their gun. Whereas the *Economist* writers used Virginia Tech shootings as the urgent impetus for their argument against gun culture in the United States, Kumeh's piece shows the leader of the group called Students for Concealed Carry on Campus using the same incident to argue in favor of guns on campus.

Kumeh's essay does not offer direct clues to why the SCCC president, Kumeh herself, or the governor of Texas believe as they do on the issue of gun control. That is, it is difficult to determine from an examination of these texts alone to what additional communities these people belong. We can make educated guesses, though; members of the National Rifle Association often take positions and make arguments similar to the SCCC leader, whereas members of the Brady Campaign to Control Gun Violence will sympathize with Kumeh's own stance. These assumptions can lead us to search engines and other research tools that will direct us toward more arguments used by those who are interested in the issue of gun control and that will allow us to define more carefully the groups that are invested in the issue.

Power Dynamics in a Rhetorical Situation

As evidenced by the "empty holsters contests," the arguments put forth in favor of guns on campus are all about power: gun users have it; people who work and study in gun-free zones (i.e., those with empty holsters) don't.

To examine and invent arguments using *kairos* is to consider the power dynamics at work in a particular issue in addition to the recent events and arguments that press on it. The questions to ask here are the following:

Which arguments receive more attention?

Who is making these arguments?

What arguments receive less attention?

Who is making these arguments?

When gun control arises as an issue, reporters often request statements from groups already organized, such as the National Rifle Association or the Brady Campaign, or in this case, Students for Concealed Carry on Campus. Organized groups often have more power to be heard in given rhetorical situations than do people who are unaffiliated with a relevant group. Government leaders, too, are asked to make known their stances on such issues. Here, for example, is an official statement containing Senator Dianne Feinstein's reaction to the Virginia Tech incident:

> My heart nearly stopped when I heard that more than 30 people had been killed at Virginia Tech today.
>
> In an instant, the hopes and dreams of students were destroyed by a cowardly and terrible act of insane violence. My deepest condolences go to all those touched by this violence.
>
> This mass shooting will be seared into our memories, alongside Columbine, 101 California, the University of Texas Clock Tower, and the shooting at a McDonald's in San Ysidro, California.
>
> It is my deep belief that shootings like these are enabled by the unparalleled ease with which people procure weapons in this country. And I believe this will reignite the dormant effort to pass common-sense gun regulations in this nation.

Feinstein represents the state of California, and so she is careful to mention incidents of gun violence that occurred in that state. Unlike other public officials, she connects the violence at Virginia Tech directly to the gun control issue, attending to the spatial dimension of *kairos*.

The arguments made by the governor of Virginia probably had more impact than those made by Feinstein, given his responsibility for the welfare of the citizens of Virginia and his relative proximity to Virginia Tech. On the other hand, we rarely hear or read the opinions of young people about gun control. Students on the campus were repeatedly asked about their emotional responses to the shootings, and they were asked as well to give factual accounts if they were in a position to do so. But reporters for the national media who wrote about the incident did not bother to ask about the opinions of those who will someday make decisions about gun control. How do we account for the absence of the voices of the young from public discourse about the issue of gun control? Could it be that this group is apathetic? Or does their status as inexperienced voters or (in some cases) nonvoters have something to do with the undervaluing of their position? All these questions and more are raised by considering the power dynamics at work in any rhetorical situation (see the chapter on *ethos* for more discussion of power relations in rhetoric).

A Web of Related Issues

Rhetorical situations are complex. A rhetor who is attuned to *kairos,* then, must demonstrate awareness of the many values and the differential power dynamics that are involved in any struggle over an issue. The stakes in an argument, or even the shape of the issue itself, can shift according to who is speaking, as is illustrated by the contrasting arguments on gun control, discussed earlier. A rhetor attuned to *kairos* should consider a particular issue as a set of differing political pressures, personal investments, and values, all of which produce different arguments about an issue. These diverging values and different levels of investment connect to other issues as well, producing a weblike relationship with links to other, different, new, but definitely related rhetorical situations. The issue of gun control is linked to the issue of violence, of course, and those who are charged to prevent violence, such as the police and the courts, have a large stake in seeing that really dangerous weapons, such as automatic handguns, are kept out of the wrong hands.

But not all arguments sparked by the Virginia Tech shootings had to do with guns. Some mental health professionals worried as well about the impact on viewers of repetitive television coverage of the event. Others wondered about the role of university faculty and administrators in seeking help for students who show signs of instability. Still others condemned NBC for airing the videotapes the killer made of himself before the shooting and then mailed on that morning. As time went on, debates began on other campuses about the need for broad and instantaneous alert systems as a security measure. These and other related issues form a web that provides seemingly endless possibilities, or "openings," for arguments.

We are not suggesting that a rhetor should address all the values and actions pressing on a particular issue at a particular time. Rather, we recommend that rhetors be aware of the issue's ever-shifting nuances, which might lead to new opportunities for rhetorical arguments. Considering the wealth of possibilities produced by attention to an issue's *kairos,* it is no wonder that Gorgias was bold enough to say to the Athenians, "Suggest a subject," and remain confident that he could make a rhetorical argument about it on the spot.

RHETORICAL ACTIVITIES

1. Survey a variety of magazines and newspapers and select a handful of articles on a given issue. How does each article draw on or create *kairos?* Is the issue so pertinent or urgent that little needs to be done to establish the

article's relevance to a time and/or a place? Do some writers or speakers use an opportune moment to "change the subject" and argue about a separate but related set of issues?

2. Using a library periodical database such as LexisNexis or the Internet, look for a few recent articles on gun control or pinkwashing. How has the *kairos* surrounding these issues changed since we wrote this book? Are people still participating in viral campaigns to raise awareness for breast cancer? What form do those campaigns take? Has talk about guns on campuses or gun control more generally faded from the national news?

3. Choose an issue and read broadly about it, keeping track of the various perspectives. Then, make a visual "map" of the arguments, tracking how the main issue gives rise to others. The map may look like two sets of lists, or it may be more sprawling with lots of offshoots, like a web. Be sure to include in the map the arguments people are making, who the people are, and what values they seem to be asserting.

4. Choose an issue and compose an opening paragraph for a paper or speech that shows how the issue matters for people you may be addressing.

WORKS CITED

Clark, Donald Lemen. *John Milton at St. Paul's School: A Study of Ancient Rhetoric in English Renaissance Education.* New York: Columbia UP, 1948.

Epstein, Edward, and Carla Marinucci. "Virginia Tech Massacre; Gun Control: Democrats, Eyes on Majority, Apt to Go Slow on Restrictions." *San Franciso Chronicle* 04/18/07. <http://www.sfgate.com/cgibin/article.cgi?file=/chronicle/archive/2007/04/18/MNGOUPAJ141.DTL&type=politics>. Accessed 05/22/07.

Ehrenreich, Barbara. "Keynote address to Breast Cancer Action Group ." April 20, 2002. full text available at: <http://www.annieappleseedproject.org/barehar.html>.

Feinstein, Dianne. "Statement of Senator Dianne Feinstein on the Mass Shooting at Virginia Tech." 01/16/07. <http://feinstein.senate.gov/public/index.cfm?FuseAction=NewsRoom.PressReleases&ContentRecord_id=fc6adefc-9b7a-525a-b67d-24447a8403fc&Region_id=&Issue_id=>. Accessed 05/22/07.

Kennedy, George. *Progymnasmata: Greek Textbooks of Prose Composition and Rhetoric.* Leiden: Brill. 2003. Print.

Kumeh, Titania. "Do Guns and College Mix?" *Mother Jones.* September 10, 2010. <http://motherjones.com/mojo/2010/09/guns-college-university-texas-concealed-carry>. Online.

Liddell, Henry George, and Robert Scott. *A Greek-English Lexicon.* New York: Oxford UP, 1996. Print.

Orenstein, Peggy. "Think Before You Pink." *The New York Times Magazine.* November 14, 2010. MM13. Print.

Analyzing Written Arguments

WHAT IS RHETORICAL ANALYSIS?

To many people, the term *rhetoric* means speech or writing that is highly ornamental or deceptive or manipulative. You might hear someone say, "That politician is just using a bunch of rhetoric" or "The rhetoric of that advertisement is very deceptive." But the term *rhetoric* is also used in a positive or neutral sense to describe human communication; for instance, *Silent Spring* is one of the most influential pieces of environmental rhetoric ever written. As a subject of study, rhetoric is usually associated with effective communication, following Aristotle's classic definition of rhetoric as "the art of finding in any given case the available means of persuasion."

Rhetoric is not just a means of *producing* effective communication but also a way of *understanding* communication. The two aspects mutually support one another: becoming a better writer makes you a better interpreter, and becoming a better interpreter makes you a better writer.

Rhetorical analysis can be defined as an effort to understand how people attempt to influence others through language and more broadly every kind of important symbolic action—not only speeches, articles, and books, but also architecture, movies, television shows, memorials, Web sites, advertisements, photos and other images, dance, and popular songs. It might be helpful to think of rhetorical analysis as the kind of critical reading discussed in Chapter 2. Critical reading—rhetorical analysis, that is—involves studying carefully any kind of persuasive action in order to understand it better and to appreciate the tactics involved.

BUILD A RHETORICAL ANALYSIS

Rhetorical analysis examines how an idea is shaped and presented to an audience in a particular form for a specific purpose. There are many approaches to rhetorical analysis and there is no one "correct" way to do it. Generally, though, approaches to rhetorical analysis can be placed between two broad extremes—not mutually exclusive categories but extremes at the ends of a continuum.

At one end of the continuum are analyses that concentrate more on texts than on contexts. They typically use rhetorical concepts to analyze the features of texts. Let's call this approach **textual analysis.** At the other extreme are approaches that emphasize **context** over text. These focus on reconstructing the cultural environment, or context, that existed when a particular rhetorical event took place. That reconstruction provides clues about the persuasive tactics and appeals. Those who undertake **contextual analysis**—as we'll call this second approach—regard particular rhetorical acts as parts of larger communicative chains, or "conversations."

Now let's examine these two approaches in detail.

ANALYZE THE RHETORICAL FEATURES

Just as expert teachers in every field of endeavor—from baseball to biology—devise vocabularies to facilitate specialized study, rhetoricians too have developed a set of key concepts to describe rhetorical activities. A fundamental concept in rhetoric is audience. But there are many others. Classical rhetoricians in the tradition of Aristotle, Quintilian, and Cicero developed a range of terms around what they called the canons of rhetoric in order to describe some of the actions of communicators: *inventio* (invention—the finding or creation of information for persuasive acts, and the planning of strategies), *dispostio* (arrangement), *elocutio* (style), *memoria* (the recollection of rhetorical resources that one might call upon, as well as the memorization of what has been invented and arranged), and *pronuntiatio* (delivery). These five canons generally describe the actions of any persuader, from preliminary planning to final delivery.

Over the years, as written discourse gained in prestige against oral discourse, four canons (excepting *memoria*) led to the development of concepts and terms useful for rhetorical analysis. Terms like *ethos*, *pathos*, and *logos*, all associated with invention, account for features of texts related to the trustworthiness and credibility of the writer or speaker (ethos), for the persuasive good reasons in an argument that derive from a community's mostly deeply held values (pathos), and for the good reasons that emerge from intellectual reasoning (logos). Fundamental to the classical approach to rhetoric is the concept of *decorum*, or "appropriateness": Everything within a persuasive act can be understood as reflecting a central rhetorical goal that governs consistent choices according to occasion and audience.

An example will make textual rhetorical analysis clearer. If you have not done so already, read "The Border Patrol State" by Leslie Marmon Silko in Chapter 11 (pp. 160–166). In the pages that follow, we use the concepts of classical rhetoric to better understand this essay.

Silko's Purpose and Argument

What is the purpose of Silko's essay? She wrote the essay well over a decade ago, but you probably find it to be interesting and readable still because it concerns the perennial American issue of civil rights. Silko's essay is especially relevant in

The statue of Castor stands at the entrance of the Piazza del Campidoglio in Rome.
A textual analysis focuses on the statue itself.
The size and realism of the statue makes it a masterpiece of classical Roman sculpture.

light of recent debates concerning the Arizona immigration bill and surrounding controversies about the enforcement of state and federal immigration laws. In this case, Silko takes issue with practices associated with the Border Patrol of the Immigration and Naturalization Service (INS). She feels they are reenacting the long subjugation of native peoples by the white majority. Silko proposes that the power of the Border Patrol be sharply reduced so that the exploitation of her people might be curtailed, and she supports that thesis with an essay that describes and condemns the Border Patrol's tactics.

Essentially Silko's argument comes down to two good reasons: the Border Patrol must be reformed because "the Immigration and Naturalization Service and Border Patrol have implemented policies that interfere with the rights of U.S. citizens to travel freely within our borders" (para. 8), and because efforts to restrict immigration are ineffective and doomed to fail ("It is no use; borders haven't worked, and they won't work," para. 16). Silko's essay amounts to an evaluation of the Border Patrol's activities, an evaluation that finds those activities lacking on ethical and practical grounds.

Silko's Use of Logos, Pathos, and Ethos

Logos

When Silko condemns the unethical actions of the Border Patrol early in the essay, she combines ample evidence with other appeals, including our sense of what is legal, constitutional, fair, and honorable. When she explains the futility of trying to stop immigration, she appeals again to her readers' reasonableness: Constructing walls across the border with Mexico is foolish because "border entrepreneurs have already used blowtorches to cut passageways through the fence" (para. 15), because "a mass migration is already under way" (para. 16), and because "The Americas are Indian country, and the 'Indian problem' is not about to go away" (para. 17).

The bulk of "The Border Patrol State" amounts to an argument by example. The single case—Silko's personal experience, as a Native American, with the border police—stands for many such cases. This case study persuades as other case studies and narratives do—by serving as a representative example that stands for the treatment of many Native Americans.

Pathos

The logical appeals in Silko's essay are reinforced by her emotional appeals.

- The Border Patrol is constructing an "Iron Curtain" that is as destructive of human rights as the Iron Curtain that the Soviet Union constructed around Eastern Europe after World War II (para. 15).

- "Proud" and "patriotic" Native Americans are being harassed: "old Bill Pratt used to ride his horse 300 miles overland . . . every summer to work as a fire lookout" (para. 1).

A contextual analysis focuses on the surroundings and history of the statue. According to legend, Castor (left of staircase) and his twin brother Pollux (right of staircase), the mythical sons of Leda, assisted Romans in an early battle. Romans built a large temple in the Forum to honor them. The statues were discovered in the sixteenth century and in 1583 were brought to stand at the top of the Cordonata, a staircase designed by Michelangelo as part of a renovation of the Piazza del Campidoglio commissioned by Pope Paul III Farnese in 1536.

▪ Border police terrify American citizens in a way that is chillingly reminiscent of "the report of Argentine police and military officers who became addicted to interrogation, torture, and murder" (paras. 3–5).

The essay's most emotional moment may be when Silko describes how the Border Patrol dog, trained to find illegal drugs and other contraband, including human contraband, seems to sympathize with her and those she is championing: "I saw immediately from the expression in her eyes that the dog hated them" (para. 6); "The dog refused to accuse us: She had an innate dignity that did not permit her to serve the murderous impulses of those men" (para. 7). Clearly the good reasons in "The Border Patrol State" appeal in a mutually supportive way to both the reason and the emotions of Silko's audience. She appeals to the whole person.

Ethos

Why do we take Silko's word about the stories she tells? It is because she establishes her *ethos*, or trustworthiness, early in the essay. Silko reminds her readers that she is a respected, published author who has been on a book tour to publicize her novel *Almanac of the Dead* (para. 3). She buttresses her trustworthiness in other ways too:

- She quotes widely, if unobtrusively, from books and reports to establish that she has studied the issues thoroughly. Note how much she displays her knowledge of INS policies in paragraph 9, for instance.
- She tells not only of her own encounters with the border police (experiences that are a source of great credibility), but also of the encounters of others whom she lists, name after careful name, in order that we might trust her account.
- She demonstrates knowledge of history and geography.
- She connects herself to America generally by linking herself to traditional American values such as freedom (para. 1), ethnic pride, tolerance, and even a love of dogs.

This essay, because of its anti-authoritarian strain, might seem to display politically progressive attitudes at times, but overall, Silko comes off as hard-working, honest, educated, even patriotic. And definitely credible.

Silko's Arrangement

Silko arranges her essay appropriately as well. In general the essay follows a traditional pattern. She begins with a long concrete introductory story that hooks the reader and leads to her thesis in paragraph 8. Next, in the body of her essay, she supports her thesis by evaluating the unethical nature of INS policies. She cites their violation of constitutional protections, their similarity to tactics used in nations that are notorious for violating the rights of citizens, and their fundamental immorality. She also emphasizes how those policies are racist in nature (paras. 11–13).

After completing her moral evaluation of INS policy, she turns to the practical difficulties of halting immigration in paragraph 14. The North American Free Trade Agreement (NAFTA) permits the free flow of goods, and even drugs are impossible to stop, so how can people be stopped from crossing borders? Efforts to seal borders are "pathetic" in their ineffectiveness (para. 15). These points lay the groundwork for Silko's surprising and stirring conclusions: "The great human migration within the Americas cannot be stopped; human beings are natural forces of the earth, just as rivers and winds are natural forces" (para. 16); "the Americas are Indian country, and the 'Indian problem' is not about to go away" (para. 17). The mythic "return of the Aztlan" is on display in the box cars that go by as the essay closes. In short, this essay unfolds in a conventional way: it has a standard beginning, middle, and end.

Silko's Style

What about Silko's style? How is it appropriate to her purposes? Take a look at paragraphs 3 and 4. You will notice that nearly all of the fourteen sentences in these paragraphs are simple in structure. There are only five sentences that use any form of subordination (clauses that begin with *when, that,* or *if*). Many of the sentences consist either of one clause or of two clauses joined by simple coordination (connection with conjunctions such as *and* or *but* or a semicolon). Several of the sentences and clauses are unusually short. Furthermore, in these paragraphs Silko never uses metaphors or other sorts of poetic language. Her choice of words is as simple as her sentences. It all reminds you of the daily newspaper, doesn't it? Silko chooses a style similar to one used in newspaper reporting—simple, straightforward, unadorned—because she wants her readers to accept her narrative as credible and trustworthy. Her tone and voice reinforce her ethos.

There is more to say about the rhetorical choices that Silko made in crafting "The Border Patrol State," but this analysis is enough to illustrate our main point. Textual rhetorical analysis employs rhetorical terminology—in this case, terms borrowed from classical rhetoric such as ethos, pathos, logos, arrangement, style, and tone—as a way of helping us to understand how a writer makes choices to achieve certain effects. And textual analysis cooperates with contextual analysis.

ANALYZE THE RHETORICAL CONTEXT

Communication as Conversation

Notice that in the previous discussion the fact that Leslie Marmon Silko's "The Border Patrol State" was originally published in the magazine *The Nation* did not matter too much. Nor did it matter when the essay was published (October 17, 1994), who exactly read it, what their reaction was, or what other people were saying at the time. Textual analysis can proceed as if the item under consideration "speaks for all time," as if it is a museum piece unaffected by time and space. There's nothing wrong with museums, of course; they permit people to observe and appreciate objects in an important way. But museums often fail to reproduce an artwork's original context and cultural meaning. In that sense museums can diminish understanding as much as they contribute to it. Contextual rhetorical analysis is an attempt to understand communications through the lens of their environments, examining the setting or scene out of which any communication emerges.

Similar to textual analysis, contextual analysis may be conducted in any number of ways. But contextual rhetorical analysis always proceeds from a description of the **rhetorical situation** that motivated the event in question. It demands an appreciation of the social circumstances that call rhetorical events into being and that orchestrate the course of those events. It regards communications as anything but self-contained:

- Each communication is considered as a response to other communications and to other social practices.
- Communications, and social practices more generally, are considered to reflect the attitudes and values of the communities that sustain them.
- Analysts seek evidence of how those other communications and social practices are reflected in texts.

Rhetorical analysis from a contextualist perspective understands individual pieces as parts of ongoing conversations.

The challenge is to reconstruct the conversation surrounding a specific piece of writing or speaking. Sometimes it is easy to do so. You may have appropriate background information on the topic, as well as a feel for what is behind what people are writing or saying about it. People who have strong feelings about the environment, stem cell research, same-sex marriage, or any number of other current issues are well informed about the arguments that are converging around those topics.

But other times it takes some research to reconstruct the conversations and social practices related to a particular issue. If the issue is current, you need to see how the debate is conducted in current magazines, newspapers, talk shows, movies and TV shows, Web sites, and so forth. If the issue is from an earlier time, you must do archival research into historical collections of newspapers, magazines, books, letters, and other documentary sources. Archival research usually involves libraries, special research collections, or film and television archives where it is possible to learn quite a bit about context.

An example will clarify how contextual analysis works to open up an argument to analysis. Let's return to a discussion of Silko's "The Border Patrol State". It will take a bit of research to reconstruct some of the "conversations" that Silko is participating in, but the result will be an enhanced understanding of the essay as well as an appreciation for how you might do a contextual rhetorical analysis.

Silko's Life and Works

You can begin by learning more about Silko herself. The essay provides some facts about her (e.g., that she is a Native American writer of note who is from the Southwest). The headnote gives additional information (that her writing usually develops out of Native American traditions and tales). You can learn more about Silko using the Internet and your library's Web site. Silko's credibility, her ethos, is established not just by her textual decisions but also by her prior reputation, especially for readers of *The Nation* who would recognize and appreciate her accomplishments.

Perhaps the most relevant information on the Web is about *Almanac of the Dead*, the novel Silko refers to in paragraph 3. The novel, set mainly in Tucson, involves a Native American woman psychic who is in the process of transcribing the lost histories of her dead ancestors into "an almanac of the dead"—a history of her people. This history is written from the point of view of the conquered, not the conqueror. "The Border Patrol State," it seems, is an essay version of *Almanac of the Dead* in that Silko protests what has been lost—and what is still being lost—in the clash between white and Native American cultures. It is a protest against the tactics of the border police. Or is it?

The Context of Publication

Through a consideration of the conversations swirling around it, contextual analysis actually suggests that "The Border Patrol State" is just as much about immigration policy as it is about the civil rights of Native Americans. The article first appeared in *The Nation*, a respected, politically progressive magazine that has been appearing weekly for decades. Published in New York City, it is a magazine of public opinion that covers theater, film, music, fiction, and other arts; politics and public affairs; and contemporary culture. If you want to know what left-leaning people are thinking about an issue, *The Nation* is a good magazine to consult. You can imagine that Silko's essay therefore reached an audience of sympathetic readers—people who would be receptive to her message. They would be inclined to sympathize with Silko's complaints and to heed her call for a less repressive Border Patrol.

What is more interesting is that Silko's essay appeared on October 17, 1994, in a special issue of *The Nation* devoted to "The Immigration Wars," a phrase prominent on the magazine's cover. Silko's essay was one of several articles that appeared under that banner, an indication that Silko's argument is not just about the violation of the civil rights of Native Americans but also about the larger issue of immigration policy. "The Border Patrol State" appeared after David Cole's "Five Myths about Immigration," Elizabeth Kadetsky's "Bashing Illegals in California," Peter Kwong's "China's Human Traffickers," two editorials about immigration policy, and short columns on immigration by *Nation* regulars Katha Pollitt, Aryeh Neier, and Christopher Hitchens. Together the articles in this issue of *The Nation* mounted a sustained argument in favor of a liberal immigration policy.

The Larger Conversation

Why did *The Nation* entitle its issue "The Immigration Wars"? Immigration was a huge controversy in October 1994, just before the 1994 elections. When the 1965 Immigration Act was amended in 1990, the already strong flow of immigrants to the United States became a flood. While many previous immigrants came to the United States from Europe, most recent immigrants have come from Asia,

Latin America, the Caribbean islands, and Africa. While earlier immigrants typically passed through Ellis Island and past the Statue of Liberty that welcomed them, most recent immigrants in 1994 were coming to Florida, Texas, and California. The arrival of all those new immigrants revived old fears that have been in the air for decades (that they take away jobs from native-born Americans, that they undermine national values by resisting assimilation and clinging to their own cultures, that they reduce standards of living by putting stress on education and social-welfare budgets). Many people countered those fears by pointing out that immigrants create jobs and wealth, enhance the vitality of American culture, become among the proudest of Americans, and contribute to the tax base of their communities. But those counterarguments were undermined when a tide of illegal immigrants—up to 500,000 per year—was arriving at the time Silko was writing.

The Immigration Wars were verbal wars. In the 1994 election, Republicans had united under the banner of a "Contract with America." Some 300 Republican congressional candidates, drawn together by conservative leader Newt Gingrich, agreed to run on a common platform in an ultimately successful effort to gain control of the House of Representatives. Among a number of initiatives, the Contract with America proposed changes in laws in order to curtail immigration, to reduce illegal immigration, and to deny benefits such as health care, social services, and education to illegal residents.

The Contract with America offered support for California's Proposition 187, another important 1994 proposal. This so-called "Save Our State" initiative was designed to "prevent California's estimated 1.7 million undocumented immigrants from partaking of every form of public welfare including nonemergency medical care, prenatal clinics and public schools," as Kadetsky explained in her essay in *The Nation*. The Republican Contract with America and California's Proposition 187 together constituted the nation's leading domestic issue in October 1994. The war of words about the issue was evident in the magazines, books, newspapers, talk shows, barber shops, and hair salons of America—much as it is today.

Silko's Political Goals

In this context, it is easy to see that Silko's essay is against more than the Border Patrol. It is an argument in favor of relatively unrestricted immigration, especially for Mexicans and Native Americans. Moreover, it is a direct refutation of the Contract with America and Proposition 187. Proposition 187 states "that [the People of California] have suffered and are suffering economic hardship caused by the presence of illegal aliens in this state, that they have suffered and are suffering personal injury and damage caused by the criminal conduct of illegal aliens, [and] that they have a right to the protection of their government from any person or persons entering this country illegally."

Silko turns the claim around. It is the Border Patrol that is behaving illegally. It is the Border Patrol that is creating economic hardship. It is the border police that are inflicting personal injury and damage through criminal conduct. Finally, it is the U.S. government that is acting illegally by ignoring the treaty of Guadalupe Hidalgo, which "recognizes the right of the Tohano O'Odom (Papago) people to move freely across the U.S.-Mexico border without documents," as Silko writes in a footnote. Writing just before the election of 1994 and in the midst of a spirited national debate, Silko had specific political goals in mind. A contextual analysis of "The Border Patrol State" reveals that the essay is, at least in part, an eloquent refutation of the Contract with America and Proposition 187—two items that are not even named explicitly in the essay!

We could do more contextual analysis here. There is no need to belabor the point, however; our purpose has been simply to illustrate that contextual analysis of a piece of rhetoric can enrich our understanding.

WRITE A RHETORICAL ANALYSIS

Effective rhetorical analysis, as we have seen, can be textual or contextual in nature. But we should emphasize again that these two approaches to rhetorical analysis are not mutually exclusive. Indeed, many if not most analysts operate between these two extremes; they consider the details of the text, but they also attend to the particulars of context. Textual analysis and contextual analysis inevitably complement each other. Getting at what is at stake in "The Border Patrol State" or any other sophisticated argument takes patience and intelligence. Rhetorical analysis, as a way of understanding how people argue, is both enlightening and challenging.

Try to use elements of both kinds of analysis whenever you want to understand a rhetorical event more completely. Rhetoric is "inside" texts, but it is also "outside" them. Specific rhetorical performances are an irreducible mixture of text and context, and so interpretation and analysis of those performances must account for both as well. Remember, however, the limitations of your analysis. Realize that your analysis will always be somewhat partial and incomplete, ready to be deepened, corrected, modified, and extended by the insights of others. Rhetorical analysis can itself be part of an unending conversation—a way of learning and teaching within a community.

STEPS TO WRITING A RHETORICAL ANALYSIS

Step 1 Select an Argument to Analyze

Find an argument to analyze—a speech or sermon, an op-ed in a newspaper, an ad in a magazine designed for a particular audience, or a commentary on a talk show.

Examples

- Editorial pages of newspapers (but not letters to the editor unless you can find a long and detailed letter)

- Opinion features in magazines such as *Time, Newsweek,* and *U.S. News & World Report*
- Magazines that take political positions such as *National Review, Mother Jones, New Republic, Nation,* and *Slate*
- Web sites of activist organizations (but not blog or newsgroup postings unless they are long and detailed)

Step 2 Analyze the context

Who is the author?

Through research in the library or on the Web, learn all you can about the author.

- How does the argument you are analyzing repeat arguments previously made by the author?
- What motivated the author to write? What is the author's purpose for writing this argument?

Who is the audience?

Through research, learn all you can about the publication and the audience.

- Who is the anticipated audience?
- How do the occasion and forum for writing affect the argument?

What is the larger conversation?

Through research, find out what else was being said about the subject of your selection. Track down any references made in the text you are examining.

- When did the argument appear?
- What other concurrent pieces of "cultural conversation" (e.g., TV shows, other articles, speeches, Web sites) does the item you are analyzing respond to or "answer"?

Step 3 Analyze the text

Summarize the argument

- What is the main claim?
- What reasons are given in support of the claim?
- How is the argument organized? What are the components, and why are they presented in that order?

What is the medium and genre?

- What is the medium? A newspaper? a scholarly journal? a Web site?
- What is the genre? An editorial? an essay? a speech? an advertisement? What expectations does the audience have about this genre?

What appeals are used?

- Analyze the ethos. How does the writer represent himself or herself? Does the writer have any credentials as an authority on the topic? Do you trust the writer?

- Analyze the logos. Where do you find facts and evidence in the argument? What kinds of facts and evidence does the writer present? Direct observation? statistics? interviews? surveys? quotations from authorities?

- Analyze the pathos. Does the writer attempt to invoke an emotional response? Where do you find appeals to shared values?

How would you characterize the style?

- Is the style formal, informal, satirical, or something else?
- Are any metaphors used?

Step 4 Write a draft

Introduction

- Describe briefly the argument you are analyzing, including where it was published, how long it is, and who wrote it.

- If the argument is about an issue unfamiliar to your readers, supply the necessary background.

Body

- Analyze the context, following Step 2.
- Analyze the text, following Step 3.

Conclusion

- Do more than simply summarize what you have said. You might, for example, end with an example that typifies the argument.

- You don't have to end by either agreeing or disagreeing with the writer. Your task in this assignment is to analyze the strategies the writer uses.

Step 5 Revise, edit, proofread

For a checklist to evaluate your draft.

BARBARA JORDAN

STATEMENT ON THE ARTICLES OF IMPEACHMENT

Barbara Jordan (1936–1996) grew up in Houston and received a law degree from Boston University in 1959. Working on John F. Kennedy's 1960 presidential campaign stirred an interest in politics, and Jordon became the first African American woman elected to the Texas State Senate in 1966. In 1972 she was elected to the United States House of Representatives and thus became the first African American woman from the South ever to serve in Congress. Jordan was appointed to the House Judiciary Committee. Soon she was in the national spotlight when that committee considered articles of impeachment against President Richard Nixon, who had illegally covered up a burglary of Democratic Party headquarters during the 1972 election. When Nixon's criminal acts reached to the Judiciary

Committee, Jordan's opening speech on July 24, 1974, set the tone for the debate and established her reputation as a moral beacon for the nation. Nixon resigned as president on August 9, 1974, when it was evident that he would be impeached.

ı   Thank you, Mr. Chairman.

Mr. Chairman, I join my colleague Mr. Rangel in thanking you for giving the junior members of this committee the glorious opportunity of sharing the pain of this inquiry. Mr. Chairman, you are a strong man and it has not been easy, but we have tried as best we can to give you as much assistance as possible.

2   Earlier today, we heard the beginning of the Preamble to the Constitution of the United States: "We, the people." It's a very eloquent beginning. But when that document was completed on the seventeenth of September in 1787, I was not included in that "We, the people." I felt somehow for many years that George Washington and Alexander Hamilton just left me out by mistake. But through the process of amendment, interpretation, and court decision, I have finally been included in "We, the people."

3   Today I am an inquisitor. Any hyperbole would not be fictional and would not overstate the solemnness that I feel right now. My faith in the Constitution is whole; it is complete; it is total. And I am not going to sit here and be an idle spectator to the diminution, the subversion, the destruction, of the Constitution.

4   "Who can so properly be the inquisitors for the nation as the representatives of the nation themselves?" "The subjects of its jurisdiction are those offenses which proceed from the misconduct of public men." And that's what we're talking about. In other words, [the jurisdiction comes] from the abuse or violation of some public trust.

5   It is wrong, I suggest, it is a misreading of the Constitution for any member here to assert that for a member to vote for an article of impeachment means that that member must be convinced that the President should be removed from office. The Constitution doesn't say

that. The powers relating to impeachment are an essential check in the hands of the body of the legislature against and upon the encroachments of the executive. [By creating] the division between the two branches of the legislature, the House and the Senate, assigning to the one the right to accuse and to the other the right to judge, the framers of this Constitution were very astute. They did not make the accusers and the judgers the same person.

We know the nature of impeachment. We've been talking about it awhile now. It is chiefly designed for the President and his high ministers to somehow be called into account. It is designed to "bridle" the executive if he engages in excesses. "It is designed as a method of national inquest into the conduct of public men." The framers confided in the Congress the power, if need be, to remove the President in order to strike a delicate balance between a President swollen with power and grown tyrannical, and preservation of the independence of the executive.

7   The nature of impeachment: [it is] a narrowly channeled exception to the separation-of-powers maxim. The Federal Convention of 1787 said that. It limited impeachment to high crimes and misdemeanors and discounted and opposed the term maladministration. "It is to be used only for great misdemeanors," so it was said in the North Carolina ratification convention. And in the Virginia ratification convention: "We do not trust our liberty to a particular branch. We need one branch to check the other."

8   "No one need be afraid"—the North Carolina ratification convention—"No one need be afraid that officers who commit oppression will pass with immunity." "Prosecutions of impeachments will seldom fail to agitate the passions of the whole community," said Hamilton in the Federalist Papers, number 65. "We divide into parties more or less friendly or inimical to the accused." I do not mean political parties in that sense.

9   The drawing of political lines goes to the motivation behind impeachment; but impeachment must proceed within the confines of the constitutional term "high crime[s] and misdemeanors." Of the impeachment process, it was Woodrow Wilson who said that "Nothing short of the grossest offenses against the plain law of the land will suffice to give them speed and effectiveness. Indignation so great as to overgrow party interest may secure a conviction; but nothing else can."

,0   Common sense would be revolted if we engaged upon this process for petty reasons. Congress has a lot to do: Appropriations, Tax Reform, Health Insurance, Campaign Finance Reform, Housing, Environmental Protection, Energy Sufficiency, Mass Transportation. Pettiness cannot be allowed to stand in the face of such overwhelming problems. So today we are not being petty. We are trying to be big, because the task we have before us is a big one.

11   This morning, in a discussion of the evidence, we were told that the evidence which purports to support the allegations of misuse of the CIA by the President is thin. We're told that that evidence is insufficient. What that recital of the evidence this morning did not include is what the President did know on June the 23rd, 1972.

12   The President did know that it was Republican money, that it was money from the Committee for the Re-Election of the President, which was found in the possession of one of the burglars arrested on June the 17th. What the President did know on the 23rd of June was the prior activities of E. Howard Hunt, which included his participation in the break-in of Daniel Ellsberg's psychiatrist, which included Howard Hunt's participation in the Dita Beard ITT affair, which included Howard Hunt's fabrication of cables designed to discredit the Kennedy Administration.

13   We were further cautioned today that perhaps these proceedings ought to be delayed because certainly there would be new evidence forthcoming from the President of the United States. There has not even been an obfuscated indication that this committee would receive any additional materials from the President. The committee subpoena is outstanding,

and if the President wants to supply that material, the committee sits here. The fact is that only yesterday, the American people waited with great anxiety for eight hours, not knowing whether their President would obey an order of the Supreme Court of the United States.

14   At this point, I would like to juxtapose a few of the impeachment criteria with some of the actions the President has engaged in. Impeachment criteria: James Madison, from the Virginia ratification convention: "If the President be connected in any suspicious manner with any person and there be grounds to believe that he will shelter him, he may be impeached."

15   We have heard time and time again that the evidence reflects the payment to defendants' money. The President had knowledge that these funds were being paid and these were funds collected for the 1972 presidential campaign. We know that the President met with Mr. Henry Petersen 27 times to discuss matters related to Watergate, and immediately thereafter met with the very persons who were implicated in the information Mr. Petersen was receiving. The words are: "If the President is connected in any suspicious manner with any person and there be grounds to believe that he will shelter that person, he may be impeached."

16   Justice Story: "Impeachment is intended for occasional and extraordinary cases where a superior power acting for the whole people is put into operation to protect their rights and rescue their liberties from violations." We know about the Huston plan. We know about the break-in of the psychiatrist's office. We know that there was absolute complete direction on September 3rd when the President indicated that a surreptitious entry had been made in Dr. Fielding's office, after having met with Mr. Ehrlichman and Mr. Young. "Protect their rights." "Rescue their liberties from violation."

17   The Carolina ratification convention impeachment criteria: those are impeachable "who behave amiss or betray their public trust." Beginning shortly after the Watergate break-in and continuing to the present time, the President has engaged in a series of public statements and actions designed to thwart the lawful investigation by government prosecutors. Moreover, the President has made public announcements and assertions bearing on the Watergate case, which the evidence will show he knew to be false. These assertions, false assertions, impeachable, those who misbehave. Those who "behave amiss or betray the public trust."

18   James Madison again at the Constitutional Convention: "A President is impeachable if he attempts to subvert the Constitution." The Constitution charges the President with the task of taking care that the laws be faithfully executed, and yet the President has counseled his aides to commit perjury, willfully disregard the secrecy of grand jury proceedings, conceal surreptitious entry, attempt to compromise a federal judge, while publicly displaying his cooperation with the processes of criminal justice. "A President is impeachable if he attempts to subvert the Constitution."

19   If the impeachment provision in the Constitution of the United States will not reach the offenses charged here, then perhaps that 18th-century Constitution should be abandoned to a 20th-century paper shredder.

20   Has the President committed offenses, and planned, and directed, and acquiesced in a course of conduct which the Constitution will not tolerate? That's the question. We know that. We know the question. We should now forthwith proceed to answer the question. It is reason, and not passion, which must guide our deliberations, guide our debate, and guide our decision.

21   I yield back the balance of my time, Mr. Chairman.

SAMPLE STUDENT RHETORICAL ANALYSIS

T. Jonathan Jackson

Dr. Netaji

English 1102

11 October 2010

An Argument of Reason and Passion: Barbara Jordan's
"Statement on the Articles of Impeachment"

Barbara Jordan's July 24, 1974 speech before the U.S. House
Judiciary Committee helped convince the House of Representatives,
and the American public, that President Richard Nixon should
be impeached. Nixon was under investigation for his role in the
cover-up of the Watergate scandal. He knew about the burglary of
Democratic Party headquarters, but denied having any knowledge
of it and illegally shielded those responsible. Jordan used her speech
to argue that the president should be impeached because his actions
threatened the Constitution and the people of the United States;
however, Jordan never explicitly states this position in her speech.
Instead, she establishes her credibility and then uses logic to set out
the evidence against the president.

> Jonathan
> Jackson
> provides
> background
> information
> in the first
> paragraph
> and his
> thesis at
> the end.

In one sense, the audience of Jordan's speech consisted of the
other 34 members of the House Judiciary Committee, gathered
together to decide whether or not to recommend impeachment.
And yet Jordan was not speaking just to a committee meeting; her
speech was very public. The Senate Watergate hearings had been
televised during the months before her speech, and millions of
Americans watched sensational testimony by a host of witnesses.
The Senate hearings produced charges that Nixon authorized break-
ins at Democratic campaign headquarters in Washington during
the 1972 election and that the White House was involved in many
political dirty tricks and improprieties.

But the accusations remained only accusations—and Americans
remained deeply divided about them—until it was discovered that
Nixon had himself collected possible hard evidence: he had taped
many conversations in the Oval Office, tapes that could support
or refute the charges against the president. Nixon engaged in a
protracted legal battle to keep the tapes from being disclosed, on
the grounds that they were private conversations protected under

"executive privilege," and he released only partial and edited
transcripts. Finally on July 24, 1974, the courts ruled that Nixon had
to turn all his remaining tapes over. That same day, knowing that
hard evidence was now at hand, the House Judiciary Committee
immediately went into session to vote whether to impeach Nixon.
Each member of the committee was given fifteen minutes for an
opening statement.

Nixon was a Republican and Jordan, like the majority of the
committee, was a Democrat. Jordan had to convince her audience
she was not biased against the president simply because of her party
affiliation. Jordan was also new to Congress, relatively unknown
outside of Texas, and a low-ranking member of the committee.
Consequently, she had to establish her ethos to the committee as
well as to the television audience. She had to present herself as fair,
knowledgeable, and intellectually mature.

> Jackson observes that Jordan had a formidable assignment in establishing her ethos in a short speech.

At the heart of Jordan's argument is her faith in the
Constitution. She begins her speech from a personal perspective,
pointing out that the Constitution is not perfect because it originally
excluded African Americans like her. But now that the Constitution
recognizes her as a citizen, Jordan says, her faith in it "is whole, it
is complete, it is total." She even implies that, as a citizen, she has a
moral duty to protect the Constitution, saying, "I am not going to
sit here and be an idle spectator to the diminution, the subversion,
the destruction of the Constitution." Jordan's emotional connection
to the Constitution shows the audience that she is motivated by a
love of her country, not by party loyalty. She establishes herself as
someone fighting to defend and protect American values.

> Jackson analyzes how Jordan's fervent allegiance to the Constitution made her appear unbiased.

Jordan describes the Constitution as the accepted authority
on the laws related to impeachment. She shows the audience how
the Constitution gives her the authority to act as an "inquisitor,"
or judge. She depicts the Constitution and the American people as
potential victims, and the president as the potential criminal. She
warns of the need to remove "a President swollen with power and
grown tyrannical."

The appeals to pathos and ethos in the opening of the speech establishes Jordan's motivations and credibility, allowing her to next lay out her logical arguments. Jordan proceeds to explain how the Constitution defines impeachment, and fleshes out this brief definition with evidence from several state Constitutional Conventions. She also quotes Supreme Court Justice Joseph Story. Using evidence from the North Carolina and Virginia Constitutional Conventions, Jordan shows that impeachment was intended only for "great misdemeanors," and that the branches of government were intended to act as a check upon one another.

Next Jordan uses quotations from James Madison, Justice Story, and others to define impeachable offenses. For each offense, Jordan provides an example of an act that President Nixon was known to have committed, and she shows how his actions meet the definition of impeachable offenses. She compares Nixon's meetings with Watergate suspects to Madison's statement that "if the President is connected in any suspicious manner with any person and there be grounds to believe that he will shelter that person, he may be impeached." She pairs Justice Story's statement that impeachment should "protect [citizens'] rights and rescue their liberties from violation" with Nixon's knowledge of the burglary of a private psychiatrist's office. She links Nixon's attempts to bribe a judge and thwart grand jury proceedings with Madison's statement that "a President is impeachable if he attempts to subvert the Constitution."

Throughout this section, Jordan repeats the historical quotes before and after her descriptions of the president's acts. This repetition makes the connections stronger and more memorable for the audience. Jordan also contrasts the formal, high-toned language of the Founders and the Constitution with descriptions that make President Nixon's actions sound sordid and petty: He knew about money "found in the possession of one of the burglars arrested on June the 17th," about "the break-in of Daniel Ellsberg's psychiatrist," about "the fabrication of cables designed to discredit the Kennedy Administration." Words like "burglars," "arrested," "break-in," and "fabrication," sound like evidence in a criminal trial. These words are not the kind of language Americans want to hear describing the actions of their president.

> Jordan uses quotations from respected figures in American history to apply to Nixon's misdeeds.

> Jordan had to confront a legal issue: Were the actions of President Nixon serious enough to justify impeachment?

Jackson 4

Jordan then adds another emotional appeal, implying that the Constitution is literally under attack. "If the impeachment provisions will not reach the offenses charged here," she says, "then perhaps that 18th-century Constitution should be abandoned to a 20th-century paper shredder." This dramatic image encourages the audience to imagine President Nixon shredding the Constitution just as he had destroyed other evidence implicating him in the Watergate scandal. It implies that if the president is not stopped, he will commit further abuses of power. Jordan also makes the American people responsible for this possible outcome, saying that "we" may as well shred the Constitution if it cannot be used to impeach Nixon. This emotional appeal has the effect of shaming those say they can't or shouldn't vote for impeachment.

Jordan concludes her speech not by calling for impeachment, but by calling for an answer to the question, "Has the President committed offenses, and planned, and directed, and acquiesced in a course of conduct which the Constitution will not tolerate?" It almost seems like Jordan is being humble and trying not to judge by not stating her position outright. However, the reverse is true: Jordan doesn't state her position because she doesn't need to. The evidence she presented led Congress and the American public inescapably to one conclusion: That President Nixon had committed impeachable offenses. Just two week later, Nixon resigned from office. Jordan had made her point.

> Jackson notes that the metaphor of the paper shredder adds emotional force.

> In his conclusion Jackson points out how Jordan shifts the focus to her audience in her conclusion.

Jackson 5

Works Cited

Jordan, Barbara. "Statement on the Articles of Impeachment." American Rhetoric: Top 100 Speeches. American Rhetoric, 25 July 1974. Web. 25 Sept. 2010.

For support in learning this chapter's content, follow this path in MyCompLab:

• Resources   • Writing   • Writing Purposes   • Writing to Analyze.

Review the Instruction and Multimedia resources, then complete the Exercises and click on Gradebook to measure your progress.

ABOUT THE VISUAL MODES OF COMMUNICATION

Do you think you need a degree in art or design to include photographs effectively in a research paper or to compose a poster for a fund-raising event?

There is certainly much more to learning to be a professional visual communicator than we present in this chapter. For example, we do not give any history of design, which could give you a sense of how visual conventions have changed over time and place. We do not ask you to spend a semester drawing lettershapes—by hand—so that you have the smart expressiveness that calligraphic work requires. We do not discuss how to prepare a document for printing or how to design interactive online interfaces: Both processes can be highly complex and require extensive technical knowledge.

What does make sense for us to offer you, however, are basic but sufficient vocabulary, concepts, and methods to help you start being as rhetorical with the visual aspects of texts as with the verbal. Almost all the texts you compose—in school or out—require you to make visual choices (even if your choices are typeface, the size of margins, and alignment). Almost all texts you encounter have been designed to have visual effects on you; you can respond to those texts analytically only if you have vocabulary and concepts to help you see how the texts are working.

We don't intend to make you an expert in this chapter; we do intend to give you resources that will help you move thoughtfully through our visually full and varied environments.

THE PLEASURES—AND COMPLEXITIES—OF VISUAL COMMUNICATION

Seeing so often brings delight. Think of how parents look at their children and of how people who are in love look at each other. Think of how enjoyable a walk in the woods is, whether we see the bright greens of early spring or the stark soft shapes of an overnight snowfall. These visual pleasures seem easy: We just open our eyes and, automatically and effortlessly, there is the world to touch with our eyes. Seeing, that is, can seem to be only physiology, a result solely of the physical processes of our bodies, unaffected by who we are, where we live, or how we've been raised.

This easiness of seeing appears to extend to the visual texts we make for each other. When we take photographs or videos or try to capture an "exact likeness" in a drawing, we might think we are capturing a bit of reality; anyone anywhere should understand what the picture is about without explanation. Think of how children's books are composed only of pictures with little or no text and how we take it as a sign of maturity when a child can read words-only books.

Because seeing and understanding photographs and drawings can seem so effortless and can be so pleasurable, some people think that visual texts are not as serious as verbal texts, which by comparison appear to require more abstract and conceptual thinking. Because of this, some people look at the increase in visual texts in this country and time—advertising, comic books, music videos, webpages, movies—and believe we are all becoming less thoughtful and complex people because we spend less time than ever reading.

In this book, however, we argue that visual texts are complex—and can be as complex and thoughtful as any purely verbal text. If someone thinks they are not, it is in no small part because our educations have encouraged us to have that attitude: We have grown up in places and times that have valued verbal texts as being more serious and worthy of educated attention than other kinds of texts.

But every visual text involves choices—just like every written text. A photograph requires the photographer to frame the picture, to decide what to emphasize and what not, what level of focus to use, and so on … and we can understand photographs only if we have some understanding of the contexts in which they are shown.

We are not arguing that our understandings of the visual aspects of texts have no connections with how our bodies work. For example, our eyes are of a certain size, they cover a certain angle of vision, and they have a certain range of focus, which changes as we age. Anyone who is designing visual objects must keep these matters in mind when making compositions for others: If you compose a poster, you want to be sure others can see its main elements from a distance; if you design a booklet for older people, you will use larger typefaces and colors that help people see contrast more clearly.

We are arguing, however, that if we don't learn to analyze and understand the complexities of visual texts and to compose thoughtful, complex visual texts ourselves, then it can seem as though we just perceive visual texts naturally and easily … and then we won't read visual texts critically, as texts made by people who arrange the text's elements to achieve specific purposes.

On the following pages, we present strategies for analyzing and composing visual texts, strategies based both on how we see physically and on how we see as participants in our cultures.

Figure provided by Daniel Simons. For more information and to view the video, visit http://www.theinvisiblegorilla.com

"Daniel Simons, a professor of psychology at Harvard, has done a … dramatic set of experiments. … He and a colleague, Christopher Chabris, recently made a video of two teams of basketball players, one team in white shirts and the other in black, each player in constant motion as two basketballs are passed back and forth. Observers were asked to count the number of passes completed by the members of the white team. After about forty-five seconds of passes, a woman in a gorilla suit walks into the middle of the group, stands in front of the camera, beats her chest vigorously, then walks away. 'Fifty percent of the people missed the gorilla,' Simons says. 'We got the most striking reactions. We'd ask people, "Did you see anyone walking across the screen?" They'd say no. Anything at all? No. Eventually we'd ask them, "Did you notice the gorilla?" And they'd say, "The what?"' Simons's experiment is one of those psychological studies which are impossible to believe in the abstract: If you look at the video (called 'Gorillas in Our Midst') when you know what's coming, the woman in the gorilla suit is inescapable. How could anyone miss that? But people do. In recent years, there has been much scientific research on the fallibility of memory—on the fact that eyewitnesses, for example, often distort or omit critical details when they recall what they saw. But the new research points to something that is even more troubling: It isn't just that our memory of what we see is selective; it's that seeing itself is selective."

from "Wrong Turn: How the Fight to Make America's Highways Safer Went Off Course." By Malcolm Gladwell. *The New Yorker*, June 11, 2001 (pp. 50–61).

VISIBLE PURPOSES, AUDIENCES, AND CONTEXTS

Visible Purposes

When should you use visual strategies for argument instead of or in addition to written or oral strategies? Whenever it is appropriate to your purpose and when the visual strategies support your purpose.

Like writing and speaking, visual communications and the purposes they can fulfill are complex and interesting because—they draw on what we know about the world because we have bodies and because we grow up in cultures. Consider how the following characteristics of visual texts shape possible purposes:

- In our culture, photographs and drawings of people can seem automatically to carry more emotion than writing. We respond because we know or can imagine what it is like to have the expression and be in the body posture shown. Including photographs or drawings in a written composition can thus attach emotions and bodily sensations to the writing—but do be alert to how different audiences can respond in very different ways.

- When we see photographs and realistic illustrations, we see and assume much more than we often are aware because of our knowledge about people and culture. We make judgments about people's ages and character and relationships, about when and where photographs were taken, and so on. These are good reasons to check how your intended audiences understand any photographs or illustrations you are considering for a composition. How we respond to photographs and illustrations also suggests that we can use them to lead audiences to think of particular times and places and of the associations they have with those times and places.

- Often when people say "image," they think only of paintings or photographs. But consider technical illustrations, charts and graphs, logos, and so on. Technical illustrations or photographs are designed to show us only the details we need to understand a process or machine. Charts and graphs show us the relations that their composers want us to see among numbers or other data. When they compose logos (the plural of "logo"), designers try to compress into them the values they want audiences to associate with a company. Each of these kinds of visual communication has purposes that can help you with particular communications you produce.

- When we learn to write, we rarely learn about visual potentials of writing. We do understand differences between handwritten and printed documents: The former seem more personal, and we often make judgments about people based on their handwriting (for example, how do you feel about the letter *i* when the dot above it is a circle or a heart?). Printed documents have the feel of being formal and professional and so distanced from us. But what about differences in the typefaces and colors you can use on a page? Like photographs and illustrations, typefaces and color can add emotional associations to a page (and, as with photographs and illustrations, this means you should always test your choices with audiences). Typefaces and color also can help with the logos of a page, helping readers differentiate levels of argument on it. Much of this chapter will help you make such choices.

In this chapter, we focus primarily on how you can use visual elements of pages (print or screen) to produce arguments. We consider the compositional strategies of posters and photographs; we look at comics and how words and drawings or photographs can work together to achieve purposes that either alone cannot.

Visible Audiences

I am 55 years old as I write this (this is Anne, one of your authors), and my eyes are different than they were when I was 20. I am one of those people you see in the aisle at the supermarket trying to read the small type on the sides of vitamins. I move the bottles nearer and farther, and eventually end up quite close—closer than my glasses can handle so I look out from underneath my lenses. I am one of those people you—who are most likely not 55 years old—should have in mind when you design visual communication for general or older audiences. If you assume that anyone can read what you design because you can, you might leave me out.

So even though writing and visual communication are the same in that you rarely see your audiences at the time they engage with your productions, there are additional attentions you need to give to your audiences when you design visual communications.

I've already mentioned eyes—and their age-bound abilities—but also consider how different audiences respond to different photographs and drawings. Not too many years ago, a software company producing page layout software put a graphic on screen while the software was opening; the graphic included the symbol at the top left of this column, the circle with perpendicular lines over it, which you might sometimes see if you use page layout applications. When a book, poster, or other text is printed on a press in hundreds or thousands of copies, its pages are often printed on paper that is larger than the document's final size and then trimmed. (This is how we get pages that have photographs that run off the edge of a page: The photograph "bleeds" off the edge of the page as it is designed to do, and then that bleed is cut away when the page is trimmed to its final size.) The symbol on this page is a registration mark that printers use to ensure that pages are all aligned properly up and down when they go to trim big stacks of the pages.

The point of all this information is that many people who bought the software we've just described complained about the registration mark because they didn't know what it was. Christians complained that the software company was profaning the cross; non-Christians complained that the software company was trying to force Christianity down their throats. Were these audiences for the software being too sensitive? Were they just stupid?

No.

You can never expect others to know everything you know—just as you hope others do not expect you to know everything they do. Judging what others value is also a dicey proposition: Even when you disagree, you probably would like others to respect what you value and not to call your values stupid or not worthy of care. Look back at the list of conditions that make argument possible; if you want arguments that do indeed engage you with others, you do need to respect their beliefs and values.

Because we cannot often predict the associations others will have with the photographs or drawings we use, it is crucial when you are making decisions about using photographs or drawings to test them with your intended audiences. Ask people what associations or ideas come up for them as they look at the photographs or illustrations or the colors you're considering. You can learn if audiences think the graphics are too childish for them, incomprehensible, or potentially distracting from your purposes.

As you design and produce visual communications, think of audiences as people with beliefs, values, and opinions you want to engage, not to alienate.

Visible Contexts

Like writing but unlike speaking, you never or rarely get to be there when audiences see visual communications you have made. And so you have to be imaginative as you produce communication that is primarily visual. Imagine the moment when others see what you produce—but also get out there observing how others look at similar productions. Find people from your audience who will help you test your productions in the contexts where they'll be seen.

One of the biggest—and most avoidable—failures of visual communication is communication that people can't see because it's been poorly designed for its context. Have you ever noticed road signs that were impossible to read as you drove by at 60 mph because they were detailed and pretty—rather than large and simple? Most failures, however, are the ones you don't see because they are easy to overlook. The next time you pass that wall on your campus or those telephone poles plastered with announcements, notice how many of the announcements you don't notice—and pay attention to how the ones that do grab your eyes do their work. If you make posters or flyers, test one (before you print 400) by hanging it in a place where it would be hung and ask someone from your intended audience to walk by: Does the person even see it? Posters and flyers are seen by people walking by 5, 6, or 10 feet away: There must be something large—really large—on the page that can catch their attention. If your page has a single feature that interests audiences from a distance, they will come closer to read the more detailed information in smaller type.

For visual communications like signs, posters, and flyers, there's an aspect of context that writings and talks don't have to work with: Signs, posters, and flyers are placed where they compete with other signs, posters, and flyers. For them to be noticeable, they have to stand out against the background of all the others. This is where you need the principle of contrast, which we discuss in this chapter. Consider the strategies for creating contrast to help you design communication that others can see.

Other visual communications—or communications that require some visual attentions, such as any printed or onscreen piece of communication—will be seen in the same contexts as people reading books or magazines. Go back and look at what we wrote about context in the writing chapter for encouragement and ideas. Most importantly, research contexts.

Or make contexts. If you have a poster, in what unexpected places can you put it so that people will see it? On the ground? Tucked into visible but uncluttered corners?

Always consider how you can shape the contexts in which your productions are seen.

TO ANALYZE

■ **DISCUSS with others:** Bring your favorite or an interesting picture postcard to class. In groups of two or three, look at someone else's postcard—but don't look at the back.

List as much as you can about the photograph on the postcard based just on what you see. When and where do you think the photograph was taken? What can you say about who or what is in it?

After about 5 minutes, share your observations with the whole group. Tell why you make the guesses you did about the postcards. (Turn over the postcard to see what information is there—how close were you?)

Were you surprised by how much everyone could say about the postcards? What can you learn from this about how we see and understand photographs?

A STATEMENT OF PURPOSE FOR A PHOTO ESSAY

Remember that in a statement of purpose, you bring together your initial sense of purpose with your knowledge about your audience and the context in which your audience encounters your text. By doing this, you sharpen your sense of what it is you hope to achieve with your text, and so you set yourself up to make crisper decisions about the strategies you will use.

FOR EXAMPLE

In addition to writing a paper based on his research, Ajay has an assignment to compose a short photo essay using his research; his first focused thinking on this assignment is on the below in his statement of purpose.

Ajay's design plan for the photo essay is on pages 127–128 and the photo essay is on pages 129–130.

Statement of Purpose for a Photo Essay

My audience includes my classmates and my teacher, and the context will be class on the next to the last day of classes (yay!) when we're going to post our photoessays on the wall. Everyone's going to be a bit wiped out from the semester and from having finished our final papers and doing our presentations, so I think everyone's looking forward to having a little fun experimenting with pictures.

But this is still graded (the professor made that very clear) based on the following qualities: The photoessay has to grow out of our research paper/oral presentation and has to creatively use at least four photographs (and captions if we want) to make a point tied to our paper/presentation. It also has to be understandable to others in class with no help from us. (The professor said the essays can be printed or online and that on the day they are due, we will post them on the wall or move from computer to computer to look at them.)

So part of my purpose is to meet those expectations—but then I also have to have a purpose specifically tied to the photoessay. As I was imagining what I could do with my argument from my research paper about students as customers, I tried to picture what students as customers looked like—and I realized how hard it is to show this. I mean, it's easy to picture someone buying a soda—but what does it mean to buy a grade? Okay, I know you can picture handing money over for a grade, but such a photograph would look weird, wouldn't it? Wouldn't such a photograph sort of creep us out because we would know that buying grades isn't right?

I need to think a bit more on how to make this work, but I think my purpose is to use photographs to show just how weird it is to try to photograph students being consumers as students—and by doing that, to suggest that (while we may try to act as customers when we are students), the reality of what we do shows that we can't really purchase a grade, a diploma, or an education.

I'm hoping that I can do all that but also maybe have my photo essay seem a little funny or weird, to work for it being almost the end of classes.

VISIBLE ETHOS, LOGOS, AND PATHOS

As with written and oral communication, visual texts have their own particular strategies we can use to compose ethos, logos, and pathos, strategies that have developed over time and through the shaping of particular cultures. Keep in mind, then, that what we offer you here about ethos, pathos, and logos in visual arrangements is appropriate for arguments that meet audience expectations in the early 21st century United States.

In visual communication—as in the general U.S. approach to how we use space and time—efficiency is now valued. Historians of visual design argue that the rise of efficiency as a value in visual communication paralleled the linked rise of industry and advertising in the 20th century. As industrialists strove to produce as many objects as possible as quickly as possible, they also needed to produce consumers for those objects. Advertising was born to encourage people to desire things and to desire them quickly, and visual communication in general therefore took on the values of quickness and directness.

What we present in the sections on the logos of arrangement in visual communication, especially, will help you compose layouts whose order supports the efficient communication of information, but keep in mind that ethos and pathos can also be visually shaped into efficiency. A photograph, for example, can show a person having a single clear emotional response to an event or can indicate more complex emotional responses. You can visually compose an ethos that shows you to be singularly focused on efficiency or you can compose an ethos that shows you to value generosity as well.

Because efficiency has been so highly valued, it can seem not to be a value but simply how things are and always ought to be. Many books that teach about visual communication teach layout principles as though efficiency—with its concordant layout values of coherence, unity, and a clear hierarchy of informative elements—is the value that should underlie all choices in layout. In the pages that follow, we hope to teach you the ability to use those values well, precisely because they are the values many of your audiences will hold. But as you read through the next pages, keep in mind that many other possible values can go into how you compose ethos, logos, and pathos on a page or screen.

Because visual communication has such strong ties to advertising, many people think that advertising is all that visual communication can do. It doesn't take much looking—whether back in time or in different places in the present—to see visual texts that use other values to shape ethos, logos, and pathos: Look at stained glass windows, weather charts, biology textbooks, tattoos, or the pages of Bibles or Korans to see those other values at work. We challenge you—both as a composer and as audience for others' compositions—to look in visual texts for ethos, logos, and pathos that advocate values such as compassion, respect for complex thinking, diversity, simplicity, and self-awareness.

Precisely because we have grown up in a culture in which such values are rarely taught through visual communication, they may look odd to us when we see them made visible. But if we wish to see more of such values in our communications, we need to make those values visible ourselves, and we need to show generosity toward the designs of others who are trying to make those values present.

ETHOS IN PHOTOGRAPHS

Which of the photographs on this page draws your attention? How have the elements been arranged or treated so that you notice one element first and then another second or third?

Photographs tend to direct our attention to other people and objects, to the "outside" world. In that way, even if they are about family members or intimate events, photographs resemble scientific essays. We would like them to show us the world just as it is.

How then could there be any ethos? What in these photographs asks you to think about the character of the photographer?

Along with showing us people or objects, photographs (even those made with automatic cameras) show us the photographer's decisions. They show us

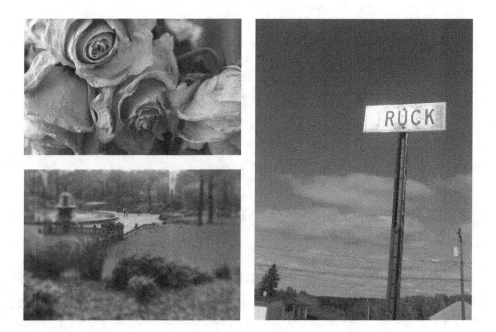

the position the photographer chose for the camera, the exposure time, and the use or not of a flash or filters—and they show us that the photographer thought there was something worth photographing.

Learning to interpret photographs, then, means acknowledging that such decisions have gone into them. Learning to interpret photographs means listing the decisions—the strategies used to take them—and asking what they tell us about the photographer and what the photographer wants us to see.

For photography, such a line of questioning matters more than for other media because photographs ask us to become the photographer. Whenever we see a photograph, we see it from the position the photographer did. Every photograph asks us to see the world as though we were seeing it through the photographer's lens and through the series of judgments the photographer made in setting up the shot and then working with the photograph because of how much can now be done digitally. In looking at any photograph, then, we need to ask why a photographer wants us to see a particular scene arranged as it is.

What sort of person would look at the world—would make the particular choices about framing and displaying—in the way the photograph asks us to look?

WHAT YOU ALREADY KNOW BECAUSE YOU LOOK—AND A PROFESSIONAL ETHOS

If you find rest or distraction in flipping through TV channels, you can probably tell, almost immediately, whether you've hit an infomercial or a network series. Without thinking, you probably register the difference in production values—in the lighting and in the quality of sound and the set—between the two genres because you've seen so many different kinds of TV shows that you've learned almost automatically what looks polished and professional and what doesn't.

Two useful-to-understanding-visual-texts qualities reside in your ability to distinguish between infomercials and other shows.

First, you Make Judgments About the Quality of Different Visual Texts all the Time—

often without being aware of the judgments. If you want to start producing your own visual texts or being even more alert to how such texts have the effects they do, noticing your existing judgments and tastes about visual texts can help you. The vocabulary and concepts we offer in this book can support you in such work.

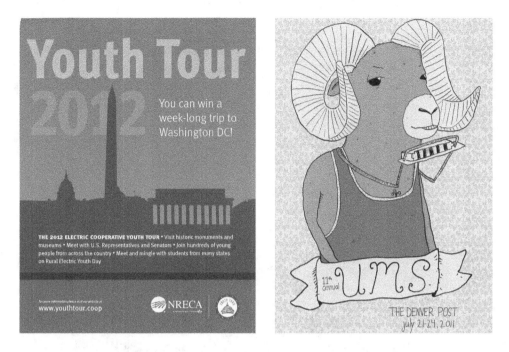

Second, the Qualities of "Polished and Professional" are Valued in our Day and Place.

As a culture, we often value communicative visual texts if they get to the point efficiently and demonstrate that their composers know how to use their materials well. A director who lets a microphone show in a scene or an actor who speaks in a monotone are the stuff of comedy for us. When texts do look "polished and professional," we tend to place a certain trust in the makers of the text and hence in the persuasiveness of the text—in most contexts.

Producers of visual texts can rhetorically use the distinction between what is considered professional and what isn't. Precisely because alt bands want to look outside the mainstream, posters for their shows are often hand drawn and, in comparison to a poster for a Katy Perry concert, they can look gentle and edgy rather than slick and mechanical.

Danny Gregory drew the page on next page, showing pictures of his son, Jack. The page comes from a (published) diary in which Gregory used drawing and writing to reflect on and come to some understanding about his life. When Jack was a baby, Gregory's wife had been run over by a subway train and paralyzed from the waist down. Gregory writes that his book "is about how art and New York City saved my life." Gregory's pages do not look "professional" because they are handwritten, but they are handwritten precisely because computer-generated pages—while professional looking—would not at all convey the heart- and hand-tied emotions Gregory needs.

As you analyze and produce visual texts, you need to learn what is generally considered professional looking, so that you can produce professional texts and can decide when nonprofessional strategies are useful.

TO ANALYZE

■ **Observe, then write:** Because "professional" is such a noticed quality in visual texts of our time and place, it is useful for you to be able to say explicitly what qualities make different texts professional or not.

Collect at least 10 samples of a certain kind of visual text. For example, you could collect examples of brochures, flyers for events on your campus, business cards, PowerPoint presentations, or resumes. For each, list any adjectives you would attach to the ethos of the composers of the sample. Do you think the composers present themselves and their work professionally? Do they seem friendly and inviting or formal and distant? Do they seem cheerful or neutral? Also decide which of your samples look most professional and which look less.

Write down the qualities of the different texts that encourage you to make your judgments. As you look and judge, consider how the samples use type as well as the quality of writing, the kind of paper used, any use of color, the size of graphics, what any photographs depict, and so on.

As you work through this chapter, you will learn other terms and concepts to use in adding to your judgments. Your lists of what visual decisions help persuade audiences to see a particular ethos in a text can help you analyze visual texts in more detail in the future—but they can also help you if you ever need to produce any of these kinds of texts in the future. Any time you need to produce a kind of text that is new to you or that you've seen many times but have never made yourself, it is useful to collect and analyze a wide range of examples of that kind of text.

PATHOS IN PHOTOGRAPHS

Obvious Pathos

When we see people in a photograph, we might identify with them: We understand the situation they are in through our own experiences. When we see happy (or sad or angry) people, we can feel similar emotions in response because we know the emotions ourselves. It is probably an obvious point to you, but this is why advertisements for cars or cookies show happy rather than perplexed people: The advertisers want you to believe you too will be happy in possession of that car or cookie.

Less Obvious Pathos

The two photographs above right are also composed to evoke emotional response from us.

When we see only part of an object, we mentally fill in what isn't shown, which can get us more engaged with the object—especially when it also takes a little time to understand what the photograph is showing us. A photograph of a storm might invoke memories of being caught in the rain, but it might also invoke the feelings of summer afternoon beauty. The context in which you see such a photograph—printed on a Christmas card or on a postcard from someone's overseas trip—and your specific cultural background will shape your own specific response.

Neither of the photographs on the right are meant to evoke the emotions of happiness, sadness, anger, or fear, but they do evoke bodily feelings— and therefore can be used rhetorically. To analyze and use the potential pathos of photographs, don't be afraid to name the emotions or bodily responses you yourself feel—just be alert to how the different backgrounds of others might lead them to respond differently.

PATHOS AND COLOR

When you analyze or choose colors for communication, keep in mind that we respond to colors because of our experiences within both the natural and cultural worlds—but our associations with color are not fixed. For example, we might associate light blue with a warm summer sky or the glow of winter ice. Black is the color people in the United States associate with death; in some Asian countries, white is the color for mourning. How people understand or respond to colors thus depends on the contexts in which they see the colors.

The colors of a photograph or page layout contribute substantially to our emotional responses. Our responses are not random but instead have much to do with what we have learned to associate with different colors.

To analyze and use color rhetorically, you need not only your cultural knowledge but also some vocabulary. "Color" is analyzed in terms of hue, saturation, and brightness:

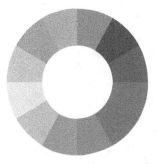

Hue

"Hue" describes what most of us think of as color: When you name the hue of a color, you are saying whether it is red or blue or yellow or.... Hues are often represented in a wheel, as above: You can use those that are next or close to each other on the wheel when you want color schemes that seem harmonious; hues that are opposite have the most contrast.

Saturation

"Saturation" describes how much of a hue is present in a color. In the colored bar directly above the colors toward the left end are unsaturated; they have no blue in them. As you move to the right in the bar, the colors become more and more saturated: They have more and more blue in them.

Brightness

"Brightness" (sometimes also referred to as "value") describes how light or dark a color is. In the colored bar directly above the color at the extreme left has no brightness; the color at the extreme right is as bright as it can be.

Hue, saturation, and brightness are present in all colors. In the three examples here, the leftmost color chip is red hued with as much saturation and brightness as possible. The color chip in the middle is not very bright but is still a saturated red hue. The color chip on the right has a blue hue, is fairly bright, but is not very saturated.

Analyzing the Rhetorical Effects of Color

The two posters to the left are the same except for their colors. The poster's purpose is to persuade people not to use dissection in biology classes. The poster's composers decided to use photographs instead of drawings or technical illustrations; they decided to use a photograph of a television personality instead of a scientist, teacher, or student; they used informal typefaces and an informal layout, with very few and large shapes.

The poster's composers thus seem to want to address their audience in a nonthreatening and humorous way about the topic—and so the poster's visual presentation should almost tickle the audience into considering the topic. Which colors best support that overall purpose?

The first example uses bright and saturated yellow and green. The second uses less bright and less saturated blues and browns. Which uses hues that you associate with humor? Which poster seems to pull you in more, and why, in terms of color? Which do you think uses color appropriately for the poster's purpose? (Notice that were you just to discuss hue you couldn't account for how the colors work fully. You need to consider brightness and saturation together with hue.)

TO ANALYZE

- **Write:** Choose any poster in this chapter. Write a short rhetorical analysis in which you explain how its overall colors (be sure to address hue, saturation, and brightness) support (or not) the purpose of the poster.

- **Discuss with others:** Discuss our use of color in this textbook. We've tried to differentiate sections and functions of the book through our use of color—color as logos—and we've also used color to (we hope) give the book appeal and depth to your eyes and to give it a look that is up-to-date—color as pathos. How effective do you think our color choices have been for these purposes? What would you change, and why?

TO ANALYZE: PATHOS AND COLOR

- **Observe and then write:** The "Eat at Bill's" examples on the right use hue, saturation, and brightness differently to create their effects. Apply one or two adjectives to each example: hard, soft, inviting, exciting, shouting, cheery, loud, energetic, quiet, and so on. Make a chart like the one below to connect the adjectives with how the color qualities are used. Because your observations depend on your own associations with color, the chart can help you decide how to use color to achieve effects for audiences that share your general background.

Adjective	Color Qualities
hard	the colors have the strongest possible contrast in hue and brightness but have similar saturation

■ **Write:** Use the discussion of pathos in photographs as well as what you've learned about color to write a short rhetorical analysis comparing the emotional effects
of two of the photographs below. First, describe how you respond to each photograph, and then describe how you think what is shown in each photograph shapes your response (be sure to mention the kinds of associations you have with what is shown in the photographs); then describe how the colors contribute to your response.

Compare your analysis with those of others in class: Do you bring the same associations to what is in the photographs as well as to the colors? When you find someone with different responses, work together to figure out how you have come to your different understandings.

THE PATHOS OF TYPE

Typography is the study of how letter shapes—on paper or on screen—work functionally and rhetorically. You need to know about typography to compose effective visual compositions with words.

In some visual compositions, such as school papers, type should not, by convention, call attention to itself: Such type should be designed so readers heed your ideas and not the letters' appearance. Such type design results from convention and our bodily practices. When you are told to turn in double-spaced pages in Times 12 point size, for example, it is because this is a typeface and a size of type that—when double spaced—many people have become accustomed to reading in school papers.

In other visual compositions—brochures, posters, webpages—we have learned to expect that type will evoke emotion and feeling. We expect to see typefaces that look boisterous, edgy, or loud because they work with the composition's other elements to create an overall effect in support of some purpose.

If you look at pages printed in earlier centuries, they look different from those printed today. In hand-calligraphed manuscripts, pages have large ornate letters. These manuscripts were usually meant to be read slowly aloud. The purpose of the type wasn't to ease the speed of an individual reading alone and quietly, which is the purpose of functional typography today.

How does Type Evoke Feeling and Emotions?

Letters' curves and straight lines can be arranged to suggest bodies or abstract shapes. Type can be:

Describing Lettershapes

Knowing the names of parts of letters and of the qualities of different typefaces can help you differentiate among typefaces, which can help you make thoughtful rhetorical choices.

A fundamental distinction with typefaces is that between serif and sans serif typefaces. Serifed typefaces have little lines at the ends of the letter strokes; sans serifed have none ("sans" means "without" in French). In the United States, serif typefaces are considered more formal and easier to read than sans serif typefaces.

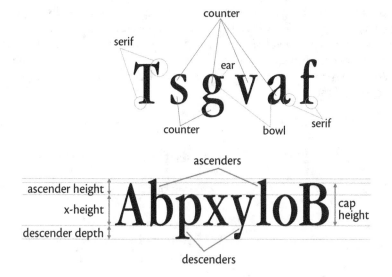

Styles of Type

Typefaces often come in sets with lettershapes that have the same basic structure but different vertical orientations and visual weights. When you want to compose a page or screen on which the elements look harmonious because they look similar, use the different styles of one typeface.

Minion

Minion Italic

Minion Semibold

Minion Semibold Italic

Minion Bold

Minion Bold Italic

Minion Black

Categories of Type

The following chart describes categories of typefaces. If you are deciding which typefaces to use in your compositions—or trying to figure out why someone else chose the particular typefaces of a layout you are analyzing—If you are deciding which typefaces to use in your compositions—or trying to figure out why someone else chose the particular typefaces of a layout you are analyzing—distinguish first between *typefaceswe see in books and other situations where we have to read at length* and *typefaces that are used to emphasize short passages like titles or a line or two*. When you produce visual communication, divide typefaces into one of these two categories first. When you produce visual communication, divide typefaces into one of these two categories first.

> the arrow means: *look on the next pages to learn more about this category*

TYPEFACES FOR EXTENDED READING

Oldstyle

This category goes back to the 16th century when people were designing typefaces for the relatively new printing press and were paying attention to creating regularity among letters' appearance. Oldstyle typefaces always have serifs and usually wide and rounded lettershapes. Notice how the serifs at the tops of the letters are usually slanted, and that the strokes are not all the same weight but have some transition from thick to thin. These typefaces look formal.

Modern

"Modern" typefaces were modern in the 17th century when mechanization picked up its pace and printing technologies supported people's desires for more precision and clarity. New printing technologies allowed type designers to make typefaces with very thin lines. Modern typefaces always have serifs—but their serifs don't slant. Modern typefaces mix very thick and very thin strokes, whose contrast can give them an elegant feeling.

Slab Serif

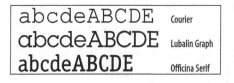

In the early 19th century Napoleon invaded Egypt. His army included historians and artists who brought back samples of Egyptian art and writing to France. This started a craze in Europe for all things Egyptian—including typefaces that looked like they came from the Nile area. These typefaces were originally called "Egyptienne." Notice how the serifs are straight slabs with no curves softening how the serif joins the body of the letter. These typefaces often look informal.

Sans Serif

In the 19th century, type designers wanted typefaces that looked modern and up-to-date to echo the streamlined mechanical wonders that were filling western factories and streets. Note how the lines in most of these typefaces are all the same weight, and that there is no ornamentation to the letters. These are straightforward-looking typefaces.

Six-of-One

abcdeABCDE	Optima
abcdeABCDE	Poppl-Laudatio
abcdeABCDE	Zapf Humanist

In the "for-extended-reading" category, you will occasionally find a typeface that has mixed features of serifed and sans serifed faces, like the ones above, with varying weights in their strokes. These faces tend to have an informal feeling.

PICTURES & SYMBOLS

	Animal
	Good Dog Bones
	Insect
	SchneeFlaken
	Sugar Coma
	Zapf Dingbats

Instead of lettershapes, these typefaces have pictures or symbols attached to each letter. These characters can be used as bullets or paragraph markers or decorative elements or… Be creative with them.

TYPEFACES FOR AT-A-GLANCE EMPHASIS

Novelty

ABCDEABCDE	Almonte Snow
ABCDEABCDE	Baby Jeepers
abcdeABCDE	Bailey's Car
ⒶⒷⒸⒹⒺ	Dialtone
ABCDEABCDE	Elwood
abcdeabcde	Jingopop
ABCDE	Shrapnel

Novelty typefaces are usually cute and lively; you might associate them with circus posters or old-fashioned advertising.

Script

Script faces look as though they were hand-drawn with a pen. Sometimes they look drawn by someone with a long-practiced hand and sometimes by a three-year-old. They can therefore give a feeling of relaxed elegance to a page—or of playfulness.

From Extended-Reading Faces

Sometimes a typeface intended for blocks of extended reading is modified to make the face bolder for using as a headline, title, or other function. If you use one of these typefaces with the typeface from which it was developed, the look will generally be harmonious because the lettershapes echo each other—but do not use these typefaces for long text blocks.

Black Letter

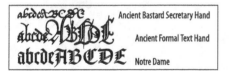

You now see black letter typefaces in goth settings, but these typefaces go back to the Middle Ages, when monks and other scribes used quill pens to write. These typefaces can look formal and elegant—or dark and oppressive—so use them carefully.

Grunge

As you might expect from their name, grunge faces appeared with grunge music: The typefaces and the music share the same quick, hard-edged garage aesthetic.

Other

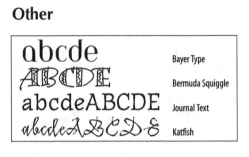

Because typefaces in the "at-a-glance emphasis" category are used in so many different kinds of documents, designers develop new typefaces all the time, and sometimes they don't fit into the other divisions of this category. These typefaces tend to be playful and energetic.

THE LOGOS OF ARRANGING VISUAL ELEMENTS

Some use "shaping someone else's attention" as a definition of rhetoric—which helps us consider aspects of logos in visual composition. Because we see where we focus our eyes, seeing is very much about attention. If we are asked to put our visual attention on one thing, we often miss other things going on. (Look back to the description on page 83 of how much we can miss seeing because of how we focus.)

And so: When you make any kind of visual layout, you work to draw your audience's eyes—and hence their attention and thinking—through your presentation in a certain order: You want the order to persuade them to take the action, think about the matters, or have the experience you hope they will. Composing visual layouts, you order your elements (alphabetic symbols, photographs, drawings, shapes, and so on) that your audience follows visually—and hence conceptually—to arrive where you want them to.

This all means, then, that your visual compositions must be arranged:

Questions (in order) that help you arrange your visual compositions:

1

Your visual compositions generally should have a limited number of elements so that your audience is not overwhelmed by detail and can see the point of your composition.

What elements do you need to include in your composition?

2

Your visual compositions should have a visual hierarchy— a visual path—that indicates to your audience what to look at first, what to look at second, what third, and so on … .

►What visual hierarchy—created from contrast and repetition— supports your purposes?

3

Your visual compositions must look like a set of unified pieces so that your audience understands that the pieces are meant to work together to make one main argument.

► What visual unity—created from repetition—can you create?

THE LOGOS OF ARRANGING VISUAL ELEMENTS
HOW MANY ELEMENTS TO INCLUDE

Which of the two layouts above feels to your eyes as though all the elements come together into one unified layout?

We're hoping you agree that the layout on the left—with a limited number of elements and a consequent visual simplicity—requires less effort from eyes and mind: When we look at it, we feel as though our eyes can take it in all at once.

With the layout on the right, however, our eyes feel pulled all over the place, not quite sure where to stop and focus. It is consequently hard to understand the relationships among the elements of the layout.

Audiences comprehend layouts like that on the left more easily because they do not require the audiences to make much visual effort. That is why the layouts seem straightforward: Audiences can look and easily see what element you want them to see first, which second, and which third; there's no need for them to figure out which element you intend to be fourth in their attentions, or fifth, or sixth, or seventh … .

Imagine you've brought home a pet rat and you have a choice of printed instructions to read about caring for the rat. Which of the two rat examples above look like instructions you could read easily and quickly? Which looks like you could find what you needed without much trouble?

The first sample has three elements—a rat, a series of lines (which you might interpret as a block of text), and cheese; the other example has those same elements plus 8 or 10 or 12 more. The second example might look as though it has more information, but could you find out on it quickly what to do when your rat starts nibbling its way through your clothes?

As you produce visual compositions, notice that many layouts use a limited number of elements to achieve their purposes. Flip through the examples in this chapter, look at the poster examples, and look at examples in magazines to analyze how many elements layouts tend to use.

When you start producing visual compositions, limit yourself to three to four elements (one picture, perhaps, a title, and one text block). This helps you to learn how to control the relationships among the elements so you can achieve your purposes straightforwardly. Doing this also shows your audience that your purpose is straightforward.

- You can have more than three to four elements, but use the strategies of repetition and proximity (which we discuss in the next pages) to make different elements look closely related. This reduces the apparent number of elements.

- Simple layouts are conventional in the sense that we see lots of them in magazines and on television. This means that, like most audiences we will address, we are accustomed to not having to do much work in figuring out visual compositions.

THE LOGOS OF ARRANGING VISUAL ELEMENTS
CREATING A VISUAL HIERARCHY

For each set of page thumbnails below, circle the composition that looks to you to have a clear visual path for your eye to follow. That is, in which of the two compositions do you have no question as to which element you are to look at first, which second, and so on?

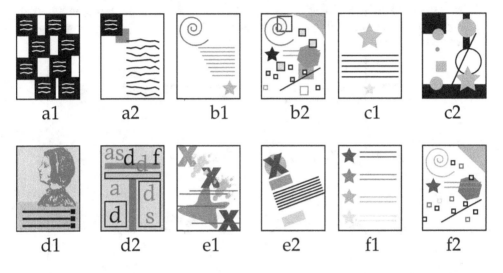

We're guessing you circled a2, b1, c1, d1, e2, and f1. In each of those, you should be able to tell which element you are intended to notice first, which second, and so on. In those layouts, in other words, there is a clear visual hierarchy. You can see immediately which elements are given most visual weight and which least.

Contrast—a design principle we discuss in the next pages—helps one element stand out against a background of repeated elements, while the repetition creates visual unity.

■ Notice that the element that first draws your attention is usually largest and darkest. When you start building visual hierarchies, begin by making obvious contrasts.

■ Notice how the elements you are to see first are often in the top left or top middle. Because we learned to read from top to bottom and left to right, we are accustomed to start reading at top left. Use that to your advantage to create a clear and unambiguous visual starting point on a page.

■ Notice how the number of elements helps you see a path. As we recommended on the preceding pages, limiting yourself to three to four elements can help you create compositions that are easy for your audiences to comprehend.

THE LOGOS OF ARRANGING VISUAL ELEMENTS
CONTRAST AND REPETITION FOR VISUAL HIERARCHY

Notice in the examples on the facing page that, in general, one element (at the top left or center) attracts your attention first, telling your eyes where to start looking. Creating one element that stands out by using contrast is easiest to do by thinking about contrast analytically, if—when you produce visual compositions—you describe in words to yourself how you create contrast. The following illustrations should help you figure this out; circle the one in each set that has one element that stands out.

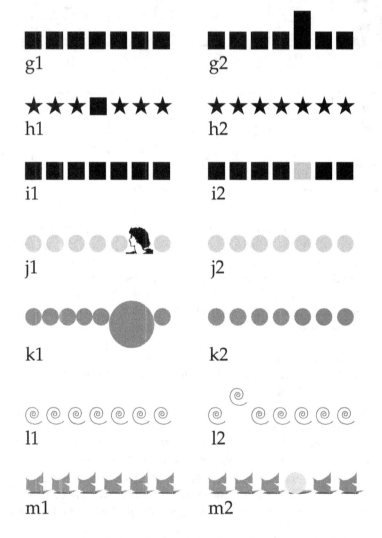

We're guessing you circled g2, h1, i2, j1, k1, l2, and m2. In each of those sets, one element contrasts with all the others.

The element contrasted because of how its **size**, **shape**, **color**, **position**, or **level of abstraction** contrasted with all the other elements. ("Level of abstraction" refers to what is going on in the "j" set: Notice how the abstract shapes create a background against which the more "realistic" face can stand out.) Contrast draws our attention to parts of visual compositions (although contrast isn't a principle for visual composition alone. Musical composers play with contrasts of tone or rhythm to create aural interest just as writers vary their voice, rhythm, or word sound).

When you compose, attend to this odd aspect of visual composition:

> No single element can stand out unless the other elements blend together, appearing all the same.

When you want to create contrast, therefore, attend carefully to creating a background of sameness against which an element can stand out. This means also that you can't make too many things different—or none will stand out.

THE LOGOS OF ARRANGING VISUAL ELEMENTS
CREATING VISUAL UNITY THROUGH REPETITION

In our time, we value unity and coherence. Newspapers put similar articles together into sections (world news, entertainment, sports), people dress in coordinated outfits, car colors do not vary much, and we expect politicians to base their decisions on a coherent set of values. Just as in those situations, unity and coherence extend to visual compositions. Unity in a visual composition isn't magic. You can design unified layouts by attending to certain concrete visual principles.

Circle the thumbnail layouts below that look to you as though all the elements are unified and built into a coherent visual composition.

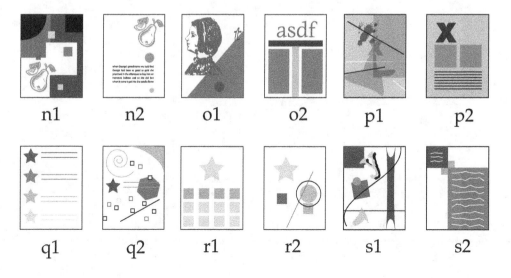

n1   n2   o1   o2   p1   p2

q1   q2   r1   r2   s1   s2

We're guessing that you circled n2, o2, p2, q1, r1, and s2. In each of those layouts, the different elements are visually linked with each other, and each element repeats something from the other elements.

Elements can repeat the **size**, **shape**, **color**, **position**, **alignment**, or **level of abstraction** of other elements. Notice that these are almost all the same qualities used to create contrast.

Repetition of elements' qualities creates visual relationship between the elements just as when you meet a friend's sister and you can tell the two are related because their faces look alike. Repetition matters in writing or speech-making, too: You show an audience you are staying on topic by using the same or similar words, phrases, and tone of voice throughout—except when you use contrast to emphasize what you want people to remember.

Repetition therefore serves two purposes in layouts:

1. Repetition creates the level of sameness against which some elements can stand out.

2. Repetition helps create the sense of unity that ties the elements together visually.

Repeating Alignment

Of all the elements you can repeat, alignment most often gets overlooked—but alignment always matters for creating a unified page. Each composition on the left above follows the guidelines we've described on the preceding pages: Each has only a few elements and strong contrast in size and shape, with a background created by color repetition. Notice, though, how the right-hand composition of each pair looks more orderly and is aligned with at least one (if not more) other element.

In the illustrations in the third column, we have added the lines to which each composition's elements align: Every element aligns with at least one other element. Alignment is thus a strategy of logos, for creating compositions whose elements have an obvious visual relationship because they all line up with each other.

Two kinds of Alignment

▧ **"Backbone" alignment.** The composition with the star and the one with the pointing blue hand have central alignment. It's as though all the elements hang off a single line, like a backbone, at page center. When you choose one line on a page as the backbone and hang everything off it, you compose layouts with a high degree of unity.

▧ **Alignment with the edges of the page.** Notice that the elements in the aligned compositions align not only with each other but also with the edges of the page: Every element is positioned vertically or horizontally, and so all the elements of these thumbnail compositions—including the pages they are on—are aligned. You may think, "Well, duh… I've been doing this all my life because this is what comes out of the printer," but if you consider this kind of alignment as a choice, you can use it alertly and purposefully in your visual compositions.

THE LOGOS OF TYPE ARRANGEMENT

The same strategies for making shapes stand out in a composition apply to typefaces: A background of sameness enables you to emphasize the words you want to emphasize.

For example, imagine that the thumbnail sketches of flyers above were posted together on a wall. Which are most likely to catch your eye? Which help you most clearly see—and differentiate—the information being presented?

Notice how clear differences in size and shape of the letterforms help you more easily see differences in what the words are conveying. Notice also how differences in color (here, whether a typeface looks black or gray) also help you see and differentiate among the elements of the layouts: This helps you more clearly tell what the flyer is about.

As we've just described, many of the same strategies for creating contrast with shapes apply to typefaces—and, on the next pages, we'll write about these strategies as well as about a few additional features of typefaces you can use to help you build contrast (and, so, clear visual hierarchy) when you are working with type:

category

size

shape

position

color

weight

When you start to produce visual compositions and try to choose and use different typefaces together, choose faces that have a lot of strong contrast—and then you want to arrange the typefaces so that the contrast is clear to your audience.

How the Different *Categories* of Type can Help you Choose Typefaces with Strong Contrast

Earlier in this chapter, you learned that typefaces can be divided into two large categories: those for extended reading and those for short blocks of text. You learned further that those categories can also be separated into serif and sans serif and then novelty, grunge, and so on. When you are choosing typefaces for strong contrast, a handy—but not foolproof—rule of thumb is to choose typefaces from different categories. That is, you can generally count on a serif and a sans serif contrasting well (but rarely will the different kinds of serifed typefaces contrast enough for you to be able to use them without some additional work).

Look at the pairs of typefaces shown above and circle the ones you think have the most contrast. Then identify the categories of those pairs to see what works for you.

Using the *Size* of Typeface to Create Contrast

Size is probably the most obvious differentiation you can make between different pieces of type. Look at the examples at the top of this column. Which of the sets of letters has the most contrast between the two letters?

As with any use of difference in type size, be sure that when you are sizing typefaces you make the contrast clear and bold; it is generally better, as you are starting out, to err on the side of more rather than less contrast. In the beginning, go for bold rather than subtle: It's easier to learn subtlety after you have the broad moves down.

Using the *Shape* of Typefaces to Create Contrast

"I have never let my schooling interfere with my education."
Mark Twain

"I have never let my schooling interfere with my education."
Mark Twain

"I have never let my schooling interfere with my education."
Mark Twain

"I have never let my schooling interfere with my education."
Mark Twain

gg gg ɡg gg

When you want to build strong contrast between two or more typefaces, look closely at how the *shapes* of individual letters contrast. This will help you choose typefaces that, on the whole, contrast strongly.

For example, look at the differences in the *g*s to the left try to describe (using the names for parts of typefaces on page 101) the differences between the letters in each of the different pairs. Then look at the phrases from Mark Twain, each of which uses the two letterfaces in one of the sets above:

Do the phrases show strong contrast between "Mark Twain" and the other words? Can you account for at least some of the contrast by the differences in the shapes of the different letters?

Using the *Position* of Type to Create Contrast

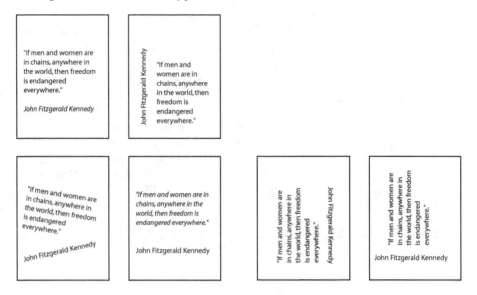

Position refers to how one piece of type is placed relative to another. In the examples at the top of this column, notice that position can also involve type's direction. Which of these examples develops the clearest contrast to your eyes—and why?

Notice that you have to make quite distinct changes in direction for this strategy to be effective.

Using the *Weights* of Typefaces to Create Contrast

This typeface is Caecilia Light.
This typeface is Caecilia.
This typeface is Caecilia Bold.
This typeface is Caecilia Heavy.

If you've chosen typefaces on a computer, you may have noticed that you can sometimes choose Roman (meaning generally that the typeface is a serif face) or light, bold, or ultra versions of one typeface. Notice, however, that in the example at the top of this column there is little contrast between the light and Roman versions or between the bold and heavy versions. If you were to use these typefaces, you would probably want to use the light and the bold versions together, or the regular face with the heavy version.

When you are using different weights of typefaces, be sure that the differences in the weights are clearly visible.

Using the *Color* of Typefaces to Create Contrast

Yet I cannot speak your tongue with ease,
No longer from China. Your stories
Stir griefs of dispersion and find
Me in simplicity of kin.
> —Shirley Geok-lin Lim

Yet I cannot speak your tongue with ease,
No longer from China. Your stories
Stir griefs of dispersion and find
Me in simplicity of kin.
> —Shirley Geok-lin Lim

Yet I cannot speak your tongue with ease,
No longer from China. Your stories
Stir griefs of dispersion and find
Me in simplicity of kin.
> —Shirley Geok-lin Lim

Color can be red, green, blue, puce, lavender, or flesh—but it can also mean the range of grays from white to black. You can apply different colors to individual letters of words to build contrast, but when you are choosing typefaces to use together, look at the "color" of the whole typeface. Designers do this by comparing paragraphs printed out in different typefaces to see how light (or dark) one typeface looks relative to another; the greater the differences in color between the typefaces as a whole, the more likely the typefaces will contrast well.

Notice how different the phrases at the top of this column look—even though the type is all set in the same size. You can use the color of type to choose typefaces that contrast well; you can also use a typeface's color to add a light or heavy mood to a visual composition.

A Note about Building Contrast with Typeface

You may have noticed you can take two approaches to building contrast with shapes:

First, you can change only one thing about a shape. For example, if you have a set of circles, you can make one of them big—but for this to work, you have to make that shape tremendously bigger for the contrast to be truly visible.

Second, you can change many things about one of the shapes: you can change its shape, size, color, and position.

The same holds for working with type:

1. You can build contrast by changing only one aspect of the type with which you are working, such as the color—but you have to make big changes for this to be visible.

2. You can build contrast by being sure the typefaces you choose take advantage of three or more of the ways to build type contrast that we've discussed in this section. If you do this, you are more likely to build effectively contrasting type.

TO ANALYZE: RHETORICAL TYPE ARRANGEMENT

■ **Write:** Write a short rhetorical analysis of the visual composition on the right. Use the evidence of the poster—its words as well as its arrangements and typefaces—to develop an idea of the audience the designer had in mind as she composed it. Characterize the audience in as much detail as you can: Describe not only the age you think characterizes the audience but also where they might live and the values and beliefs they might hold. Use evidence from the poster to support any claim you make.

These tips from Women In Media & News (WIMN), a New York-based media-monitoring, training, and advocacy group, can help you make the leap from righteous indignation to effective critique.

how to write a

PROTEST LETTER
by Jennifer L. Pozner

You flip to your local Clear Channel station to find a shock jock "joking" about where kidnappers can most easily buy nylon rope, tarps, and lye for tying up, hiding, and dissolving the bodies of little girls. Reuters run an important international news brief about a Nigerian woman sentenced to death by stoning for an alleged sexual infraction—in its "Oddly Enough" section, where typical headlines include "Unruly Taxi Drivers Sent to Charm School."

When California Democrats Loretta and Linda Sanchez became the first sisters ever to serve together in Congress, the Washington Post devotes 1,766 words in its style section to inform readers about the representatives' preferences regarding housekeeping, hairstyles, and "hootchy shoes." (Number of paragraphs focusing on the congress women's political viewpoints: one.) Nearly a million demonstrators gather in cities across the country to protest impending war on Iraq; America's top print and broadcast news outlets significantly undercount protestors' numbers...again.

So, what else is new? Sexist and biased fare is business as usual for all too many media outlets - but what do you do when hurling household objects at Dan Rather's head just isn't enough?

Be firm but polite Make your case sans insults, rants, and vulgarity. Nothing makes it easier for editors and producers to dismiss your argument than name-calling. Good idea: "Your discussion of the rape survivor's clothing and makeup was irrelevant, irresponsible, and inappropriate. Including those details blames the victim and reinforces dangerous myths about sexual assault." Bad idea: "Your reporter is a woman-hating incarnate of satan!"

Be realistic but optimistic Calling for the New York Times to transform itself into a socialist newspaper will get you nowhere; suggesting that quotes from industry executives be balanced by input from labor and public-interest groups is more likely to be taken seriously.

Choose your battles While we'd all like to see fewer female bodies used to sell beer, asking the networks to reject such ads is a waste of time. (A letter-writing campaign to the companies that produce those ads is another matter.) However, its worth the effort to pressure telecom and cable giant Comcast to air the antiwar ads it censored during Bush's State of the Union speech.

Correct the record For example, remind media outlets discussing "partial birth abortion" that this imprecise and inflammatory term doesn't refer to an actual medical procedure but is, rather, a political concept fabricated by conservative groups to decrease public support for abortion rights. Focusing on facts is more persuasive than simply expressing outrage: "Christina Hoff Sommers's quote contained the following inaccuracies ..." is better than "Anti-feminists like Christina Hoff Sommers should not be quoted in your newspaper."

Expose biased or distorted framing Look at whose viewpoint is shaping the story. In light of the Bush Administration's assault on affirmative action, for example, Peter Jennings asked on World News Tonight: "President Bush and race: Does he have a strategy to win black support?" Let ABC producers know that you'd rather they investigate the economic, academic, and political implications of the president's agenda for African-Americans then the effects of race policy on Bush's approval rating.

Keep it concise and informative If your goal is publication on the letters page, a couple well-documented paragraphs will always be better received than an emotional three-page manifesto. Sticking to one or two main points will get a busy editor to read through to the end.

Avoid overgeneralization Don't complain that your local paper "never" reports on women's issues or "always" ignores poor people. Even if stories on topics like welfare are infrequent or inaccurate, their very existence will serve as proof to editors that your complaint doesn't apply to their publication.

Address the appropriate person Letters about reportorial objectivity sent to editorial columnists or opinion-page editors will be tossed in the circular file.

Proofread! Nothing peeves an editor faster than typos or bad grammar.

Finally, give 'em credit Positive reinforcement can be as effective as protest. Be constructive whenever possible, and commend outlets when they produce in-depth, bias-free coverage.

Jennifer L. Pozner is WIMN's founder and executive director.

THE LOGOS OF USING WORDS AND PICTURES TOGETHER

When you use words and photographs or illustrations together, they can interact in three ways:

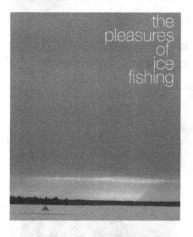

1

The photograph or illustration "explains" the words. The words, that is, wouldn't make much sense without the photograph or illustration.

For example, does "smell friends" make sense to you as anything other than a very odd command—until you see the words paired with an illustration of dogs? Then, based on your knowledge of how dogs interact, the words probably make perfect sense.

2

The words "explain" the photograph or illustration.

In the middle example above, would you have any idea what that triangle on the ice is if you didn't see the words? (In case you have only lived in warm climates, know that the triangle is an ice fishing tent.) Notice also how the words direct your attentions away from the light and clouds to focus on the tent.

3

The words and photograph or illustration work together to have a stronger effect than either alone has. In the third example, the connection between the word and the photograph is not quite as direct as in the first two. Instead, you—the viewer—have to figure out whether the word asks you to think of the leaves as clothing for some animal or to rethink your notion of clothing (as covering) based on the leaves, or both. There is more room for viewer interaction when the connection between word and photograph is not so obvious.

Naming the Relationships

French theorist Roland Barthes named the first two relationships on the facing page "anchors": The words and pictures tie each other down in the same way an anchor keeps a boat in one place. "Relay" is how Barthes named the relationship shown in the third example where, as in a relay race, the function of the pairing is to move us along rather than tie us down.

Rules for Putting Words and Pictures Together?

Because our responses to photographs and illustrations depend on our bodily and cultural experiences of the world, there are no hard and fast rules for using words and pictures together. Instead, attend to their rhetorical functioning: How do particular audiences in particular contexts respond to particular combinations of words and pictures? Testing your compositions—through asking audiences how and why they have the responses they do—will show you if your word + picture combinations work.

TO ANALYZE

■ **Write and discuss:** Under the two bird photographs above, write captions that encourage others to understand the photographs as differently as possible.

■ **Discuss with others:** Use the three categories of word and photograph interaction to analyze the strip above. If you were to see just the photograph or just the words, how would you respond? How do the words typed on paper scraps contribute to the overall effect? Imagine different typed words; what words will most change your response to the strip?

ANALYZING VISUAL ARGUMENTS

Visual Analogies

Analogies compare two objects, events, or processes so that the more familiar can explain the less familiar. The two posters below help us see how this can work visually.

The red poster is from Great Britain in the 1940s, during World War II. As in the United States, so many men were away at war that factories needed workers; efforts were directed at women to encourage them to leave home and go to work constructing war equipment—work traditionally considered inappropriate for women. By showing women patching fabric, sewing, and peeling potatoes and then showing the women in almost exactly the same postures but working with drafting tools and industrial equipment, this poster argues that because the postures are the same, women have the abilities to do industrial work. The argument of this poster isn't "You can do it!" but—by analogy—is "You are already doing it, so get yourself into the factories!"

The second poster is also from the 1940s but from the United States. You can probably see how its purpose, like the previous example, is to get women into factories: Similarly to the first poster, women are shown doing two different tasks to demonstrate that, if they can do one, they can do the other. Here, however, the analogy works across time, showing a woman in clothing from the time of the Revolutionary War loading a musket to argue that contemporary women could work with power tools. This poster uses pathos—evoking the emotion of patriotism—to bring women into the industrial workforce.

In the first poster, the viewer is directly addressed as "you," Women are the audience, and the argument for going to work is aimed directly at them. In the second poster, audiences are to understand the words as spoken by women ("us") but addressed to men ("Mister!"). Perhaps this poster is addressing two different audiences: Women are asked to identify with others across time who have done patriotic work so that they have justification for going to work, while men—husbands, fathers, and brothers who might resist women working—are asked to see industrial work as a patriotic tradition.

In these examples, visual analogies are used to help a composer encourage an audience to look differently (literally and figuratively) at a situation. The analogies help audiences understand what would have been strange and unseemly—factory work—is equivalent to the work of home or the work of defending the country.

Visual Symbols

If you've ever left soup to bubble on the stove for a while, you've experienced how flavor intensifies as the soup condenses. Symbols are like that left-to-bubble soup: They contain emotions and understandings condensed into a drawing or object.

For example, Valentine's Day is awash in the symbol of the heart, meant not only to evoke thoughts of love but also the diffuse but usually lovely emotions connected with love.

The flag of the United States—like that of any country—is a symbol. It can represent the emotions of patriotism or the country's strength. Its colors represent blood and valor; the stars represent not only the states but all that stars can evoke—aspiration, light, glory. The number of stripes represents the original 13 states. Even when the flag is represented inaccurately, its power as a symbol still holds, and it can be used to bring people together around common causes or to cause divisiveness as people argue over what counts as allegiance. Because symbols condense so much emotion and understanding, they have that power to unite or divide.

When you use visual symbols, recognize that they will not mean the same thing to everyone. Different cultures have different symbols, and the symbols with which we have grown up are usually ones we do not question because they have been such a part of our lives.

Symbols are linked to what they represent through resemblance (the way the majesty and power of the bald eagle are supposed to represent the majesty and power of the United States) or convention (as the apple is meant to represent temptation). You cannot make your own symbols; you can only use the symbols you inherit through living in a particular time and place.

The poster on the right demonstrates a symbol working visually. Without explanation and with only a few words, the poster links sex with the devilish evil of Eve's temptation in the Garden of Eden. The poster overlays sex with a Biblical history and the loss of paradise. The poster can do this because chances are that—if you've grown up in the United States—you've learned that an apple and a snake together mean that original temptation. With the addition of "AIDS," the poster makes clear its purpose: The designer wants viewers to see the danger lurking around the red pleasure.

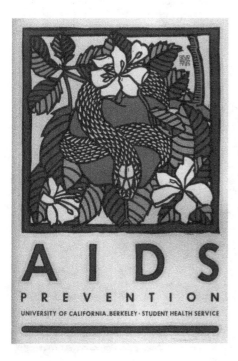

A question to ask about symbols in visual arguments, then, is whether you think the linking of symbol with its purpose is appropriate. Regarding this poster, we can ask whether sex should be linked with the original temptation. Because symbols work without explicit statement of their emotional weight, they can cause us to carry away many more associations and emotions than might really be necessary for the argument to be made. When you compose arguments that use symbols, you need to ask yourself whether you are doing too much.

Visual arguments using symbols work because they equate some situation (in this case, AIDS) with a whole set of undescribed emotions and understandings we've learned by growing up in a particular time and place. When you want to bring the weight of a culture's beliefs or emotions to bear on an issue, then consider what symbols you can use.

Visual Accumulation

To *accumulate* is to pile up objects that are similar or the same.

The photograph on the right is of an artwork titled "Whale" from the series "Running the Numbers II: Portraits of global mass culture"; its original size is 44" x 82". The person who made the piece, Chris Jordan, uses photography to document human resource consumption. The artwork uses "50,000 plastic bags, equal to the estimated number of pieces of floating plastic in every square mile in the world's oceans"; the words come from Jordan's website, where you can see more of his work: www.chrisjordan.com. In the closeup following the photograph, you can see how plastic bags have been shaped into the whale.

What might such an accumulation of plastic bags, so photographed, tell us about our use of plastic? What might it tell us about our consuming habits? Why might Jordan have shaped the bags into the whale?

How would the effect of this visual argument be different if Jordan had photographed each bag separately and hung all the photographs on a wall?

Visual accumulation can make visible and concrete a large number of elements or make visible a pattern that can then perhaps be broken. In this artwork, a number is given emotional weight.

In what argumentative contexts do you think such strategies will be most effective?

TO ANALYZE: VISUAL ARGUMENTS

■ **Observe, then write:** Look through magazines and online sites to find other examples of visual analogy, accumulation, or symbols. Do the examples you find support our descriptions of when these different arrangements seem most effective? See if you can find examples that show other arguments that these arrangements can help build, and then write a short paper that argues how these visual arguments work, as we did with the examples in this chapter.

■ **Discuss with others:** Look through writing examples—essays, poems, opinion pieces—to find word examples of analogy, accumulation, and symbol. When these arrangements are built of words, how are the arguments of which they are part similar to or different from visual arguments that use these structures?

■ **Write:** Look at the websites of candidates running for national office, members of Congress, or the presidential administration. You'll find many symbols at work in the websites, including (often) the U.S. flag. Write a short rhetorical analysis of one such site, arguing how any symbols used support its overall purposes and focusing on how you think the site designers thought about their audience(s). Use your analysis as a lens for considering the website of someone who takes different political positions.

■ **Discuss with others:** The photograph above shows an accumulation of photographs that are all the same size and that are mostly in the same format, a closeup of someone's face.

General Augusto Pinochet was president of Chile from 1973–1990; during this time, thousands of people were detained by the military, never to return. In 1998, General Pinochet was arrested under an international warrant issued by a Spanish judge and charged with the crime of torture. The photograph above, printed in *The New York Times*, shows a 2003 exhibition in Chile of photographs of the missing. The accumulation of so many similar photographs allows the audience to see—literally see—at once how many people are missing. The audience can see individual faces and think about individuals who are missing, but always as part of the accumulated weight of how many all together are missing. How is seeing this exhibit different from reading, "Thousands of people disappeared during General Pinochet's presidency"?

(Notice too how the photograph has been structured so that you cannot see how high up the wall the photographs go, or how long the walls are. Why do you think the photographer chose this particular framing? To learn about *framing* as a rhetorical strategy for directing attention.

A DESIGN PLAN FOR A PHOTO ESSAY

Remember that a design plan integrates the following in the order that makes sense to you:

- your statement of purpose. (See Ajay's statement of purpose on page 89.)
- a description of your overall strategies with justifications based on your statement of purpose.
- your choice of medium or media with justifications based on your statement of purpose.
- your ideas about arrangement with justifications based on your statement of purpose.
- a description of how you will produce the communication.
- a plan for testing the communication.

You write a statement of purpose to help you think about how to proceed with a text, so a statement of purpose is not a test and can be more or less formal. Generally, however, a fairly informal statement of purpose will be most useful because you want to focus on your own thinking, not on how you are communicating your thinking to anyone else. You want to ask questions of yourself, get possible ideas down, think about what others have said about your concerns, and start to imagine the whole text you are about to produce.

FOR EXAMPLE

Below is Ajay's design plan for his photo essay—which you can see on pages 129–130.

Design Plan for a Photo Essay

PURPOSE: As with all my research for this class, I want mostly to raise questions about how we think of ourselves while we are in college. *Are we students—or consumers? How are we supporting students in college so that everyone gets the best possible education? What happens when students think of themselves as consumers?* Because of what I wrote in my statement of purpose, I know that I want to use photographs to show that we can talk as though we are consumers when we are in school. But looking at pictures of "buying a grade" or "buying a diploma" will show (I hope!) how weird it is really to do that. I hope that, by seeing how weird it is really to show what it looks like to buy a grade, maybe we'll think differently about how we earn our educations.

MEDIUM & PRODUCTION: I am using photographs. I am not the best photographer, but—because of my purpose—I know that I need to focus on someone buying things. I need to show someone buying regular stuff and then someone buying a grade. I need to figure out how to show buying a grade or an education because it's just so hard to picture what that actually looks like. (And I need to plan: Pictures of people buying stuff will be easy, but I'm going to have to find a teacher— oh, and I think my friend Mia will help me by being the student in the photographs.) I also will probably need to take a whole bunch of photographs in order to get a couple that work. I need to ask Jamshed if he will help me learn how to get photographs off my phone so I can print them.

STRATEGIES

ETHOS: Even though I am raising serious questions, I don't want to come across as someone who thinks my position is the only one or as though I'm yelling about my position. I think the ethos that best supports my purpose—to get others to question—will have me come across as questioning rather than assertive.

PATHOS: What I wrote about purpose and ethos makes me think I should keep the essay simple and focused. But also I'd like it to seem kind of lighthearted and funny (especially since it's the end of the semester). I want the essay not to look too polished because I want people in class to be sucked into thinking that this is all easy and the questions are relaxed. Maybe then they'll take the questions home with them. (And I was thinking about using captions—so I want them to look handwritten.)

LOGOS: My argument is based on comparison. I am going to put a photo of someone buying regular stuff next to a photo of someone "buying" a grade. I hope the comparison makes people think about how weird the second photo is.

But as I picture all this in my head, I think I am going to need to put a caption with each comparison because the second photograph in the comparison won't make sense on its own: We just don't see people buying grades. And because I know I want to have a questioning rather than a demanding or yelling ethos, I think I need the captions to be questions—and that also means that people might really ask themselves the questions and go home thinking about them (which is my purpose). I wonder how many sets of comparisons will be enough? The assignment says at least four photos, but that's only two sets; I don't think that's enough. I think I need at least three sets—three comparisons—in order to make enough of a pattern for people to remember.

ARRANGEMENT

Because writing about logos helped me see that my argument is about comparison, I will probably have four pages for my essay: A title page and then three pages, each of which has two photos on it for comparison. Having the photo sets on separate pages means my audience has to move through them page by page, so they will move through the photos more slowly rather than see them all at once.

TESTING

If Mia will be in my photos, I'll show them to her after I put them on their pages with their captions to make sure she can understand what is in them. She'll know what I am trying to do and so can help me test the wording of my captions.

TO ANALYZE

■ **Compare with others:** With a classmate or two, compare Ajay's design plan for his photo essay with his design plan for his research paper and his oral presentation.

What do you see in the design plans—in both what Ajay wrote and also how he wrote the plans—that most seemed to help him? How might such approaches help you in your own composing work?

A PHOTO ESSAY

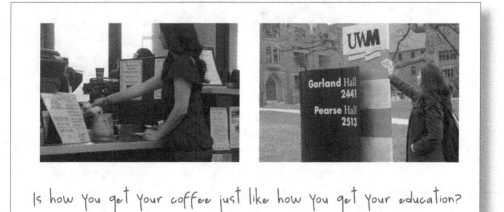

how alike are buying and learning?

photo essay • Ajay Chaudry • June 8, 2012

- Here and on the next pages are Ajay's photographs and captions for his photo essay. Given what he wrote in his statement of purpose (on page 89), we know that the assignment for which he made the essay says that these pages are meant to be understandable to others without help from Ajay. Do you think he has achieved that?

- Given what Ajay wrote in his design plan (on pages 127–128), do you think his essay's opening page appropriately prepares his audience for his purposes? Do you think the photograph and title are appropriate for his purposes?

Is how you get your coffee just like how you get your education?

▨   Do you think Ajay has framed and cropped his photographs to help his audience see what he wants them to see? What might you have done differently with these photographs if you were making his essay?

Is how you get your gum just like how you get a grade?

▨   Are Ajay's captions doing the work he hoped they would do as he described in his design plan (on pages 127–128)?

▨   How would Ajay's captions have worked as statements or assertions rather than questions? Would the photographs have worked without captions?

▨   Would you change any of Ajay's photographs?

Is how you get your soda just like how you get your diploma?

▨   Do you think Ajay has enough photographs to achieve the purposes he described in his statement of purpose (page 89) and design plan (pages 127–128)? Why?

▨   How well has Ajay achieved the overall purposes he set for himself?

TESTING AND EVALUATING VISUAL TEXTS

A Self-test for Visual Texts you Produce—and the Fundamental Questions to ask of any Visual Text

As with any text in any medium that you produce for communicating with others, look at the text when you think it is finished (or almost finished); pretend that you are a member of your audience and answer the following questions based on what you see in the text.

- Who specifically is the audience for this text? Does the text treat the audience as appropriately complex people? (For example, has the text avoided defining the audience simply as adults or teenagers?)
- What is this text's purpose? What is this text trying to do?

If you cannot answer those questions from what you see in the text (and not based on what is in your head), then your text needs more work to clarify its purpose for its audience.

Also always ask:

- Do I want to be the person whose ethos is constructed in this text? Do I want to hold these opinions and ideas? Do I want to have the relationships with other people that this text establishes?

Because different kinds of visual texts depend on different visual strategies, here are other questions you might use in evaluating particular visual texts whether you or someone else has made them.

Some of the following criteria can be used for multiple kinds of texts.

A Brochure Designed for a Nonprofit Organization

- Has writing that develops an appropriate ethos for the nonprofit organization.
- Has writing that addresses its audience using pathos appropriate to the purpose.
- Uses strategies that address the audience respectfully.
- Has writing that has been visually presented to be easy to read.
- Uses photographs or illustrations that are clearly relevant to the brochure's purpose.
- Makes thoughtful and purposeful use of contrast, typefaces, color, and so on.
- Is crisp and professionally produced.
- Uses verbal text that is all correctly spelled and grammatically appropriate.

A Short Comic on a Social Issue

- Uses comic book/graphic novel conventions appropriately in developing its purpose.
- Uses comic book/graphic novel conventions creatively in developing its purpose.
- Has text that treats its audience as people who think and feel.
- Uses writing that is respectful of its audience (even when humorous).
- Reflects the composer's ethos, which is appropriately authoritative and thoughtful but nonetheless fits the comic medium.
- Uses illustrations and/or photographs that are appropriate for the argument being made.
- Uses a layout that encourages the audience to approach the material thoughtfully.
- Uses writing and illustrations that have appropriate pathos appeals for the audience.
- Uses appropriate grammar and spelling.

A Documentary Photography Book

- Has an argument that makes a statement or claim about its topic and supports the statement or claim with reasons.
- Has an argument that is worth making, is new for its audience or creatively presented, or offers an old argument in a newly compelling manner.
- Orders photographs to build an argument over time.
- Uses visual strategies (typography, page arrangement, etc.) that are appropriate to the argument.
- Presents photographs that are relevant to the argument.
- Includes only text that is relevant to the argument.
- Has text that supports the photos, not vice versa.
- Introduces its audience to its topic appropriately.
- Has text or captions that are perfectly spelled and use appropriate grammar.

An Argumentative Poster

- Shows that thought has been given to how the poster's appearance support its purpose.
- Uses pictures or other visual strategies that are unambiguous and easy for its audience to understand.

- Includes pictures that are clearly relevant to the poster's purpose.
- Uses words that are unambiguous and easy for its audience to understand.
- Makes thoughtful and tied-to-its-purpose use of contrast, typefaces, color, etc.

A Short Video Public Service Announcement

- Is created so that, after seeing it, the audience will know the sponsoring organization and how to contact it.
- Develops an appropriate ethos for the organization being represented.
- Doesn't put an overly emotional spin on its topic.
- Uses only audio and video effects that support the purpose of the video.
- Uses audio that is clear and easy to understand.
- Is engaging for its audience, who will want to see it again.

TO ANALYZE

- **Evaluate and reflect:** According to the assignment Ajay was given for his photo essay, his essay would be evaluated on the following criteria:

  - The photo essay has to grow out of the research paper and/or oral presentation.
  - The photo essay has to make a point tied to the paper and/or presentation.
  - The photo essay has to creatively use at least four photographs (and captions if needed).
  - The photo essay has to be understandable to others in class with no help from us.

  What evaluation would you give Ajay's photo essay based on these criteria?

  What other criteria to the left might you use to evaluate Ajay's photo essay? Why?

- **Evaluate:** Find samples for any of the visual texts listed to the left. Evaluate the samples using the criteria on the left.

  What on other criteria might you use for evaluation?

DESIGNING SLIDES TO SUPPORT ORAL PRESENTATIONS

The title at the top of this page gives the most important advice for designing slides: Slides should rhetorically support the arguments you make. Slides should not stand alone but should come to life only with your words and explanations.

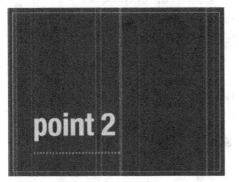

Put on a slide only the absolute minimum for making your point. You want what is on the slide to be memorable for your audience.

Your audience has come to hear you talk, not to read your slides. If your slides are full of stuff, the audience will read and look, not listen.

Choose (or make) and stay with a slide template that works with your purposes. Unless incoherence suits your purposes, using the same theme throughout gives your presentation coherence.

Your slides should contain only elements that are relevant to your presentation. You do not need to decorate slides—although a relevant graphic can help explain or make information memorable.

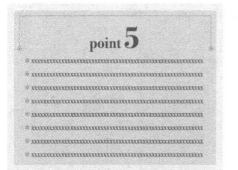

Go easy on bullet points. If you must use them, keep them short and do not use more than three to four. (Remember point 2, to the left.) (Go easy on text, in general.)

Choose typefaces that are easy to read and large enough to be readable at the distance where your audience will sit. Test your slides by projecting them ahead of time and trying to read them from your audience's distance. (See pages 101–106 on choosing type.)

Choose colors to support your purposes. Make sure that the type color contrasts crisply with the slide's background color so that your audience can read the type. (See point 6 for advice on checking the readability of slides, and see pages 96–99 for help with color.)

Photographs that are large and uncluttered generally are the most easy for audiences to understand—and all photographs should relate to your purposes.

Slide transitions are fun—but they can make audiences dizzy. Transitions *between* slides should support your argument's movement: For example, does your argument seem to move up, or down, or sideways? Transitions *on* a slide—as bullet points come on, for example—should also tie to your purposes.

Just as a beginning memorable slide will help pull your audience into your presentation, a final slide should offer a memorable takeaway. What is the last point you wish your audience to remember about your presentation?

TO ANALYZE

■ **Develop criteria:** Using the points we have listed here as well as the criteria for testing and evaluating visual texts on pages 131–133, develop a rubric for evaluating slides for a presentation.

■ **Evaluate:** Look back over the slides that Ajay used to support his oral presentation.

How well do Ajay's slides take into account the advice we offer on these two pages? If you developed criteria in response to the prompt above, use your criteria to evaluate Ajay's slideshow.

■ **Reflect:** From your experiences watching others' presentations, do you have other points to add to what we have listed on these two pages? Are there aspects of those slideshows—and the presentations they supported—you would like to remember for your own work in the future?

THINKING THROUGH PRODUCTION

▨ Using any technologies available to you, produce two to three posters for an upcoming event. (Be sure to compose a statement of purpose and design plan as you work.) Each poster should have exactly the same illustrations or photographs, the same text, and the same layout—but choose very different color schemes for each poster. Ask your classmates to describe their responses to the colors. Record the strategies that seem most effective for the context, audience, and purpose of the poster.

▨ Use whatever materials and technologies you have available to produce your own visual argument—for any purpose, context, and audience—based on analogy, accumulation, or a symbol. Look again at the examples and our analyses of them to think about the contexts in which these formal arrangements are most effective, in order to decide which to use for the audience and purpose you choose.

▨ Look at the "Spoof Ads" at the Adbusters website (http://www.adbusters. org/spoofads). (Look especially at the tobacco, fashion, McDonald's, and corporate spoofs.)Choose two or three of the spoofs that you find most successful, and write a short analysis of what you think makes them successful. Then use whatever materials you have available to you to make your own ad spoof.

▨ Produce a visual timeline* that presents the changes over time in some aspect of our lives. You could show how a company's logo has changed since the company began, how women's dresses or men's pants differ from generation to generation, or how the design of cars, cereal boxes, or newspapers has varied over decades. But don't just show pictures of the changes: Annotate them to argue how the changes are in response to other cultural or technological changes.

You'll need to do research. Find examples of the visual artifact you're studying, and research why it has changed. Come to your own position on why the changes you see have occurred and support it with evidence.

When you produce the timeline using any medium available to you, integrate into your presentation annotations that explain what the visual aspect is, how it has changed, and why you think it has changed. (Be sure to take advantage of the layout of your timeline to help you make your argument.)

* An example of a timeline to help you think about what you might do is in the chapter "Graphic Design in America" in *Design/Writing/Research* by Ellen Lupton and J. Abbott Miller, which your library might have or can get for you. Many examples of interactive timelines are online.

▨ Take a short paper you've already produced, and re-produce it twice. Each time, use a very different typeface (you might use a sans serif typeface in one and a grunge face in the other) as well as different spacing between the lines of type. If you have headers in the paper, make them be a very different typeface from the body of the paper. Revise the visual structure of the paper, keeping in mind what we've described about using layout rhetorically. Give your papers to others for reading and response. Compare the responses you receive: Do readers appear to give less serious attention to papers printed in typefaces that are unusual in academic circumstances?

▪ Take a short paper you've already produced and re-produce it as best you can by using photographs. Afterward, write a short paper in which you reflect on differences between writing and photography: *Given your paper's arguments, what were you able to show photographically—and what not? What do you think you were able to argue more effectively through words, and what through photographs? What was impossible to do in photographs?*

Compare your conclusions with others in class. As a group, try to develop some general statements about how we use words and pictures differently in our time and place, and why.Do you think you need a degree in art or design to include photographs effectively in a research paper or to compose a poster for a fund-raising event?

ACHIEVING STASIS BY ASKING THE RIGHT QUESTIONS

Every subject which contains in itself a controversy to be resolved . . . involves a question about a fact, or about a definition, or about the nature of an act, or about . . . processes.

—Cicero, *De Inventione* I iii 7

STUDENTS WHO WANT a systematic way of asking questions about rhetorical situations can use the ancient **stases,** which help rhetors determine exactly what any argument is about; use of the stases also ensures that rhetors investigate an issue fully. The term *stasis* (Latin *status* or *constitutio*) is derived from a Greek word meaning "a stand." Thus a stasis can refer to the place where one rhetor takes a stand. If two rhetors disagree, the stasis marks the place where they come to rest, where they can agree that they disagree. Hence the appropriateness of the Latin *constitutio,* which can be translated as a "co-standing" or a "standing together." But although finding the point of stasis is an important first step, this resting place is temporary, suspended as it is between conflicting movements until a writer or speaker begins the actual argument.

The most satisfactory modern equivalent for stasis seems to be the term **issue,** which we define as the point about which all parties to an argument can agree that they disagree: this is what is at issue. This point of agreement is important because all parties to an argument must know the precise issue on which they disagree; otherwise, they may just talk past one another. This failure to agree on the point of disagreement often results in frustration for all concerned parties, and thus it may be one reason why people don't like to argue.

Determining the point of stasis is crucial to any rhetorical argument. However, figuring out the stasis is sometimes more difficult than it may seem at first

139

glance. Most people who are engaged in arguments want to advance their own position as quickly and forcefully as possible. Thus they do not want to take the time to find all the available arguments, as ancient means of invention require. However, this hasty approach can lead to stalemate (or shouting or violence), as has happened in public arguments over abortion.

Happily, the stases also provide rhetors with a set of questions that, when asked systematically, can help them to determine the arguments that are available in a given rhetorical situation. Rhetors who do take the time to find all the available arguments can be assured both that their position is defensible and that they have found the best evidence to support it. The very old systematic investigative procedures described in this chapter were used for thousands of years to help rhetors figure out what arguments are available to them, and we hope that they will help you to determine the issues you want to argue, as well.

ON INVENTING: HOW TO PROCEED

We recommend that you begin your work with the stases by trying to answer the questions outlined next. Consider all the statements you generate to be potential propositions. If you work systematically and thoroughly, you should produce a full and useful analysis of the issue you have chosen to examine. Doing all this intellectual work has several advantages. Rhetors who work through the questions raised by this heuristic in systematic fashion will find that

1. It clarifies their thinking about the point in dispute.
2. It forces them to think about the assumptions and values shared by members of their targeted audience.
3. It establishes areas in which more research needs to be done.
4. It suggests which proofs are crucial to the case.
5. It may point the way toward the most effective arrangement of the proofs.

What this or any heuristic will not provide, however, is a draft of a paper or speech. Ancient rhetors spent a good deal of time in preparation for writing or speaking, trying out one method of invention or another. They did not mind if these trials produced false starts because they knew that the false starts turned up in one case could most likely be used in some other rhetorical situation. Contemporary debaters work in a similar fashion, preparing all relevant arguments in advance in case they ever need to use them, and to limit the chance that a skilled opponent will use an argument they are not prepared to answer. It is important to remember, then, that practice with this (or any heuristic) also supplies the rhetor with *copia*. Proofs generated in practice with any heuristic may prove useful at some other time.

One additional caution: heuristics do not work as reliably as mathematical formulas do. In many cases, you will continue to refine the issue and to develop nuances of your proposition as you work through each of the rhetorical canons. In fact, invention can begin all over again during late stages of the composing process—arrangement, revision or even editing. However, attention to the heuristics described in this book will certainly enrich your stock of arguments—your verbal *copia*. And systematic, thoughtful consideration of the issue at hand just may provide you with precisely the proposition you are looking for, as well as arguments you can use to support it.

THE IMPORTANCE OF ACHIEVING STASIS

Contemporary public discourse about abortion provides a good example of an argument that has been sustained for many years but that shows no sign of being resolved. Public debate on this issue began in earnest nearly forty years ago, when the Supreme Court legalized the practice in 1973. Ever since that time, those who oppose the availability of abortion, usually on moral grounds, have employed a number of tactics to get the procedure banned, while at the same time, those who support the availability of abortion have fought to keep the practice, as they say, "safe, legal, and rare." Those who oppose abortion are called "pro-life" because of their belief that abortion is murder; those who support it are called "pro-choice" because they believe that women should be able to choose their methods of controlling reproduction.

Ever since *Roe v. Wade,* the 1973 Supreme Court decision that legalized abortion, proponents and opponents of abortion have battled one another in both the judicial and legislative arenas. In 2005, for example, the state legislature of South Dakota passed a bill making it a felony for a doctor to perform an abortion anywhere in the state. The legislation allowed no exceptions whatever: abortions were not permitted when a mother's health was at stake (unless her life was in danger), and citizens of South Dakota who had suffered rape or incest were denied this option as well. The law had been expressly designed by its advocates to produce a test case that would challenge *Roe v. Wade.* Then, in 2006, abortion rights activists succeeded in placing a resolution on the ballot that would strike down the 2005 legislation, and the people of South Dakota supported it. Legislation similar to the 2005 bill that banned nearly all abortions appeared on the ballot again in 2008, and once again voters in South Dakota defeated it.

Clearly this issue is hotly contested in South Dakota, as well as in other states. One reason that the argument over abortion has not been resolved is that it cannot be, as long as the central propositions put forward by those involved in it are not in stasis. People who oppose the legalization of abortion ordinarily offer the following statement as their major proposition: Abortion is murder. People who argue that abortion should maintain its current status as a legal operation put the following statement forward as their major proposition: Women have the right to control their reproductive practices. Keeping in mind that reaching stasis means finding the place where opponents agree to disagree, even a cursory examination of these statements shows that they are not in stasis.

A rhetor who wishes to find stasis with someone who believes that abortion is murder should argue (a) that abortion is not murder, or (b) that abortion is legal so therefore it cannot be murder because murder is illegal in America, or (c) that abortion is not murder because a fetus is not a human being, or some other proposition that defines abortion in such a way that it can be excluded from the category "murder."

Stasis Achieved: Rhetors Can Now Agree to Disagree

A. Abortion is murder.

B. Abortion is not murder.

A rhetor who wishes to find stasis with someone who believes that women have the right to control their own reproductive practices, on the other hand, must argue that (a) women do not have that right, at least when they are pregnant, or (b) that the right to life of a fetus outweighs a woman's right to choose what happens to her body, or (c) that the right to life extends to fetuses and takes primacy over any other human right, or some other similar proposition about the priority ordering of human rights.

Stasis Achieved: Rhetors Can Now Agree to Disagree

A. Women have the right to decide what happens to their bodies, including terminating a pregnancy.

B. Women do not have the right to decide what happens to their bodies when they are pregnant because a potential life is at stake.

Although the propositions we turned up in our stasis analysis do appear in contemporary discourse about abortion, they are seldom offered in the systematic, head-to-head way we have listed them here; that is, they are seldom put in stasis. But the act of putting them in stasis establishes that the participants in this argument are usually arguing right past each other. That is to say, the major propositions they put forward do not address the same issue.

Interestingly enough, the statements that would achieve stasis in this argument are not very persuasive to opponents: pro-choice advocates do not often directly address the pro-life position by saying, "Abortion is not murder." Nor do pro-life advocates often say in public forums that "women do not have the right to determine what happens to their bodies." This reluctance to state the implications of its propositions may be another reason why the argument is not in stasis. Those who frame the abortion issue as a question of murder are compelled to argue that abortion, defined as murder, outweighs a woman's right to determine when or if she will have children. They frequently support their position by making reference to religious, moral, or natural laws. Those who support legal abortion, on the other hand, must either argue or ignore the claim that abortion is not murder, and to do so they have recourse to the political discourse of rights, arguing that individuals have a right to conduct private business without interference from the state.

This argument assumes further that deciding to have an abortion is a private, not a public, matter.

Another way to articulate this failure to achieve stasis is to say that people who oppose abortion are arguing from philosophical or theological assumptions about the point at which life begins; people who defend women's rights are arguing from political grounds about the rights of individuals and the relation of those rights to the good of the community. The point to be made here, however, is that as long as the major propositions in this discourse remain out of stasis, the argument will continue. To date, those who argue about this issue in these terms have ordinarily been unwilling to meet one another on the same ground.

THEORETICAL VERSUS PRACTICAL QUESTIONS

Ancient rhetoricians divided questions into two kinds: theoretical and practical. Some questions concern what people should do (action), but these are always related to questions about why people should do something (theory). Cicero gave this example of a theoretical question in his treatise called *Topics* (xxi 82): Does law originate in nature or in some agreement and contract between people? This is the sort of abstract theoretical question that is discussed today by law school professors and their students when they talk about what grounds or centers the law. It is an important question because certain practical actions follow from any answer that may be given. If law is grounded in nature it cannot easily be changed; for instance, it is futile to argue that the law of gravity is wrong, or ill-suited to the times, or that it supports one party to the detriment of another. A rhetor's only option in this case is to argue that the law in question is unnatural. To get an idea of how difficult this is, imagine yourself arguing in court that gravity is unnatural. The theoretical argument from nature is used on occasion: motorcycle riders who opposed legislation requiring them to wear helmets argued—without much success—that such laws violate the natural human desire for freedom from restraint.

If law results from human contract, on the other hand, it is much easier to justify alterations to laws because a rhetor can appeal to the expressed opinions or desires of the majority as support for her argument that a law should be changed. Someone who advocates against a helmet law for motorcycle riders, then, can simply provide as proof a survey showing that some percentage of riders (preferably more than 50%) prefer to ride unprotected by a helmet; someone who advocates the practice of abortion can cite polls showing that the majority of Americans want *Roe v. Wade* to stand (which can be tricky because the percentage of Americans who support or disapprove of abortion changes from poll to poll, depending, in part, on who is taking the poll).

Unlike theoretical questions, which address the origins and natures of things, practical questions always concern proposed actions, what people should do. Cicero gave this example of a practical question: Should a philosopher take part in politics? Notice that this question asks what people who study philosophy ought to do; it does not raise questions about the nature or aim of philosophy or politics, as a theoretical question would. The English word *theory* derives from a Greek word (*theorein*), which literally meant "to sit in the highest row of the theatre." More freely translated, the term meant something like "to observe from afar." A theoretical question, then, allows rhetors to view questions "from afar," as though they had no immediate relevance for daily affairs and putting aside for the moment their practical effects. Many times theoretical investigations will provide positions on more practical issues. But they also take rhetors far afield from everyday events. Take this very practical (and very specific) question, for instance:

> Should I drop engineering and major in history instead?

To answer this question, a rhetor needs to consider the reasons why he decided to study engineering (interest, good job opportunities) and why he now might prefer to study history (interest, he wants to become a teacher or archivist). He also needs to consider the consequences attached to each choice (If I change majors, will it take me longer to graduate? What sort of work is available to a history major? and so on). Another way to think about the difference between theoretical and practical questions is to consider the **level of generality** at which an issue may be addressed. Greek rhetoricians used the term *hypothesis* to name a specific question that involved actual persons, places, or events. They used the term *thesis*, on the other hand, to name general questions having wide application—matters suited to political, ethical, or philosophical discussion—which don't refer to actual persons or events. The classic example of a general question was:

> Should anyone marry?

The classic specific question was:

> Should Cato marry?

Here are some contemporary examples of general and specific questions:

1. *General:* Is it legal to protest at funerals?

   Specific: Should members of the Westboro Baptist Church be allowed to protest at funerals for soldiers killed in the line of duty?

2. *General:* Should people convicted of murder be put to death?

   Specific: Should Timothy McVeigh have been put to death for blowing up the Murrah Building in Oklahoma City on April 19, 1995, an act that resulted in the deaths of 168 people?

3. *General:* Should the sexual orientation of couples who want to marry be taken into account?

   Specific: Should our state legalize gay marriage?

   More Specific: Should Joan and Annette be allowed to marry?

The ancient distinction between a theoretical question and a question of action is a binary distinction—that is, it allows for only two possibilities. However, as the last example demonstrates, general and more specific questions are more helpfully thought of as lying along a spectrum or range from very general to very specific. There are many levels of generality and specificity at which any issue can be stated. Hence the generality or specificity of a given claim is never absolute; it follows that statements of a question are general or specific only in relation to each other. For example:

> *General:* Is conservation of the environment more important than economic development? (*This is a theoretical as well as a very general question—stated this way, the question raises issues for contemplation and discussion rather than action*).
>
> *More Specific:* Should the United States sacrifice industries that negatively affect its environment—logging, manufacture of certain chemicals and plastics, nuclear power plants—to conserve the environment? (*This question, although still general, is no longer simply theoretical; answers to it imply actions to be taken by the United States.*)
>
> *Even More Specific:* Should the City Council of Ourtown reject an application to build a large discount department store if this requires clear-cutting five acres of forest?
>
> *Very Specific:* Should I take time to recycle plastics, paper, and aluminum even though to do so costs money and time? (*The last three versions of the claim raise practical questions, insofar as they imply human actions, but each successive claim involves fewer people, so each is more specific than the one preceding it.*)

The level of generality at which a question or issue is stated determines the amount of research needed and the kinds of proofs that must be composed to argue it persuasively. More general questions require broader knowledge, and they usually require a longer and more complex treatment. To answer the general question about conservation given here, for example, would require at least a book-length discussion. On the other hand, the very specific question, involving a personal decision, at minimum requires some private reflection and a bit of hands-on research. To answer the very specific and very practical question whether I should take time to recycle only requires me to recycle plastics, glass, paper, and aluminum for awhile to see how much time and/or money is required to recycle these substances and to compare these results to the time and money required in having unsorted garbage hauled away by the city. A paper or speech answering this question could simply state a proposition ("Recycling is expensive and time-consuming for me") and report the results of this research.

As you can see, though, answers given to this very specific question depend on answers given to more generally stated questions, including the first, very general, question stated earlier. Whether you recycle or not depends, ultimately, on your values: Is preservation of the environment more important to you than your time or your budget? (Here we've restated the very specific question just a bit more generally).

The relation of general to specific issues was a matter of debate among ancient rhetoricians. As Quintilian pointed out, every special issue presupposes a general one: for example, the question of whether Cato ought to marry really couldn't be answered satisfactorily unless the general question, "Should a person marry?" had also been considered (III v 13). Too, there are questions that hover somewhere between the very general and the very specific: for example, "Should an older person marry?" For ancient rhetoricians, questions like these were ethical ones, having to do with a person's character and the right course of conduct for certain characters. Ethical questions still concern us, of course. We regularly read or hear arguments about whether young people ought to marry, for example, or whether gay people ought to be allowed to marry. Often these arguments are cast as personal or financial choices, but they have ethical aspects, too, because decisions about marriage and reproduction affect many people, not just those who make them.

Of course any decision you make about the level of generality at which you will pursue an issue is always affected by the rhetorical situation for which you are composing. Who is the audience for the paper or speech? What is the setting? How does the audience feel about the issue? What do they know already, and what will the rhetor have to tell them?

THE FOUR QUESTIONS

The process of asking questions does not conclude once the point of stasis has been identified. Ordinarily, the determination of the question for debate will give rise to other questions. Ancient rhetoricians devised a list of four questions or stases that would help them refine their grasp on the point at issue.[1]

1. CONJECTURE (*stasis stochasmos*)—"Is there an act to be considered?"
2. DEFINITION (*stasis horos*)—"How can the act be defined?"
3. QUALITY (*stasis poiotes*)—"How serious is the act?"
4. POLICY (*stasis metalepsis*)—"Should this act be submitted to some formal procedure?"

If someone is accused of theft, for example, the first question that must be raised is **conjecture:** "Did she do it or not?" If all parties agree that she took the property in question, the stasis moves to a question of **definition:** "Was it theft?" (She might have borrowed it). And if everyone agrees that the act can be defined as theft, the stasis becomes: "Was it right or wrong?" (The theft might be justified on any number of grounds—she took liquor from the house of a friend who is an alcoholic, for instance). Some ancient teachers called this stasis "quality," and we will use this term as well. Last, if the question of quality is agreed on, the stasis then becomes: "Should she be tried for the offense?" This last stasis is the question of procedure or **policy.**

THE FOUR QUESTIONS

Conjecture: Does it exist? Did it happen?

Definition: What kind of thing or event is it?

Quality: Was it right or wrong?

Policy: What should we do?

Cicero and Quintilian insisted that only the first three questions were necessary to the preparation of arguments to be used outside the courtroom. Nevertheless, the fourth stasis, policy, is sometimes useful in nonlegal settings. People who deliberate in city councils or student assemblies often have to decide how to regulate practices: Should we put a crosswalk on Elm Street to eliminate jaywalking there? Should we lobby the administration for faculty library privileges for graduate students?

Cicero recommended that speakers and writers work through the questions in order. This approach has several advantages: the process of working through questions of conjecture, definition, and quality, in order, will help rhetors to find the points about which they and their audience agree; it will also establish the point from which they must begin the argument—the point where they disagree.

In the first stasis, conjecture, the rhetor determines whether or not he and his audience agree about the existence of some being or thing or act or idea. If they do, this stasis is no longer relevant or useful, having been agreed to—waived—by both parties.

In the second stasis, definition, the rhetor determines whether or not he and his audience agree about the classification of the being or thing or idea or the act; if so, the stasis of definition may be passed by.

In the third stasis, quality, the rhetor determines whether he and his audience agree about the value of the thing or idea or being or act. That is, what is its importance to the community as a whole? Cicero explained the function of the third stasis as follows: this stasis comes into play when there is both agreement on what has been done and certainty about how the act should be defined, but there is a question nevertheless about how important it is or about its quality: for example, was it just or unjust, profitable or unprofitable? (*De Inventione* I viii 12). Use of this stasis required rhetors to think hard about values that are widely held in their community, values such as loyalty and responsibility, thriftiness and benevolence, heroism or self-control.

In the fourth stasis, policy, there is controversy about what should be done in a given situation: Should citizens pass a property tax increase? Should the students at State University establish policies opposing the expression of bigotry? Should I drop engineering and major in art instead? As you can probably guess, the point of agreement is often much easier to establish in the first and second stases than in the third and fourth.

A Simple Example

During the midterm elections in 2010, citizens of Florida were asked to vote on a proposition that would raise class sizes in Florida's public schools. Here is an article from the Fort Myers *News-Press* about voters' decision, written by Dave Breitenstein:

> Florida's public schools must adhere to strict class-size caps after a provision to relax standards couldn't muster enough support.
>
> Statewide, 55.3 percent of voters wanted to calculate class size by using school-wide averages, as opposed to individual classroom limits. However, the constitutional amendment needed 60 percent to become law.
>
> The rejection of Amendment 8 means core classes—math, English, science and social studies—still cannot exceed 18 children in pre-kindergarten through third grade, 22 students in grades four through eight and 25 in high schools. Caps do not apply to art, music or physical education classes . . . .
>
> Class-size reduction has been a costly initiative. In Lee [County] alone, the district spent $535.5 million through last year to hire more teachers and build additional classrooms, and $92.4 million was budgeted this year.
>
> Lee estimates the negative vote will cost an extra $30.3 million annually to create overflow classrooms for extra students. School districts can be fined if they're not in compliance.
>
> In 2002, 52.4 percent of Florida voters approved class-size limits. Initially, the state used district averages, then school averages, and individual classroom caps were implemented in August. The amendment proposed capping classes at 21, 27 and 30 students for the three grade levels, respectively.

Obviously, when a ballot proposition receives just over 50% of the vote, an issue exists. That is, the people of Lee County disagree about the importance of class sizes in public schools. Some possible arguments about this dispute emerge when we consider the four questions of stasis in regard to it:

Is there a question of fact or conjecture? Yes. In 2002 Florida voters approved class-size limits, and then in 2010 they rejected a proposal to raise those limits. Does anyone disagree that these events occurred? Probably not. So this question can be agreed to, or waived, and participants in this discussion can move to the second question.

Is there a question of definition? That is, what kind of thing, idea, or act is at issue here? The stasis of definition is clear in this dispute: What is at issue is a previous vote to limit class sizes; that is, a ballot proposition. It is doubtful that any party to the discussion would deny this definition of the act, although the minority who voted against it might object to its having been placed on a ballot at all. But this objection is not relevant under the head of definition; it is instead a policy question and should be raised under the fourth stasis.

As is often the case, the third and fourth stases yield more interesting, and more controversial, arguments. Even a cursory examination of the third stasis, questions of value, suggests that there are at least two values at stake in this dispute. The first is educational excellence: all parties to the discussion must agree that limiting class size is a good thing. Those who do not agree must offer evidence that counters the many studies supporting this point, or, they may take issue with this claim on some other ground. It appears, for instance, that some school districts have had difficulty raising enough money to support the extra classrooms and teachers that are required by smaller classes. It is, after all, cheaper to assign 30 or 40 students to a single teacher using one room than it is to find space and teachers for more, smaller, groups of 18 students each. People who voted against the ballot proposition in 2010 apparently valued educational quality over economy; that is, they believed that limits on class size improved educational quality sufficiently to offset the additional cost. So the values at stake here include at least quality of education and economic expediency. We have chosen a relatively simple case for illustrative purposes, so rhetors will ordinarily find more than two competing values at work within the complex issues that people face in their daily lives.

Let us move on to the fourth stasis. Is there a question of procedure? Yes. The ballot proposition itself is a proposal to eliminate a program that was established eight years earlier. No doubt the legislators who struggled with this issue in 2010 examined alternative policy suggestions, which could include raising class sizes only in high schools, where students can be expected to need less help than do elementary students. Or they might have proposed a tax increase to pay for the reduction in class size. Or, they might have offered a different kind of proposition that required only a majority vote to pass, rather than trying to amend the Florida constitution, which requires 60% support. When the four questions are expanded and specified, as recommended by ancient teachers, they ordinarily create additional propositions like these.

EXPANDING THE QUESTIONS

Each of the four questions can be expanded into other sets of questions. According to Cicero, there are four ways of dealing with a question of conjecture (*Topics* xxi 82). One can ask

Whether the thing exists or is true
What its origin is

What cause produced it

What changes can be made in it

Some modern rhetoricians call the issue of conjecture "the question of fact." However, the Greek term *stochasmos* is more literally translated as "a guess" or "an inference." Today the term *fact* connotes hard physical evidence, but this reading is misleading here (see the chapter on extrinsic proofs for more information about factual evidence). The stasis of conjecture does not establish anything at all about the truth or fact of the matter under discussion; rather, it represents an educated guess about what might be, or what might have occurred. And because reality may be perceived very differently by people who occupy different social and political positions, people may paint very different pictures of that reality. For example, people who opposed federal legislation about health care in 2010 worried that it mandated "death panels"—committees of doctors that would condemn elderly people to die without medical care. Proponents of the measure, on the other hand, pointed out that the legislation only contained a provision providing insurance for anyone who wanted to make a living will in consultation with a doctor. People on both sides of this issue offered conjectures about the way the legislation would work, or how people would behave were it to pass. In these examples of conjecture, each party to the dispute has some stake or **interest** in picturing the legislation in the way that they do. Their disagreement about these facts is what renders conjecture rhetorical.

Questions of Conjecture

Does it exist? Is it true?

Where did it come from? How did it begin?

What is its cause?

Can it be changed?

For example, let's say that a rhetor named Lisa Simpson wants her city, Springfield, to pass a dark-sky ordinance. Under the question of conjecture, she can ask:

Does light pollution exist in Springfield?

What is the origin of the pollution?

What causes it?

What will change it?

When she tries to answer these questions, Lisa learns that she will probably need to provide evidence that light pollution does indeed exist. She will also need to provide evidence that the pollution is not natural (that is, that it doesn't originate from moonlight or starlight). She will have to establish that the pollution is caused by billboards and streetlights, and she will need to establish further that elimination of these two sources will produce a level of light that will make astronomic observation possible.

Use of the stasis of conjecture is often productive in just this way—that is, it demonstrates to rhetors what evidence they need to mount their arguments. Sometimes, use of the stasis of conjecture also establishes that there is no issue, or that a rhetor has framed the issue incompletely, or that he wants to change his mind about the issue. Because heuristics often produce surprises—that is what they are for, after all—rhetors must be prepared for shifts in their thinking. When using the stases—or any means of invention—rhetors should always remain aware that invention may cause them to change their minds about an issue.

If all parties to the discussion agree about the conjecture—the description of the state of things—the search for stasis moves on to matters of definition.

Questions of Definition

What kind of thing or event is it?

To what larger class of things does it belong?

What are its parts? How are they related?

Definitions are rhetorical because they can determine on whose ground the question will be taken up (see the chapter on the sophistic topics for advice about composing definitions). In this case, Lisa Simpson can take advantage of the rhetorical aspect of definition to compose one that suits her interest. Lisa and the astronomers at the local observatory are probably the only parties, other than thieves and lovers, who have an interest in diminishing light pollution.

Definition requires that Lisa name the particular or proper quality of light pollution and divide that quality into its constituent parts. Let's say that she defines light pollution as "those levels of light that are sufficient to interfere with astronomical observations." She might then divide such light levels into

Light caused by billboards

Light caused by streetlights

Light caused by home lighting

Light caused by natural sources such as the moon

This **division** demonstrates to her that she needs evidence that establishes the level of pollution caused by each of these sources. It tells her further that if the evidence demonstrates that natural light is not an important factor in creating light pollution, she can concentrate her major arguments on the other sources of light, all of which can be mitigated by a dark-sky ordinance. As it does here, the stasis of definition will sometimes produce a way of dividing up the discourse—producing what ancient rhetoricians called the **partition** (see the chapter on arrangement for more about partitions).

Other parties concerned about this issue might return to the question of conjecture to assert that there is no such thing as light pollution, in an attempt to render Lisa's definition irrelevant. If they succeed in this, she too will be forced to return to the stasis of conjecture if all parties wish to continue the discussion. If they accede to her definition, on the other hand, the argument is in stasis, and all parties can turn to the next stasis: quality. If, on the other hand, they do accept that light pollution exists, and that it can be defined as she asserts, Lisa has been able to set up the discussion in terms that favor her interest.

Questions of Quality: Simple or Complex

Simple questions of quality attempt to determine the worth of the issue—its justice or rightness or honor—or how much the community desires it. Comparative questions of quality put the issue in the context of other qualities, comparing it with other values to determine its priority among the community's values. If asked simply, then, the question of quality is, "Is light pollution a good or a bad thing?" If asked comparatively in this case, the question could become, "Is the safety of citizens more important than the needs of astronomers?"

According to Cicero, there are three kinds of simple questions of quality:

what to seek and what to avoid,

what is right and what wrong,

what is honorable and what base (*Topics* xxi 84).

Simple Questions of Quality:
Is it a good or a bad thing?
Should it be sought or avoided?
Is it right or wrong?
Is it honorable or dishonorable?

Comparative Questions of Quality
Is it better or worse than something else?
Is it more desirable than any alternatives?
Is it less desirable than any alternatives?
Is it more or less right than something else?
Is it more or less wrong than something else?
Is it more honorable than something else?
Is it less honorable than something else?

Is it more base than something else?

Is it less base than something else?

Thus Lisa might ask the following simple questions of quality:

Should lower levels of light pollution be sought, or should they be avoided?

If the lower levels of light affect other situations, like citizens' safety, should they then be avoided?

Is it right or wrong to ask for lower levels of light?

Is it honorable to put the needs of astronomers above those of ordinary citizens?

Is it dishonorable to deprive citizens of a source of safety?

Thinking comparatively, the rhetor compares the importance of her issue to other related issues. In Lisa's case, for example, a general comparative question of quality is

Should the present state of affairs, which includes light pollution, be preferred to a state of affairs in which light pollution has been lessened?

A comparative specific question is

Should the present state of affairs in Springfield, which includes lighted billboards, be maintained in preference to an imagined state of affairs (or the actual state of affairs in the town down the road), where lighted billboards have been eliminated so that astronomers can see better?

Because questions of comparison are of two kinds—similarity and difference—Lisa can ask herself what differences will be brought about in her observations of the night sky if light pollution is reduced. She can argue from similarity that astronomers in the town down the road enacted legislation to control light pollution, and the quality of their observations of the night sky improved.

If she is systematic in her use of the stases, Lisa must produce all the available arguments, even those that oppose her position. She can be sure that those who disagree with her will produce these arguments, and so she must be prepared to answer them. For example, her use of the stasis of comparative difference may produce this question: Will the reduction of light pollution alter our previous descriptions of the night sky because it gives us a clearer view? In other words, will astronomers be forced to revise our earlier work if we can see better?

As this example makes clear, the stases of quality are ordinarily very productive. Using them, Lisa has generated some questions that can show her which arguments are available in a given situation. In some cases the stases may force rhetors to articulate assumptions they previously held more or less unconsciously, and which may be controversial to others. For example, any astronomer might simply assume, without giving the issue much thought, that other citizens value a dark sky as much as he does. Other citizens, however, will not take this proposition for granted. The police will be concerned about safety, and billboard companies will be concerned about possible loss of revenue if they cannot light their advertising signs at night. Use of the stases, then, demonstrates that a rhetor must prepare arguments that defend his proposition, should it become necessary to do so.

Questions of Policy

The fourth stasis, policy, is relevant to Lisa's case as well. In questions of policy, the rhetor proposes that some action be taken (or not) or that some action be regulated (or not) by means of a policy or law. Questions of policy are usually twofold: they are both **deliberative** and **forensic**. That is, a rhetor who wishes to put forward a question or issue of policy must first deliberate about the need for it and then argue for its implementation.

Deliberative Policy Questions

Should some action be taken?

Given the rhetorical situation, what actions are possible? Desirable?

How will proposed actions change the current state of affairs? Or should the current state affairs remain unchanged?

How will the proposed changes make things better? Worse? How? In what ways? For whom?

Forensic Policy Questions

Should some states of affairs be regulated (or not) by some formalized policy?

Which policies can be implemented? Which cannot?

What are the merits of competing proposals? What are their defects?

How is my proposal better than others? Worse? When Lisa considers the questions of policy, she will ask herself some hard questions. She has already decided that some action should be taken. She needs now to ask herself whether her proposal to enact a dark-sky ordinance can be implemented (for instance: How much will it cost? What changes in technology or equipment will need to be made?) and whether it is a good thing for the community it will affect. She needs to consider changes that its implementation might bring about—loss of revenue to Springfield, possibly dangerous situations for citizens—and determine whether the seriousness of these changes outweighs the merits of her proposal. If anyone has made an alternative proposal, she needs to compare that to her plan and find arguments showing that her proposal is superior.

Lisa can find arguments for implementing her proposal by showing how it will improve the current state of things, by showing how alternative proposals are not as satisfactory as her own, and by showing that implementation of her proposal is entirely possible. For example, she should try to counter the opposing argument that lowered levels of light can endanger citizens' safety (in other words, this argument requires **refutation.** See the chapter on arrangement for information about refutation). If possible, she should point out in her proposal that current levels of light from streetlights do not pose a problem to astronomical observation.

Once she has considered all the questions raised by the policy questions, Lisa can draft a proposal of her dark-sky ordinance. The draft demonstrates the depth of her concern about the situation because she took the time to compose it. It also strengthens the possibility that her audience will use part or all of her draft when they actually write the ordinance, as busy people are likely to make use of work that has already been done.

So if you wish to recommend that a policy or procedure be implemented, you should first compose it. It will help if you can find out how similar policies are enacted in similar situations and compose a similar plan for implementing the one that you suggest. You should also determine how the policy that you recommend can be enforced. If you are recommending, on the other hand, that some public practice be changed, you must first compose your recommendation. Then find out who can make the changes you suggest, and find out what procedures must be followed to make the recommended change. You should also try to find out how your recommended change can be implemented and enforced, and offer suggestions for achieving this.

USING THE STASES

The stases still prove surprisingly useful for beating a path through the thicket of issues that often surround a controversy. We suggest that rhetors begin by considering the issue under each the four stases: conjecture, definition, quality, and policy. Then compare the arguments generated under each head: Do any seem to capture the point at issue? Do any hold out the possibility of helping you with further investigation? Do any tell you something about issues that might be raised by a member of the audience, or by someone who disagrees with you? Do any help you to begin to develop an argument? Remember that this procedure is only intended to help you decide where to start. Its use does not guarantee that you will generate any useful proofs, much less that you can begin to draft a speech or paper at this stage of your preparation.

In the sample analysis that follows, we used the stases to find out what issues reside in the controversy surrounding abortion.[2] The example is intended to demonstrate how this heuristic can help someone who is just beginning to think about a rhetorical problem. We did no formal research on the issue before we began this analysis, although of course we had heard it discussed in conversation and had read news articles about it. Many more propositions and arguments are available within these issues than those we found during this trial run. However, even a preliminary use of this heuristic discloses its rich argumentative possibilities and points out as well the amount of the research and composition that are necessary to argue it persuasively. Our example cannot be followed slavishly because it does not model all possible uses of the system. The rhetorical situations that gave rise to controversies always differ from one another, and so the stases can never be applied mechanically. The issues or problems it turns up will differ from situation to situation, so any rhetor who uses it must be alert to all the possibilities it raises in any case. Rhetors should always be ready to follow any tangent thrown up by their consideration of the stases.

In other words, we use stasis theory here as a heuristic—a means of discovery. We state the issue both theoretical and practically and consider what happens when we state its available propositions at various levels of generality. Then we subject its available propositions to the four questions to see if we can discover persuasive arguments that may be useful on occasions when we wish to enter into discussions about abortion.

Step 1: *Decide whether to formulate the question in theoretical or practical terms.*

Possible Theoretical Questions:

Seen "from afar," or theoretically, what is the nature of abortion?

What are its origins? Its ends?

Possible Practical Questions:

Where and when do abortions occur? Who is involved?

Why do people practice abortion?

What and whose interests are served by the practice of abortion?

What and whose interests are denied by the practice of abortion?

Your answers to these questions may yield propositions that you wish to support or reject. If you try to answer the theoretical questions, you will probably discover that you do not know all that you need to know about this issue to argue responsibly about it. To answer the first theoretical question, for example, you need a medical dictionary that will tell you just what this procedure entails. Answers to the second require you to know something about the history and contemporary use of the practice.

Answers to the practical questions lead to **lines of argument**—the related issues that we discussed in the chapter on kairos. For example, the second practical question might be answered as follows: people practice abortion as a means of birth control. This answer suggests a line of argument: Because there are other means of contraception available, why do people resort to abortion for this purpose? Is there some feature of the state of affairs that keeps people from using these other means?

Step 2: *Decide whether to formulate the question generally or specifically.*

Possible General Formulations of the Question:

> Do abortions occur? (conjecture)
>
> What is abortion, exactly? (definition)
>
> Is it a good or a bad thing? (quality)
>
> Should abortion be regulated? (policy)

Possible Specific Formulations of the Question:

> Do abortions occur in Ourtown? (conjecture)
>
> Can the abortions done in Ourtown be classified as medical procedures? Murders? Methods of contraception? (definition)
>
> Is the availability of abortion a good thing or a bad thing in Ourtown? (quality)
>
> Should the practice be regulated in Ourtown? (policy)

This analysis reveals something about the scope or size of the available arguments on this issue. That is, a rhetor who undertakes this exercise learns how much research will be necessary to tackle the question on either a theoretical or practical level. To answer the theoretical question of conjecture requires empirical research. Additional research would be necessary to determine, for instance, the number of abortions practiced prior to *Roe v. Wade*. Answers to the second theoretical question require the composition of a definition suitable to the rhetor's position on the issue, although a careful rhetor will look for definitions advanced by others as well so that he is prepared to argue for the superiority of his own definition. (See the chapter on the sophistic topics for advice about composing definitions). The third and fourth theoretical questions require at least book-length examination, and indeed, many books have been written about both of them. The practical and specific questions cover less daunting amounts of space and time and hence require a rhetor to do less research. The specific questions may also be more interesting to the immediate community of Ourtown.

Step 3. *Decide which of the four stases best describes the point at issue in the rhetorical situation at hand.*

In arguments over abortion both the conjectural and the definitional questions are very much at issue. People who are pro-choice conjecture abortion to be among the rights granted to citizens. Those who are pro-life find this position unacceptable. The second stasis, definition, is crucial for the pro-life position because the pro-life definition of abortion as murder is precisely the point at issue in this argument. Other definitions thrown up by the stasis of definition (abortion is a method of contraception; abortion is a medical procedure) are not acceptable to the pro-life position, and any rhetor who argues that position should find arguments against both during invention because opponents will surely use them. Pro-lifers and pro-choicers also struggle over the definitional issue when they contest how, exactly, to define a fetus. Is it a human life even though it cannot survive without the woman who carries it? The question of quality often forms the point of stasis in this argument as well, as when the question arises whether the ready availability of abortion is a good or a bad thing for a given community. The question of policy has already been decided in American courts of law (abortion is currently legal), although pro-life advocates are seeking to change the policy. It is hard to generalize about which question will prove most useful in a given case because the rhetorical situation dictates which of the propositions yielded by the stases will prove most useful to a rhetor (see the chapter on kairos for more about rhetorical situations).

We are now in a position to determine which of the four stases best represents the point at issue. Remember that our analysis is cursory; we have not by any means exhausted the interrogative possibilities raised by the stases.

Conjecture: Questions to Ask

1. Does abortion exist? Pro-life people sometimes attach a number to abortion, saying say that over four million "babies" have been "killed" since *Roe v. Wade* became law. (We put the words "babies" and "killed" in quotation marks because use of these words already presupposes the pro-life position). Is this figure correct? Is it current? Under what conditions are abortions performed? Because of pressure from antiabortion activists, fewer doctors and hospitals will perform abortions. Are private clinics still performing abortions? If so, how many are there? How many pregnant women opt for adoption instead of abortion? In short, consideration of this question demonstrates the sort of factual information that is required to argue this question usefully.

2. How did it begin? Abortion has been used as a method of birth control for thousands of years. Recently, however, safer and more effective means of birth control have been found, and the use of abortion as a means of contraception has become increasingly controversial. Can the practice of abortion be ended? What would be the result?

3. What is its cause? In some cases, of course, abortions are performed because they are required to save women's lives. Although contested, this cause does not seem to be so controversial as cases in which abortion is used as a means of birth control. Here the question of cause asks us to consider what causes people to choose abortion rather than other available means of contraception. Those who support the legality and availability of abortion suggest a number of causes for its use: lack of education about birth control, lack of access to birth control, women's fear of rejection or abuse if they use other

means of birth control, and women's lack of control over their reproductive choices—the most glaring example of which is rape. Those who oppose abortion conjecture its causes quite differently: as irresponsibility, lack of the correct values, and disrespect for tradition.

4. Can it be changed? It is an interesting question whether the practice of abortion will ever cease, or whether the number of abortions, legal or illegal, can be changed by regulation. Abortion has been legal in America for almost forty years, which suggests that it can be made illegal again. States have limited access to abortion by mandating a twenty-four-hour waiting period or parental counseling, for example. And on the national level, opponents of abortion rights have attempted to outlaw certain kinds of abortions. These are legal means of seeking change, as are demonstrations and parades and petitions. Some antiabortion actions have on occasion been found to be illegal, such as protests in which property is damaged, clients are harassed, or clinical staff are injured or killed. Conjecture about the possibility of change in this case raises further interesting questions: Can illegal procedures— such as the bombing of abortion clinics or murder of doctors who perform abortions—effect a change in law? If not, why do the perpetrators of such acts engage in them?

Definition

How can the act be defined? As we have seen, this is a crucial stasis in the debate over abortion. In this issue the question of definition requires rhetors to examine their moral positions—something that is ordinarily very difficult. Perhaps the question of definition is seldom raised in public discussion about abortion because of the difficulty and seriousness of the questions it raises. If a rhetor accepts the definition of abortion as murder, she can argue propositions that treat abortion like other instances of murder. It would follow that similar punishments should be meted out to those found guilty of performing the act. A rhetor who supports abortion rights cannot allow the argument to be taken up at the stasis of definition if his opponents argue that abortion is murder. If he does, he will inevitably find himself in the unenviable and untenable position of defending acts of murder. If he accepts some other definition of abortion, certain other consequences follow. If he defines it as a woman's right, for example, he can compare it to other rights enjoyed by citizens, such as the right to vote and the right to free speech. If he defines abortion as a woman's health issue or as a reproductive issue, other arguments appear. If abortion is defined as a feature of health care for women, for example, a rhetor can argue that its practice ought to be supported legally and perhaps even financially.

Definition Questions to Ask

1. What kind of a thing is it? Is abortion an act of murder? Is it a medical practice? A means of birth control? An affront to family values? A feminist issue?

2. To what larger class of things does it belong? Does the term "prenatal care" include abortion? Is a fetus a human being with all the rights to which humans are entitled? Or is a fetus not human if it is not viable outside the womb? What is a human being, anyway? What is the essence of "being human"? Is abortion a crime against humanity? Is resistance to legal abortion part of a disabling set of patriarchal prescriptions against women?

3. What are its divisions? Currently, federal law proscribes medical intervention into a pregnancy beyond the first trimester (three months), unless some overriding concern (such as the mother's life or health) warrants this. Is this the best temporal division that can be devised? There are other ways to apply division to the issue of abortion—who practices it, places where it is illegal and for whom, and so on.

Quality

How serious is the act? Answers to questions of quality always depend on the values maintained in the community. Few issues currently under public debate so deeply involve community values as abortion does. For many religious people who oppose abortion, its practice is a sin. But people who support legalized abortion take the issue seriously, too, arguing that its practice is part of the larger issue of women's control of their reproductive lives.

Simple Quality Questions to Ask

1. Is abortion good or bad? No one who is party to this argument thinks that abortion is a good thing. Those who oppose it want it banned completely. Those who support it want it to be safe and legal, but they would prefer that women not have to resort to it as a means of birth control.

2. Should abortion be sought or avoided? Are there any cases in which abortion ought to be sought? Or should abortion always be the choice of last resort?

3. Is abortion right or wrong? Those who oppose abortion say that the practice is always wrong. Can you imagine a hypothetical situation in which this is not the case? In other words, are there any situations in which abortion is the right choice?

4. Is abortion honorable or dishonorable? Those who are opposed to abortion have tried to shame doctors who perform the procedure by convincing them that it is a dishonorable act. Some doctors refuse to perform the procedure, whereas others consider it a mark of courage and pride that they are willing to continue performing abortions under frightening and sometimes dangerous conditions. Are they behaving honorably or dishonorably?

Comparative Questions of Quality

1. Is it better or worse than some alternative? A pregnant woman has only a few alternatives to abortion: parenthood, adoption, or abandonment.

Given that situations differ, can these alternatives be ranked in terms of their relative goodness and badness?

2. Is it less or more desirable than any alternative? Most parties to this discussion think that abortion is the least desirable alternative of those listed. Can you think of situations in which abortion may be the most desirable alternative?

3. Is it more or less right or wrong than any alternative? Those who support abortion rights often argue that abortion is preferable to bringing an unwanted child into the world. In other words, they say that abortion is less wrong than giving birth to an unwanted child. Is this argument valid? With whom might it be effective?

4. Is it more or less honorable or base than some alternative?

Policy

Abortion is currently a legal medical procedure. However, there is much contemporary debate about policies related to abortion (for example: Should so-called partial-birth abortions remain legal? Should women under the age of 18 be forced to tell their parents about a planned abortion?) As is the case with any issue, rhetors who wish to advocate or oppose adoption of a policy must first deliberate the need for the policy or procedure, and second, they must study how it would be implemented (or removed).

Deliberative Questions of Policy

1. Should some action be taken? Should abortion remain legal? Should it be made illegal? Should it be made illegal in some cases only? Pro-life supporters have tried to extend the definition of "childhood" to the moment of conception. Should this be done? Is it possible?

2. Given the rhetorical situation, what actions are possible or desirable? Is it possible to outlaw abortion?

3. How will the proposed actions change the current state of affairs? Or should the current state of affairs remain unchanged? Or, is the status quo satisfactory? Desirable? Will these changes be desirable? Satisfactory? To whom?

4. How will the proposed changes make things better? Worse? How? In what ways? For whom? The proposed redefinition of "when life begins" will force reconsideration of *Roe v. Wade* and other legislation related to the practice of abortion that depends on the division of pregnancy into trimesters. It could also affect the practice of contraception because the argument could be made that if life begins at conception, any means of contraception is murder. If any of this happens, will the world be a better place? How so?

Forensic Questions of Policy

1. Should some state of affairs be regulated (or not) by some formalized procedure? The practice of abortion is currently legal, although it is regulated

by a variety of state and local laws. Those who oppose abortion, obviously, would like to see it made illegal so that all the regulatory procedures that attend illegal operations (the police, courts, prisons) can be brought to bear on those who participate in abortion.

2. Which policies can be implemented? Which cannot? Given the current ideological climate in America, the legality of abortion must be defended against those who would outlaw it. So it does not seem likely that a proposal that recommends free abortions for everyone will be readily accepted. Rather, proposals intended to limit or deter access to abortion have been successful in recent years.

3. What are the merits of competing proposals? What are their defects? Those who support abortion rights have often argued that better and more widely available sex education and wide distribution of free contraceptives would markedly reduce the number of abortions that are performed in this country. Are they right? If their proposals were adopted, could abortion then be made illegal?

ENDNOTES

1. The system of questions given here does not appear in the work of any ancient thinker. We have generalized the four questions we feature out of primary and secondary classical sources (for an illuminating if complex account of competing ancient traditions of stasis, see Quintilian's painstaking discussion in the third book of the *Institutes*). Our system is a hybrid, although it is the same one that George Kennedy reconstructs for Hermagoras' lost treatise (307–08). In particular, our consideration of policy along with the other three stases is a departure from ancient thought because the ancients usually classed policy with questions of law (forensic rhetoric), whereas the first three stases we discuss were ordinarily associated with deliberative rhetoric.

2. We are aware that some readers may find this topic too sensitive to discuss in the detail required by the stasis heuristic. If so, we recommend that such readers find another issue with which to practice using the stases. And we would remind readers that, according to Aristotle, the point of engaging in rhetoric is to find *all* of the available arguments, whether we agree with them or not, whether we find them distasteful or not.

WORKS CITED

Breitenstein, Dave. "Amendments: 1, 4, 8 Fail; 2, 5, 6 Pass." <dbreitenstein@news-press.com>. November 2, 2010. Accessed 11/04/10.

Clark, David Leman. *John Milton and St. Paul's School*. New York: Columbia UP, 1948.

Lowen, Linda. "Ten Arguments for Abortion and Against Abortion." <About.com>. Accessed 11/04/10.Chapter 3

CONVERSATION
AND DISCUSSION

John Gastil

Conversation is the soul of democracy.
        —Joohan Kim,
    Robert Wyatt, and
        Elihu Katz[1]

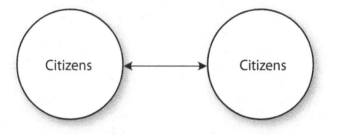

LET'S JOIN AN ONLINE CONVERSATION already in progress. And, yes, the following exchange is real. . . .

Eric shouts in frustration. He has just read a newspaper head-line about New Jersey's troops that have died in the Iraq War: "Jersey's share of a somber toll: 53 who won't see home again." So he puts his fingers on his keyboard and writes his 1,997th post at conservative-talk.com. The point of that headline, he surmises, "was that, even if it had been worth it to end the rule of Saddam Hussein, there didn't seem to be a good reason why troops remain to secure a democratic Iraq. The subtler message was that their lives had been wasted." After comparing the Iraq coverage to reporting from World War II, he calls out to his fellow conservatives, "I think in order to get the [conservative/pro-war] movement some more momentum, we will have to eventually deal with the media. Thoughts?"

The first reply comes from a sympathetic reader going by the handle Mobile Vulgus: "I think Americans ARE 'dealing with the media,'" he says wryly. "Newspapers are falling apart in readership. The Network News is a shadow of its former self in viewership, and news magazines have lower subscription rates every year."

The next reply, however, challenges Eric's main points. Ken's posting offers historical perspective by way of his own experi-ence. "Eric," he writes, "I remember sitting at the radio listening to the grim facts of war. 'Today we lost a hundred and twenty aircraft over Germany' was typical. The movie news reels showed Tarawa beaches awash with Marine dead. [World War II] was started because we were attacked; we knew who was responsible." By contrast, Ken argues, the Iraq War is now officially being waged "to remove a dictator (who we placed in power, just as we did to Pinochet and Noriega). We have lost two thousand people for what, to establish democracy? Why don't we go after Malaysia—there you can get five years for not being Muslim but being Christian or Jewish. I think they need democracy, too, don't you? Let's invade them."

WIRichie1971 quickly comes to Eric's aid and offers this challenge to Ken: "Okay Kenny [sic], I call bs: where are your links supporting the claim the CIA installed Saddam in power? Every biography I have ever read about him claimed he murdered his way to the top."

As I write, Ken has not yet taken up that challenge.[2] I briefly consider whether to jump into the fray or maintain my professional distance. A quick search on Google confirms my recollection that the PBS program *Frontline* explored early links between Saddam and the Central Intelligence Agency (CIA),[3] but I don't want to register at conservative-talk.com to make that point. I have enough junk e-mail as it is. Instead of posting, I return to my day job—writing this book.

Conversations like these happen every day, more likely every minute, in the online community, just as they have happened face to face for millennia. In a democratic society, informal discussions make up a large percentage of the universe of political communication messages that people produce. Though political talk itself is ancient, how we talk, whom we talk with, and what we discuss has varied considerably. Like most of our other basic social practices, from standing quietly in elevators to wearing black at funerals, talking about politics is a cultural accomplishment that requires a set of general rules that we learn through childhood socialization and have come to take for granted as adults. Our knowledge of those rules is tacit in that we cannot always articulate them, but they are real, whether or not we can see them at work.[4] To understand the hows and whys of modern political discussions, such as the one that took place between Eric, Mobile Vulgus, Ken(ny?), and WIRichie1971, it is useful to begin with a bit of history.

HISTORICAL NOTES ON POLITICAL CHATTER

If the early political history of human civilization was one of repression and intolerance, it is fair to say that deliberative political conversation is on the upswing since those ages. As Susan Herbst has observed, "The hallmark of an oppressive society is the absence of a rich and varied public sphere where citizens can convene to debate vital questions of the day."[5]

Where open, unfettered political conversation first became the norm remains unclear, but we do know some early forerunners of modern conversational practices. As early as 1617, the French developed salons in Paris, not for haircuts and spa treatments but for conversation among the social elite outside of the palace or other places of government. In this setting, conversation was refined as an art, purposeful in its ends but open in its structure. Satisfying and effective conversation required the advance planning and graceful facilitation of a hostess, or salonnière, typically a woman of high social standing.

Herbst offers us this quick peek into one such conversation, culled from the notes of Mademoiselle Quinault, who was leading a group through reflections on religion. At one point, Monsieur Duclos asked the group, "Where does this nation keep its reasoning capacity? It scoffs at people of other lands, and yet is more credulous [ready to believe] than they." Monsieur Rousseau replied, "I can pardon its credulity, but not its condemnation of those whose credulity differs from its own." Mademoiselle Quinault interjected that "in religious matters, everyone was right," but "all people should stick to the religion in which they were born." Rousseau countered that they should certainly not stay with their inherited faith "if it is a bad religion, for then it can only do much harm." In the exchanges that followed, Mademoiselle Quinault decided that her own point of view lacked merit. The others, she recalled, "refuted me with arguments which did, as a matter of fact, appear to be better than mine."[6] These conversations were not trivial intellectual or theological exercises because they provided at least a thin slice of French society the space in which they could explore new ideas that would, ultimately, challenge the power of not only the church but of the king himself.

Appropriately enough, it would be the Frenchman Alexis de Tocqueville, who would come to recognize a new kind of civic discourse taking place in the still-young United States. Americans had discovered their own brand of spirited exchange, but what made it particularly remarkable in de Tocqueville's eyes was how far the Americans had gone toward overcoming the stiff reserve of the English:

> If two Englishmen chance to meet where they are surrounded by strangers whose language and manners are almost unknown to them, they will first stare at each other with much curiosity and a kind of secret uneasiness; they will then turn away, or if one accosts the other, they will take care to converse only with a constrained and absent air, upon very unimportant subjects. Yet there is no enmity between these men; they have never seen each other before, and each believes the other to be a respectable person.
>
> In America where the privileges of birth never existed and where riches confer no peculiar rights on their possessors, men unacquainted with one another are very ready to frequent the same places and find neither peril nor advantage in the free interchange of their thoughts. If they meet by accident, they neither seek nor avoid intercourse; their manner is therefore natural, frank, and open. . . .

What made white American men different from their English counterparts, whom most counted as their ancestors? The answer, de Tocqueville reasoned, was "their social condition"—the relative indifference to social rank and class.[7]

The cultural contours of conversation have ebbed and flowed in the United States, as elsewhere. One particularly important trend was the early 19th century movement from informal, one-on-one conversation to structured group discussion. Roughly one hundred years ago, it became fashionable to debate and discuss ideas in large groups, such as a debate club, an open forum, or a town hall.[8]

As the popular affection for discussion grew, educators adapted their pedagogy away from lecture toward a more interactive method of instruction. In 1928, two influential books appeared, *Public Discussion and Debate* and *The Process of Group Thinking*.[9] These works helped to formalize emerging practices into a set of rules and procedures for effective discussion.

As recounted by communication scholar Ernest Bormann, discussion advocates insisted that "the individual citizen has an innate worth and dignity," which means that they are not to be manipulated for the state's purposes. Thus, each citizen should be free to discover his or her own opinions, and "public discussion gives citizens a chance to hear all sides of important public questions." Specifically, discussion should deploy "the scientific method" to conduct a rational analysis after discussants have "purged themselves of all emotional prejudices, interests, and biases." In the end, this process would benefit not only the individual but also the society, for "in the long run the majority of informed citizens would make the right decision."[10]

This rational model of discussion is still with us today, and it shapes the way many Americans think about conversation and discussion. Most of all, it has a profound influence on modern conceptions of what it means to have a deliberative conversation.

IMAGINING A DELIBERATIVE CONVERSATION

The Ideal Speech Situation

Modern deliberative democratic theory comes directly from the cultural tradition that Bormann calls the public discussion model. Among the most influential works setting the stage for modern theories of deliberation are two works by German philosopher Jürgen Habermas, the *Structural Transformation of the Public Sphere* and *Communication and the Evolution of Society*.[11] In these works, Habermas tried to conceptualize an "ideal speech situation," in which two or more persons could infinitely question one another's beliefs about the world until each perspective had been fully scrutinized, leaving only a limited set of valid statements on which to base one's conclusions about an issue. Behind the abstract, at times impenetrable, philosophical language of Habermas's theory was none other than the public discussion model—the ideal of a rational exchange of views resulting in enlightened understanding.

There is no question but that this is part of what ideal deliberative conversation entails. In fact, the analytic process described in the left-hand column of Figure 8.1 conforms to this rational ideal to a degree. After all, gathering data and analyzing it systematically using consistent criteria is a relatively rigid way of deducing a solution.

Democratic Conversation

Deliberation, however, is more than this. Around the same time that Habermas was shaping his political theory, Benjamin Barber was capturing the imagination of scholars and citizens alike with his popular polemic *Strong Democracy*. Barber's book was an indictment of thin democracy, a bland soup of legal rights and institutions lacking in human connection and any tangible sense of a public. "At the heart of strong democracy," Barber insisted, "is talk."[12] By *talk*, Barber was not referring to the cold exchange and aggregation of individuals' predefined interests into a majority preference; rather, he imagined a more complex mix of imagining, wondering aloud, listening, and understanding. If thin democracy

General Definition of Deliberation	Specific Meaning for Conversation/Discussion
Analytic Process	
Create a solid information base.	Discuss personal and emotional experiences, as well as known facts.
Prioritize the key values at stake.	Reflect on your own values, as well as those of others present.
Identify a broad range of solutions.	Brainstorm a wide variety of ways to address the problem.
Weigh the pros, cons, and trade-offs among solutions.	Recognize the limitations of your own preferred solution and the advantages of others.
Make the best decision possible.	Update your own opinion in light of what you have learned. No joint decision need be reached.
Social Process	
Adequately distribute speaking opportunities.	Take turns in conversation or take other action to ensure a balanced discussion.
Ensure mutual comprehension.	Speak plainly to each other and ask for clarification when confused.
Consider other ideas and experiences.	Listen carefully to what others say, especially when you disagree.
Respect other participants.	Presume that other participants are honest and well intentioned. Acknowledge their unique life experiences and perspectives.

FIGURE 8.1

Key Features of Deliberative Conversation and Discussion

reduced talk to "the hedonistic speech of bargaining," then strong democracy would celebrate conversation.[13]

By *conversation* Barber meant a more open-ended process that was as much about mutual discovery as problem solving. In Barber's more florid prose, "A conversation follows an informal dialectic in which talk is used not to chart distinctions in the typical analytic fashion but to explore and create commonalities."[14] Talk of this sort must be open, inclusive, and free flowing: "Because conversation responds to the endless variety of human experience and respects the initial legitimacy of every human perspective, it is served by many voices rather than by one and achieves a rich ambiguity rather than a narrow clarity."[15]

With that in mind, look at the right-hand column in Figure 8.1 and notice that the analytic process includes personal and emotional experiences as well as facts. It involves introspection on subjective values, rather than merely objective analysis. It also includes open-ended brainstorming, holding more than one perspective at a time, and possibly never reaching a decision. In other words, it may be enough to just talk and listen for a while.

The social process in Figure 8.1 draws on both the Habermasian and Barberic conceptions of talk. Equal access, comprehension, and consideration have a rationalist side, but the social process of deliberation also speaks directly to Barber's interest in mutual respect and the consideration of "the other" as a whole person—more than just a source of ideas and information that happens to be human. Philosopher John Weithman describes this process as follows:

> Citizens taking part in public deliberation should be willing to offer considerations in favor of their positions that will enable others to see what reasons they have for them. They must be appropriately responsive to the reactions and replies those considerations evoke. They must be appropriately responsive to the considerations put forward by others in favor of their positions. And they must respect at least those other participants who show that they are willing to comply with the norms of well-conducted deliberation.[16]

Gricean Maxims

Lest the deliberative model of conversation sound like a political philosopher's ungrounded abstraction, we should notice the many ways in which it corresponds to the universally taken-for-granted assumptions of human conversation. Linguist H. Paul Grice posited a series of rules or maxims that we all unconsciously follow as listeners to make sense of everyday conversation.[17] Figure 8.2 transposes each of the maxims into common expressions used in vernacular English. They can be summarized even more succinctly in the statement "Briefly tell me the complete truth I need to hear." The deliberative variant could be similarly summarized as "Let's briefly exchange the truths we need to share."

Maxim of Quality: Truth
- Do not say what you believe to be false ("Don't lie").
- Do not say that for which you lack adequate evidence ("Don't go out on a limb").

Maxim of Quantity: Information
- Make your contribution as informative as is required for the current purposes of the exchange ("Let's hear the facts").
- Do not make your contribution more informative than is required ("Too much information!").

Maxim of Relation: Relevance
- Be relevant ("Stay on topic").

Maxim of Manner: Clarity
- Avoid obscurity of expression ("Make some sense").
- Avoid ambiguity ("Don't waffle or be vague").
- Be brief ("Keep it short").
- Be orderly ("Keep it organized").

FIGURE 8.2
Gricean Maxims in Plain English

One of the ways we have confirmed that these maxims are at the core of our rules of speech is by watching the linguistic behavior of autistic children. Children with a specific language impairment have difficulty recognizing the violation of maxims, and this makes normal conversation tremendously difficult for them, both as speakers and listeners.[18]

In practice, we frequently violate the maxims to varying degrees. Normally, their violation simply prompts the listener to make an inference, such as when a truncated comment ("I'm tired") prompts the listener to construct a more complete thought, based on the context ("I'm too tired to go out to a movie"). Other times, though, the accidental or careless violation of the maxims results in confusion, misunderstanding, and frustration. Their willful and malicious violation can result in manipulation or deception. And, more happily, their intentional, playful violation can result in comic genius.

For our purposes, not only do the maxims parallel some of the principles of deliberative conversation, they also provide another illustration of what a conversational ideal looks like. It is important to remember, as we read about how people talk about politics in everyday life, that the deliberative ideal of conversation and discussion is just that—an ideal. Like democracy, the conversational ideal is something that we can use as a critical standard for judging the quality of actual talk, but it is not something humans can live up to, at least not all the time. Moreover, the deliberative ideal is something that—even if not always clearly articulated—is widely recognized, as shown in a pair of inductive studies on how professional facilitators or lay jurors understand the term.[19]

INFORMAL CONVERSATION

In this chapter, we consider two kinds of talk—casual political conversations and more organized group discussions. Both are informal processes, and neither has a direct link to official decisions. Conversation, however, has less structure and, more rarely, an orientation toward formal problem solving. We begin by studying the flow and content of conversation, but when we turn to look at the process of discussion, we examine a slightly different kind of deliberation.

Drawing on Media and Personal Experience

Sociologist William Gamson broke new ground in 1992 with *Talking Politics*, a careful account of how small groups of friends and acquaintances discuss political issues in informal chats. He used a modified focus group research method to bring together not strangers but small peer groups to participate in loosely moderated conversations on a variety of current affairs. He transcribed thirty-seven discussions involving 188 diverse working-class participants. Afterward, he concluded, "Listening to their conversations over a period of an hour or more, one is struck by the deliberative quality of their construction of meaning about these complex issues." He saw the participants in the peer-group conversations "achieve considerable coherence in spite of a great many handicaps, some flowing from limitations in the media discourse that they find available and others from their own lack of experience with the task."[20]

The first point Gamson made in *Talking Politics* is that the conversations were deliberative. At the time he wrote his book, Gamson did not make an explicit link to work on deliberative democracy; rather, he used the term in its vernacular meaning. Nonetheless, it is striking how many of Gamson's specific findings highlight aspects of the definition of deliberative conversation in Figure 8.1. For example, Gamson's research often explores the development of opposition—how dissent can congeal into organized resistance to dominant ideas and institutions. In the study detailed in his book, he explored the balance between themes and counterthemes. For example, two contrasting technology themes are making "progress through technology" and maintaining "harmony with nature."[21] In the deliberative framework, discussing themes and counterthemes constitutes weighing alternative evaluative criteria or reflecting on your own values, as well as those of others present. Gamson found that groups readily drew on opposing themes or values in their discussions, implicitly considering each and weighing them against one another. In other words, Gamson's research showed evidence that everyday political conversation is, indeed, often deliberative.[22]

Gamson's second point was that the quality of a group's conversation comes from drawing on its available resources, no matter how limited. Two principal sources of information and ideas in peer conversations are media content and personal experience. Probably the most common interpretation of Gamson's work is that he found out how, in more concrete detail, media content frames how citizens talk about issues.[23]

For example, the citizens Gamson observed drew on media coverage to inform their discussions of nuclear power. Participants discussed the catastrophic 1986 accident at the Chernobyl nuclear power plant, in which a nuclear reactor collapsed and deadly amounts of radioactivity spread into the surrounding environment.[24] That they mentioned the topic is unremarkable, as it was a gripping current event. What was more noteworthy was that participants latched on to particular facts or arguments presented in the media to frame their understanding of nuclear power. For instance, one fact that had come up in media discussions of Chernobyl came into a conversation in this way: Ida, a bookkeeper in her late sixties, argued that Chernobyl should not make Americans worry about our own power plants. "You see," she explained, "our plants are built better than that one." She then added that "it didn't have the safety features that our plants already have." In a separate conversation, Joe, a firefighter in his fifties, interjected, "Look at Chernobyl. They're comparing it to the nuclear power plants in the United States. They can't do that! . . . That plant's antiquated. Know what I mean?"[25]

The plant comparison Ida and Joe heard in the media was not just an idle bit of trivia. Rather, it was an important piece of information that helped them understand a problem and, ultimately, judge the value of maintaining the nuclear power program in the United States. In the next chapter, we consider whether media coverage of issues such as these is "fair and balanced." For now, it is important only to notice how conversations can help citizens broaden their base of information by facilitating the exchange of information they learn through the media.

A less widely recognized finding in Gamson's work is that people's conversations draw on personal experience as much as they do on media content. This is particularly true for certain issues, such as affirmative action, which directly touch on people's daily lives. But personal knowledge came into discussions of every issue Gamson studied. Returning to the issue of nuclear safety, Gamson admitted, "Initially, I thought that the issues of nuclear power . . . were so far removed from people's daily lives that it surprised me to find a substantial minority introducing experiential knowledge. . . ."[26] In one such conversation, two discussants in their early twenties had this exchange:

Rich: From my window at school, I could see the Yankee—no, what was it? What was the one in Vermont? Vernon, the Vernon power plant.

Pat: You could see that?

Rich: Yeah.

Pat: You could see the lights of the plant?

Rich: You can see the lights—about eighteen miles down the river. And they were busted every three or four months for venting off the steam, which is really illegal. You're supposed to cool it with the water tanks and everything. But it cost a lot of money, and they didn't care. I mean, they're run so lax.[27]

As this example illustrates, referring back to the definition of deliberation in Figure 8.1, political conversations like these touch on "personal and emotional experiences," as well as "known facts." In Gamson's terms, conversations like these pull together personal and cultural knowledge to understand or "frame" issues. Gamson observes that "there is a special robustness to frames that are held together with a full combination of resources"—when conversants effectively marshal all their experiences and recollections.[28] In this way, conversation can help people analyze problems and arrive at judgments. By talking with others, they broaden their information base and the range of arguments they can consider; however, as we will see later, there is no guarantee that the conversation will include a diverse set of participants.

Community Bonding Through Conversation

Whatever its merits as an analytic process, political conversation serves other functions. Foremost among these is developing a sense of community, what Barber calls "exploring and creating commonalities."[29] The recent research of political scientist Katherine Cramer Walsh helps us understand this process. She spent three years with "the Old Timers," a group of politically conservative, retired white men at a corner store in Ann Arbor, Michigan. Her goal was to better understand what informal political conversation accomplishes for its participants. At the conclusion of her study, she wrote a personal letter to the Old Timers. She explained her research to the corner store gang in these words:

> Many political scientists believe conversation is the soul of democracy. . . . The idea is that by talking to each other, Americans can create a "better" society and learn to get along with many different kinds of people. By spending time with you (as well as a group of women who get together every week at a local church), I came to a different conclusion. When most people talk informally about politics, they aren't doing it to solve the world's problems. Their intent is not to improve democracy or foster brotherly love. Instead, their conversations are a way of sharing time, figuring out the world together, and feeling like part of a community.[30]

Walsh acknowledged that she, along with many others, read that finding as a "pessimistic conclusion" because it implies that conversation reinforces borders between social groups rather than bridging them. The men at the corner store provide each other with a palpable sense of community, and that alone is valuable. To the extent that conversation builds strong, isolated communities, however, it cannot function to bring a diverse society together into a coherent public.[31]

Diversity in Conversation

Turning away from her detailed case study, Walsh looked to survey data to find out whether other voluntary associations were as homogenous as the Old Timers. To her chagrin (but not surprise), she found that men tend to affiliate with men—not women—when they join senior groups, fraternal or service organizations, book clubs, civic groups, and the like. Women are even more likely to seek out fellow women. Moreover, racial or ethnic homogeneity in such groups is even greater. Thus, for example, sixty-one percent of women reported that their most important and active voluntary group had no racial diversity, and forty-one percent said their groups included no men. Even in the many associations with diverse memberships, the problem is that all too often, people tend to affiliate with members more like themselves and then place greater value on those particular affiliations.

Political communication researchers Diana Mutz and Paul Martin addressed this question more precisely.[32] Their survey data focused on conversations, per se, rather than the voluntary associations in which such exchanges take place. They also focused not on the diversity of participants' backgrounds but on the diversity of their political viewpoints. Their survey asked respondents to report their own political point of view and then compare that view with those they hear in a range of communication settings. Results showed that the setting in which participants were least likely to hear different views was in talking with their "primary discussant." Others' views begin to diverge significantly from one's own only after leaving discussants and voluntary associations and entering the workplace setting. Ultimately, it is the media sources that offer contrary points of view, and this underscores the importance of considering the potential value of mediated deliberation.

Conversations and voluntary associations, however, are more politically homogenous for some than for others. Mutz and Martin found that Republicans tended to talk with Republicans to an even greater degree than Democrats kept to their own, and this was true both for individual discussants and voluntary associations to which respondents belonged. Independents, by contrast, had a harder time finding like-minded voices anywhere: primary conversation partners tended, on balance, to share their views, but in every other setting, independents found contrary points of view to be the norm.[33]

Disagreement and Persuasion

If conversations are so often among like-minded persons, can they really be deliberative? This was one of the questions motivating the research of Robert Huckfeldt, Paul Johnson, and John Sprague. They reasoned that "the benefits of deliberation," such as promoting tolerance, compromising, and increasing political engagement, "depend on disagreement, which is defined in terms of interaction among citizens who hold divergent viewpoints and perspectives regarding politics." If we only talked with like-minded citizens, deliberation would become difficult because we would miss important information; misconstrue, forget, or overlook important alternatives; or never know others' value priorities. Even if people chatted with people whose views differed from their own, there is no guarantee that they would, in fact, deliberate. After all, "individuals may ignore, avoid, or dismiss politically disagreeable viewpoints."[34]

Huckfeldt and his colleagues set out to understand what gives rise to "effective" political conversation (mutual "comprehension," when phrased in deliberative terms) and "persuasive" conversation, which results when people change their mind on an issue. A key consideration in studying conversation is an individual's partisanship. Strong partisans are those who hold the firm conviction that their political party is best. One variety of a strong partisan, for example, is the "yellow dog Democrat." The term comes from the 1928 presidential election, in which a prominent Democratic senator from Alabama broke with his party to support Republican Herbert Hoover. Angry Alabama Democrats showed their party loyalty by boasting, "I'd vote for a yellow dog if he ran on the Democratic ticket."[35]

Let's imagine that you are alternately conversing with Susan, with the "S" signifying a strong partisan, and Wendy, with the "W" representing her relatively weak partisanship. With regard to mutual comprehension, you might guess that relative to Wendy, Susan is a poor conversational partner because she tends to be bombastic, stubborn, and unwilling to listen to you. Quite to the contrary, Huckfeldt and his colleagues found that people are no more likely to avoid or misjudge people like Susan than they are anyone else. Susan is just as likely to be a good listener as Wendy, and Susan is more likely to be an effective communicator in that she will make more clear, memorable statements about her own views. Moreover, if you and Susan disagree, this is unlikely to upset or disturb you, because you come away from conversations with Susan more clear in your own views than if you had just spoken with Wendy.[36]

Another important difference between weak and strong partisans is in their susceptibility to influence through political conversation. If you are trying to persuade Susan to change her vote, you are unlikely to make any progress. If you then try to persuade Wendy, you will be successful, so long as Wendy has other discussants who share your view. In other words, weak partisans might change their mind if numerous people in their social network try to convince them to change their vote to a rival candidate. One nudge is not enough, but when people get strong signals from different corners of their social network, the individual nudges add up to a sufficiently powerful push.[37]

Huckfeldt's research team also found that both weak and strong partisans, along with independents, typically converse in interlocking networks. For example, Susan and Wendy might be the two people you most often turn to when you want to talk about politics, but you are not the only one they seek. Susan has two other friends and a co-worker with whom she frequently converses on public issues, and Wendy has a classmate she talks to, in addition to you and Susan.

This pattern of small, interlocking political conversation networks can make deliberative conversations a powerful force for changing attitudes. Figure 8.3 illustrates this process in the case of three connected conversation networks—A, B, and C. Imagine a series of conversations happening over the course of three years. In Year 1, the person who participates in networks A and B (person A3/ B1) is influenced by the three Democratic partisans because this person's network consists of two strong Democrats (A1, B2), one weak Democrat (A2), and one independent (B3). During this same year, there are no other strong influences: the other independent (B3/C1), in particular, has a more mixed network consisting of two strong Democrats (B2, C2), one strong Republican (C3), and a fellow independent.

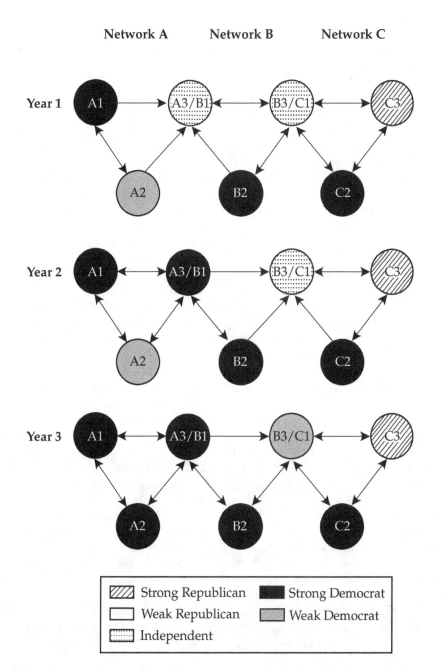

FIGURE 8.3

Changing Patterns of Partisanship Over Three Years of Hypothetical Conversations

Turning to Year 2, person A3/B1 has become a strong Democratic partisan as a result of Year 1 influences. Now the remaining independent is getting more consistent pressure to swing to the left because his or her former independent ally (A3/B1) is now a strong Democrat. Three-quarters of the person's conversants are Democratic, and that is enough to convert him or her to a weak Democrat by the beginning of Year 3. This former independent may never become a strong Democrat, owing to the steady counterarguments coming from C3, but without a change in the size or composition of the individual's network, he or she is likely to remain a Democrat indefinitely.

Something else is happening in Year 2 as well. The weak partisan Democrat A2 is now being persuaded by Al and A3/B1 to firm up his or her convictions. By Year 3, A2 has moved from weak to strong Democrat.

At this point, all three networks in this diagram stabilize, with no further shifts to the left or the right. Notice, though, that even this diagram is a simplification of the interlocking nature of conversation networks. For instance, it is likely that persons Al and A2, along with B2, C2, and C3, have additional conversational partners not shown in Figure 8.3. In other words, the effects of shifts in these three networks could radiate out even farther. As Huckfeldt and his colleagues concluded, "The conversion of any single individual to a particular candidate's cause is not only important in terms of a single vote or a single unit of social influence. It is also important in terms of the enhancement and attenuation effects that it creates throughout the networks of relationships within which the individual is imbedded, quite literally transforming entire patterns of social influence."[38]

This is not to say that it is conversations alone that change people's attitudes. Quite to the contrary, recall from the work of Gamson that the ideas and information people receive from the media constitute much of the meat in their conversations. Add to this a separate study's finding that people who get issue-specific news from the media are also the most likely to engage in issue-specific and general political discussions and one can see more clearly the media-conversation connection.[39] As Huckfeldt and his fellow researchers concluded, "Political interdependence among citizens might actually *magnify* the importance of events in the external political environment."[40]

As a final note, it appears that the conversational influence Huckfeldt and others found in the United States is common in European nations. A study of Britain, Germany, Spain, and the United States found that spouses, relatives, and friends influenced voting choices in each country during elections in 1990–1993, with the strongest influence coming from persons in the communication network who were closest to the respondent (e.g., spouses and close personal friends).[41]

MOVING FROM CONVERSATION TO DISCUSSION

To this point, we have examined the informal political conversations that occur among family, friends, and acquaintances. One of those conversational settings included the Old Timers, who met each morning over coffee in Ann Arbor. Their conversational ritual was unusual in that it occurred regularly in a public setting. Most political conversations occur spontaneously in more private settings, such as the home, work site, or office.[42] Even in a public venue, however, it was still a closed conversation among friends.

Public discussions are a bit different. Participants in these discussions can include complete strangers, their occurrence is more programmed, and sometimes their process is managed by a facilitator or otherwise governed by a set of explicit ground rules. Discussions are important forms of political talk, but they are so varied that it is useful to look at discussions one setting at a time. We begin with one that is half conversation, half discussion—the online chat room or discussion board.

Cyberchatting

Let's return to the exchange that began this chapter, the exchanges about Iraq involving Eric, Mobile Vulgus, Ken, and WIRichie1971. That conversation could be categorized as many things—socializing, seeking information, debating, or venting frustration, among others. These things can take place during both conversations and discussions, but what gives us the first glimpse of a discussion is a stricter requirement of topical coherence and the presumption that the exchange is "public." In the opening excerpt, Eric was not sure who would reply to his initial post, but he was reasonably sure his suggested topic would generate discussion. In fact, he could not be sure anyone would reply. Not every topic posted on a discussion board or offered in a chat room has takers because there is no social sanction against lurking silently or ignoring other visitors in cyberspace.

Because the Internet is a relatively new communication medium, extensive research on its use as a means of generating discussion does not exist. It is common knowledge that Internet users are disproportionately younger, as is typical of any new communication technology. A representative telephone survey of Americans' Internet use patterns suggests a less obvious finding—that the Internet may be drawing young people into politics and civic affairs who would otherwise be unlikely to engage in such activities.[43] Though it is clear that the Internet is yet another medium for politically active persons to express themselves and obtain political information, it appears that the Internet may draw in some of the nonvoting, politically disaffected younger demographic, which includes anyone less than thirty years of age.

Another indirect piece of evidence for the impact of Internet use is how information exchange online sparks social capital—the network of personal associations and mutual trust that are essential for democratic society.[44] A national survey found that casual Internet use for entertainment and socializing had no connection to one's social capital or political participation, but the use of the Internet for information exchange did have such a relationship.[45]

What about the content of online discussion? Little research has investigated the subject, but at least one finding is very encouraging. A concern addressed in more detail in the next chapter is the spiral of silence, whereby people choose not to express their opinions when they perceive that theirs is the minority or dissenting point of view. A comparison of face-to-face and online groups found that in both cases persons in the minority were willing to speak their minds on the controversial subject of abortion.[46]

Even if one person in the minority is reluctant to speak, so long as another speaks up, the view is brought into the discussion; in an online discussion, it is not always easy to see how many people are present, so it is even more ambiguous whether one view or another is being underrepresented in the discussion. Moreover, members of the majority, more so than those in the minority, may choose not to speak up simply because they have already had their view articulated by others.[47] From the standpoint of deliberation, what is more important than hearing every person's voice is hearing every perspective, and in this sense it appears that online discussions are at least as valuable as those that occur offline.

That is good news because there are a growing number of sites appearing on the Internet devoted to promoting online discussion. One of those is e-thePeople. org, which first appeared online in August of 2000. Every day, hundreds of new articles and comments are posted on this site, and the subjects range from longstanding political debates to issues of the day, such as hurricanes, international crises, and political scandals. A study of the site conducted in 2002 found that the most common reasons for participating in the e-thePeople discussions were "to voice my opinion" and "to influence policy makers," specifically the elected officials who sometimes take part in e-thePeople's discussions. In addition, more than a third of users reported coming to the site "to listen to others," which is encouraging from the standpoint of deliberation. More than a quarter of the regular users of the site, in fact, reported that participating in online discussions gave them greater "awareness of viewpoints" and helped them follow the news and current events. Those are central purposes for traditional political conversation, so e-thePeople is likely extending the same habits and benefits of political talk to its users.[48]

From the standpoint of the organizers of e-thePeople, there are also some disappointing findings about their site. More often than not, it is replicating the offline reality of homogenous conversation: fifty-seven percent of its users rate the other users whom they interact with as "like-minded" people. More discouraging is the finding that only seven percent of the thousands of conversations begun in the past year were "successful," as measured by a decent popularity rating and at least twenty or more replies.[49] Thus, most of the conversations are like the Iraq thread that Eric began at conservative-talk.com, a perfectly interesting topic that attracts some attention but then essentially ends, often in what would seem to be the middle of a discussion.[50]

National Issues Forums

From the most critical standpoint, cyberchatting is a glorified form of political conversation, and as such it is usually unqualified to call itself a true discussion.

Michael Schudson takes the position that public discussion distinguishes itself from mere political conversation by being more strictly rule governed and goal directed (i.e., oriented toward solving public problems, choosing policies, or arguing on behalf of one's principles, rights, or interests). In his view, conversation is not the soul of democracy because it is too often aimless, unstructured, and inconsequential, and it typically fails to bring together sufficiently divergent views to really call it an inclusive, public activity.[51]

Fortunately, there exist a wide range of public discussion projects active in the United States.[52] Each provides a glimpse of the kind of power that discussion can have, even when it is not strictly oriented toward decision making. The best contemporary political discussion programs address public issues of immediate local or national relevance. Since 1990, the number of modern discussion programs has proliferated, and two of the most widely used and influential are the programs developed by the National Issues Forums (NIF) Institute.

The NIF is a decentralized public discussion program for which thousands of conveners have received training. Political deliberation is the central concern of NIF, which promotes the idea that citizens must make hard choices and take responsibility for the public judgments at which they arrive through deliberation. All of the national issues that NIF addresses, such as health care and criminal justice, are those that "engage our most deeply held convictions about what we value." On these issues, "policy options pull and tug on our values." Real "choice work" forces us to acknowledge the negative implications of our favored choices and the positive value of alternatives; we must see the effects of policies on ourselves as well as others. Through careful and empathic listening, we force ourselves to come to understand and respect other people's perspectives, and we combine diverse viewpoints to create "a sense of the whole." When we engage in this kind of deliberation, political "conflict is not only among us, it is within us."[53]

NIF presumes that the best context for doing this kind of work is face-to-face deliberation among fellow citizens. In NIF parlance, deliberation is "the act of weighing carefully. . . . It's a process for determining what action is in the best interest of the public as a whole." During a forum, we have the opportunity to "talk through" an issue with peers; we begin "talking to understand our options, face up to our limitations, and put ourselves in a position to make a serious choice." After a forum, citizens continue talking and thinking about both facts and values, further developing their views on the issues they discussed in the forums. Eventually, preferences evolve into choices and private opinions become "public judgments." Judgment is distinct from mere opinion because it "rests on what we think the second time—after we have talked with others, considered the consequence of our options, and worked through the conflicts that arise."[54]

Does NIF, in fact, teach participants how to develop more informed and reflective opinions on current policy issues? More broadly, does it achieve its goal of educating citizens in the art of public deliberation? Considerable research has been done on NIF, and the balance suggests that it does, indeed, have some of the anticipated impacts on the people who take part in the forums. Among its effects are broadening participants' outlooks, causing them to think beyond their narrowly defined self-interests to arrive at more well-conceived judgments on public issues. In addition, NIF appears to teach participants new ways of participating in groups and talking about politics. Though NIF may not make people ideal deliberators, it does appear to reduce the likelihood that they will be domineering or unwilling to listen when talking about politics with fellow citizens.[55]

So many people want to improve the quality of discussion in their communities that NIF has become remarkably popular. During 1993, for example, by NIF's best estimate, forums were convened by approximately 1,440 adult literacy programs, 2,600 high schools, and 1,360 civic organizations.[56] Given the success of NIF's book publishing, the number of forums has likely grown in the years since.

In the end, even the NIF forums are like political conversations in that they often involve like-minded, self-selected participants exchanging information and ideas in a way that arrives at no final conclusion. Moreover, there is evidence that people leave NIF forums more convinced of their original views than newly aware of a publicly shared common ground.[57] Even in these cases, though, it is clear that participants learned something about themselves, their own views, and deliberation itself. There is also evidence that participants can then apply those lessons outside the forums to change how they talk about and address public problems.[58]

DIALOGUE AND DELIBERATION

Before you reach the back cover, this book will provide many examples of deliberative innovations that aim to improve how we talk to one another—conversationally, in more formal discussions, and in official meetings. Almost always I emphasize decision making, which is appropriate given the decision-oriented meaning of deliberation. At the level of conversation and discussion, though, this decision requirement can be relaxed somewhat, and participants can orient themselves more toward an open-ended dialogue.

This idea of having a dialogue holds great appeal for many civic reformers and citizens, many of whom worry that focusing exclusively on policy debate could cause us to overlook the important work that must be done before we can deliberate effectively. In their book *Moral Conflict*, communication scholars Barnett Pearce and Stephen Littlejohn argued that there are many instances where people come to public meetings unprepared to deliberate because they do not yet understand how other parties in a conflict reason and talk, let alone what views these other participants might have on the issue at hand. In these situations, dialogue might help to develop a kind of "creole language in which one side can communicate with the other."[59]

The Public Conversations Project

To get an idea of the power of dialogue, consider the case of the Public Conversations Project, an entity that weaves together the virtues of conversation and discussion into a single process. Since 1989, the project has tried to help apply the principles of family therapy and alternative dispute resolution to public conflicts. In their official materials, project staff define dialogue as "any conversation animated by a search for understanding rather than for agreements or solutions. It is not debate, and it is not mediation."[60]

Though they advocate an exploratory, open-ended conversation, one should not get the impression, however, that the project's approach to dialogue is loose. On the contrary, dialogues set up by the project follow a complex sequence of steps, as dialogue can be difficult to generate in the midst of bitter personal, partisan, and often moral or ideological conflict. Though each instance is unique in one or more respects, the project generally begins with these steps:

1. In response to an initial request, project organizers assess whether the participants in the conflict have the time and resources necessary to engage in dialogue.

2. Project staff research the issue and speak with conflict participants to learn the contours of the debate they are stuck inside, as well as those moments— if any—when they appeared to be having more fruitful exchanges.

3. Staff then create a meeting design and clear meeting objective, which is then communicated to the invitees from all parties involved in the conflict. Only those who agree to abide by the meeting's ground rules—or at least try to do so—are encouraged to attend.

4. The dialogue occurs in one meeting or a series of meetings, which always begin with a reiteration of the meeting's goals and rules. Thereafter, the structure of the conversations varies considerably, but there is always emphasis on asking questions, listening carefully, and taking turns speaking—the basics of an open-ended, exploratory conversation. Professional facilitators help participants stick to the rules and purpose of the meeting, but participants do the hard work of speaking frankly and listening attentively, even when hearing words that hurt or offend them.

Consider the case of abortion—the issue that sparked the Public Conversations Project.[61] The idea of bringing together prochoice advocates and pro-life activists may sound crazy to anyone who has seen these factions clash outside an abortion clinic or at a public rally. One side stands for personal liberty, grounded in the principles of liberal political philosophy and the principle of sexual equality advanced through the women's rights movement, whereas the other is led by its understanding of biblical scripture to oppose all threats to the life of the unborn and to challenge the spiritual health and morality of abortionists and the women who turn to them. Not fertile ground for dialogue, it would seem.

Since 1990, the project has used its approach to address this issue in Massachusetts and elsewhere. The questions posed to participants are deceptively simple:

> (1) How did you get involved with this issue? What's your personal relationship, or personal history with it? (2) We'd like to hear a little more about your particular beliefs and perspectives about the issues surrounding abortion. What is at the heart of the matter for you? (3) Many people we've talked to have told us that within their approach to this issue they find some gray areas, some dilemmas about their own beliefs or even some conflicts. Do you experience any pockets of uncertainty or lesser certainty, any concerns, value conflicts, or mixed feelings that you may have and wish to share?[62]

Questions such as these can get a conversation started, which invariably leads to both parties in the conversation acknowledging the issue's complexity and the difficulty they have talking constructively with their respective opponents. Consider how this comment from an online conversation moves from expressing hurt at being personally attacked to seeing some basis for common understanding:

> I certainly have felt stereotyped over the years. The pro-life community is very aggressive; I've had friends called "baby killer" and been told that we are "damned by God." Many people on both sides of the issue see it in very black and white terms—which, of course, is the ultimate silliness, since all reality is merely shades of gray.[63]

In moments like these, speakers move from reciting their own experience of being stereotyped and misunderstood to acknowledging, even if only fleetingly at first, the problems created by "people on both sides of the issue."

Once again, the purpose of such dialogue is not to resolve the abortion debate. Dialogue, instead, aims to promote understanding, appreciation, and respect. Instead of debating the issue of abortion, participants in these dialogues have—sometimes for the first time in their public lives—the experience of listening to the other side. As a result, common ground can be found on occasion, such as in improving prenatal care for low-income pregnant mothers or in providing women with birth control to prevent unwanted pregnancies. If the parties in the debate continue to debate, but more deliberatively and honestly, with a newfound respect for one another's views and commitments, the project has done its job.

Narratives and Storytelling

One of the most striking effects of dialogue is the personal stories that emerge. These stories, which sometimes include very detailed narratives about people's lives and their policy-relevant experiences, can arise in any number of deliberative settings, but processes that are too solution oriented and heavily facilitated tend to snuff them out.

For instance, when communications scholar David Ryfe conducted a study of the NIF, he was struck by participants' eagerness to tell stories, as well as the way forum facilitators cut stories short. "Strong facilitators," Ryfe concluded, "tend to short-circuit the storytelling process." They control the flow of conversation "by asking questions like, 'What bothers you about that?' and, 'What is your reaction to that?'" Seemingly helpful summarizing can also strip stories of their power. When facilitators continue to interject themselves into conversations, "forums tend to have a rapid-fire, scattershot quality. Participants tend to say less, to tell fewer stories, and to talk more directly to the facilitator ... and there is less of the thinking-out-loud."[64]

By contrast, many stories emerge in a series of online forums about what to build at the site of the former World Trade Center in New York City. Ryfe found the NIF stories helpful in getting participants down to the business of deliberating, and communications scholar Laura Black found that this was also the case in the online forums. Black distinguished among Introductory, Adversarial, Unitary, and Transformation story types.[65] Introductory stories served to engage participants in the task of deliberation by connecting abstract issues with their lived experiences. The two most common story types (Adversarial and Unitary), however, served as relatively straightforward means of argumentation. The Adversarial story amounts to an often emotional narrative argument for one side of an issue, whereas the Unitary story argues more tentatively and in a way that aims to include all participants. Consistent with Ryfe's findings, Black found that these stories can serve as a kind of evidence, furthering the deliberation on the policy question at hand.

Black also theorized that narratives can help groups work through values conflicts and form a shared identity—larger tasks that address the problem. Qualitative and quantitative analyses of the stories participants told showed that each of these types of story serve a powerful purpose for online discussion groups. Black found that the Unitary stories "can be useful to help group members move beyond the limitations of seeing their differences as simply a two-sided debate."[66] Though told from one person's own experience, these stories had the power to evoke a shared experience—in this case, that of a great sense of loss in the collapse of the Trade Center buildings. That, Black explains, can serve to bring participants together and lead them to "find areas for compromise or consensus within the group."[67]

A more uncommon variety of narrative Black encountered earned the label of Transformation stories. These stories are characterized by "mixed, contradictory, or changing emotions" entailed in "personal and social transformation." A typical Transformation story tells how a person "has changed his or her perspective" on the matter at hand, and it invites other participants to consider the fluidity of their own positions. Consider this example of a participant who changed her own sense of what would be an appropriate replacement for the Twin Towers:

> In the days after nine eleven I put up pictures of the Towers in my apartment. Coffee table books were returned to the coffee table and opened to those glorious pictures of downtown. . . . And then, after several weeks, the Towers—my beautiful Towers—began to look like two giant tombstones. It took a while for this to sink in, but it happened. A pair of tombstones standing over a soon-to-be cemetery. How ironic. And again I cried because I knew I would never be able to look at them the same way again. Yes, I'd love my Towers rebuilt. I'd love to go back to nine ten. But it can't happen. Everything is different. The terrorists "win" if we live in the past. Our spirit will not be broken. We will turn adversity into strengths. We will move on.[68]

Typical of this genre of story, the teller moves toward an inspirational tone, asking listeners to understand the transformation as a positive move to a place of greater serenity and clarity. It is not a smooth argument for a particular position because the teller is able to empathize with conflicting points of view. The telling of such a story makes it safe for other participants to express uncertainty. It provides others with the freedom to openly explore their own doubts and shifts in their thinking. And that, in the end, is one of the points of a dialogue—helping participants move from fixed positions in a tense debate to more flexible reflections open to discovery.

CONCLUSION

There is no inevitability to the occurrence of such dialogue, let alone more conventional political conversation and discussion. Though we can take discussion for granted as a common practice in a free society, it is just that—a practice, an activity that is socially constructed to be done a certain way, with certain people, at certain times, and in certain places. The historical record shows that modern political discussions, study circles, and issues forums are something that a culture invents and practices over the years, sometimes abandoning old practices in favor of new ones. National Issues Forums take us back to past ways of holding public discussions, and online chats are likely a sign of how we will discuss politics in the future, for better or worse.

Whatever form conversation and discussion take in the future, it is certain that they will both remain connected to other communication channels, particularly mass media. Whether in coffee shops, chat rooms, or issues forums, participants bring to their discussions things they have picked up from television, newspapers, radio, Web sites, and other media. In the next chapter, we consider just what those mediated messages add up to. If conversations and discussions can sometimes sustain one kind of deliberation, can the media produce another?

ENDNOTES

1. Kim,Wyatt, and Katz (1999, p. 362).
2. This conversation is posted online at http://forums.conservative-talk.com/tl764-treacherous-journalism.html. To protect the innocent, the grammar has been changed (a little).
3. See *Frontline* (http://www.pbs.org/wgbh/pages/frontline/shows/saddam/interviews/aburish.html).
4. This conception of tacit knowledge comes from Giddens (1984).
5. Herbst (1999, p. 187).
6. Quoted in Herbst (1999, pp. 192–93).
7. Tocqueville (1835/1961, book III). There is no doubt that in many respects, de Tocqueville idealized American society. If Americans of today seem more guarded and class conscious than these romanticized cultural pioneers, it is partly because the past is routinely lionized as a period of great civic spirit. Thus, Michael Schudson (1998) observed that "intellectuals have complained that 'we no longer have citizens' since at least 1750," when French political philosopher Jean-Jacques Rousseau lodged this very complaint about his own era (p. 295). There is little hard evidence tracking political conversational habits over long periods of time, so the question remains unsettled. As one exception, Huckfeldt, Johnson, and Sprague (2004, p. 44) cite a 1972–1990 longitudinal data set that shows decreasing correspondence between social networks and political preference. That might signal an increase in disagreement within conversations, but in the United States, increasingly sharp partisanship could signal the opposite trend (Abramowitz and Saunders, 1998).
8. See Mattson (1998), Levine (1990), and Gastil and Keith (2005).
9. Baird (1928) and Harrison (1928), respectively.
10. Bormann (1996, pp. 101–3).
11. Habermas (1979, 1989).
12. Barber (1984, p. 173).
13. Ibid., p. 179.
14. Ibid., p. 183.
15. Ibid., p. 185.
16. Weithman (2005, pp. 282–83). In Weithman's view, these are aspects of democratic character. I prefer to describe these as behaviors enacted during deliberation, not requiring that they reflect an ongoing disposition toward particular interactive norms. As long as one behaves in this way during a discussion, we can say deliberation took place without having to judge the underlying character of the participants.
17. Grice (1975).
18. Surian (1996).
19. On forum facilitators, see Mansbridge et al. (2006); on jurors, see Sprain and Gastil (2007).
20. Gamson (1992, p. 175).
21. Ibid., p. 136.
22. On the link between media use and deliberative conversational habits, see Moy and Gastil (2006).
23. Scheufele (1999, p. 106).

24. For background on this incident, see http://www.nrc.gov/reading-rm/doc-collections/fact-sheets/chernobyl-bg.html.
25. Gamson (1992, pp. 120–21).
26. Ibid., p. 131.
27. Ibid., p. 132.
28. Ibid., p. 128.
29. Barber (1984, p. 183).
30. Walsh (2004, p. 233).
31. Ibid., p. 234.
32. Mutz and Martin (2001). The authors also validate the accuracy of self-reported estimates of other points of view by comparing independent ratings of other sources (newspapers, discussants) with self-reported ratings and finding a remarkably good fit.
33. Ibid., pp. 101–2. Similar research on presidential voting in 2000 found that, on average, forty-eight percent of those who voted for Bush had conversation networks consisting exclusively of Bush voters, whereas forty-two percent of Gore voters had exclusively Gore-voting networks (Huckfeldt, Johnson, and Sprague, 2004, pp. 38–39).
34. Huckfeldt, Johnson, and Sprague (2004, pp. 13–14). See also Huckfeldt, Mendez, and Osborn (2004). On the benefits of conversational network diversity, and disagreement, for democracy, see Mutz (2006) and Scheufele et al. (2006).
35. Modern yellow dog Democrats are celebrated at http://www.yellowdogdemo-crat.com.
36. Huckfeldt, Johnson, and Sprague (2004, pp. 68–97).
37. Ibid., pp. 54–60.
38. Ibid., pp. 121–2.
39. Kim, Wyatt, and Katz (1999, pp. 371–73).
40. Huckfeldt, Johnson, and Sprague (2004, p. 122).
41. Schmitt-Beck (2004).
42. Wyatt, Katz, and Kim (2000).
43. Krueger (2002).
44. On social capital, see Putnam (2000).
45. Shah, Kwak, and Holbert (2001).
46. McDevitt, Kiousis, and Wahl-Jorgensen (2003).
47. Ibid., p. 466.
48. Weiksner (2005, pp. 220–25).
49. Ibid., pp. 220–21, 225.
50. For research on organized online deliberation, see Muhlberger and Weber (2006) and Price and David (2005).
51. Schudson (1997).
52. For overlapping reviews of public discussion programs, see Button and Mattson (1999), Button and Ryfe (2005), and Ryfe (2002).
53. McAfee, McKenzie, and Mathews (1990, pp. 10–15).
54. Ibid., pp. 17–22.
55. Melville, Willingham, and Dedrick (2005). See also Gastil and Dillard (1999a), Gastil (2004), and Gastil, Black, and Moscovitz (forthcoming). A study of the deliberative poll used methods similar to the Gastil and Dillard study and did not find evidence of increased sophistication (Sturgis, Roberts, and Allum, 2005). For more on deliberation and thinking in terms of the public good.
56. National Issues Forums (1990, 1992).

57. Gastil and Dillard (1999b). Schkade, Sunstein, and Hastie (2006) also found evidence of polarization, which Sunstein (2002) views as a common result of deliberation. My own research suggests that polarization occurs only in a limited range of circumstances (Gastil, Black, and Moscovitz, forthcoming); for a critique of Sunstein's view, see Kahan, Slovic, Braman, and Gastil (2006).
58. Daugherty and Williams (2007).
59. Pearce and Littlejohn (1997, p. 123).
60. This and other material come from the project's Internet archive at http://www .publicconversations.org. Those interested in reading more about the project's work should refer to Chasin et al. (1996). On how the project's work fits into the larger dialogic approach to conflict, see Gergen, McNamee, and Barrett (2001), Pearce and Littlejohn (1997), and Tonn (2005).
61. On this particular aspect of the project's work, see http://www.publicconversations.org/pcp/resources/resource_detail.asp?ref_id=97.
62. Gergen et al. (2001, p. 687).
63. Excerpt from project online dialogue available at http://www.publicconversations.org/pcp/index.asp?page_id=194&catid=66#Q2response.
64. Ryfe (2006, p. 88).
65. Black (2006) also identified Introductory stories, which are similar to some of the stories Ryfe (2006) identified as serving to get participants engaged in the task of deliberation. Note that Black refined her story typology in the second of two qualitative case studies.
66. Black (2006, p. 252).
67. Ibid. McBride (2005) points out a logical implication of deliberation's tendency to promote a shared civic identity—its threat to more group-specific identities. Thus, deliberation may threaten politically salient identities, which entitle minority groups to special recognition as underrepresented constituencies or voices.
68. Black (2006, p. 130).

THE "NASTY EFFECT:" ONLINE INCIVILITY AND RISK PERCEPTIONS OF EMERGING TECHNOLOGIES

Ashley A. Anderson
Center for Climate Change Communication, George Mason University
University of Wisconsin-Madison Nanoscale Science and Engineering Center in Templated
Synthesis and Assembly at the Nanoscale

Dominique Brossard
Department of Life Sciences Communication, University of Wisconsin-Madison
Center for Nanotechnology in Society at Arizona State University
University of Wisconsin-Madison Nanoscale Science and Engineering Center in Templated
Synthesis and Assembly at the Nanoscale

Dietram A. Scheufele
Department of Life Sciences Communication, University of Wisconsin-Madison
Center for Nanotechnology in Society at Arizona State University
University of Wisconsin-Madison Nanoscale Science and Engineering Center in Templated
Synthesis and Assembly at the Nanoscale

Paper forthcoming in *Journal of Computer-Mediated Communication*

All correspondence regarding this manuscript should be addressed to the first author in the Center for Climate Change Communication, George Mason University, Mail Stop 6A8, 4400 University Drive, Fairfax, VA, 22030 ph: 703-993-8368; e-mail: aander24@gmu.edu.

This material is based upon work supported by a grant from the National Science Foundation to the UW-Madison Nanoscale Science and Engineering Center in Templated Synthesis and Assembly at the Nanoscale (Grant No. SES-DMR-0832760). Any opinions, findings, and conclusions or recommendations expressed in this material are those of the authors and do not necessarily reflect the views of the National Science Foundation.

Michael A. Xenos
University of Wisconsin-Madison Nanoscale Science and Engineering Center in Templated
Synthesis and Assembly at the Nanoscale
Department of Communication Arts, University of Wisconsin-Madison

Peter Ladwig
Department of Life Sciences Communication, University of Wisconsin-Madison
University of Wisconsin-Madison Nanoscale Science and Engineering Center in Templated
Synthesis and Assembly at the Nanoscale

Uncivil discourse is a growing concern in American rhetoric, and this trend has expanded beyond traditional media to online sources, such as audience comments. Using an experiment given to a sample representative of the U.S. population, we examine the effects online incivility on perceptions toward a particular issue—namely, an emerging technology, nanotechnology. We found that exposure to uncivil blog comments can polarize risk perceptions of nanotechnology along the lines of religiosity and issue support.

Key words: blogs, online comments, incivility, nanotechnology, risk perceptions

doi:10.1111/jcc4.12009

INTRODUCTION

Because of its ability to disseminate information and reach large audiences, the Internet and communication technologies that utilize it may provide an excellent forum for interpersonal discussion surrounding issues that may not be widely covered in traditional media. The Internet has the potential to foster discussion and deliberation among far-reaching audiences in spaces such as the comments section of news items and blog posts. However, such discussions are not always rational. Discussions on the Internet can take an uncivil route, with offensive comments or replies impeding the democratic ideal of healthy, heated discussion (Papacharissi, 2004; Shils, 1992).

The question remains as to whether online incivility affects the opinions of "lurkers," or people who read online discussions without participating in them. Smith and his colleagues (2009) argue that lurkers are in fact participating in deliberation when reading others' comments because a large part of rational discussion consists of reflecting on others' opinions, which may or may not coincide with lurkers' own opinions. In other words, audiences reading uncivil language in blog comments may find the messages hostile and make judgments about the issue based on their own preexisting values rather than on the information at hand. This may develop polarized perceptions on issues among different audience segments that hold different values.

The purpose of this study is to examine how uncivil online interpersonal discussion may contribute to polarization of perceptions about an issue. We examine these dynamics in the context of nanotechnology, which is an interesting case because it is a largely unfamiliar topic that offers a rare chance to examine attitude formation and development. The majority of the public does not have a clear understanding of nanotechnology, and tend to use mental shortcuts—or heuristics, such as value predispositions or knowledge about science—when forming attitudes about it (Brossard, Scheufele, Kim, & Lewenstein, 2009; Lee & Scheufele, 2006; Scheufele & Lewenstein, 2005). Nonetheless, more than 1,300 consumer products containing nanotechnology are currently on the market (Project on Emerging Nanotechnologies, 2011). Thus, nanotechnology is representative of advanced technologies that individuals increasingly have to manage and form judgments about in their daily lives. Yet, given that it is an issue of low familiarity, it is likely people invoke cognitive shortcuts when they encounter it in the context of incivility. Thus, the mental shortcut may mitigate the effects of incivility. For instance, high familiarity with an issue may attenuate any effects exposure to incivility might have on forming negative perceptions about an issue. Furthermore, a value-based predisposition, such as religiosity, can provide a vehicle for forming an opinion about a low-familiarity topic (Brossard et al., 2009). Thus, people who draw upon such a predisposition may rely on it more rather than the new information they encounter, and this may temper the effects of incivility.

In this study, we utilize an online experiment given to a sample representative of the U.S. population to examine whether people are influenced by online incivility in blog comments when forming risk perceptions of a presumably unfamiliar topic—nanotechnology. We also examine whether online incivility has polarizing effects on risk perceptions when individuals rely on various predispositions when forming these perceptions, including issue familiarity, issue support, and religiosity.

THE FORMATION OF RISK PERCEPTIONS

Most current definitions of risk share the underlying notion that natural or human activities have the potential to bring about an adverse state of reality (NRC, 1983). Although the concept of "risk" has been explicated differently by a number of academic disciplines, the sociological, cultural, and psychological perspectives of risk are all important in the context of this study because they have all integrated communication into their approaches. Taken together, these perspectives suggest that social, political, and environmental factors, in addition to individual factors such as cognition levels, can contribute to variation in risk perceptions (Kasperson et al., 1988). Thus, while communication messages from media certainly play a role in how people perceive risk, various predispositions also play a role (e.g., Kahan, Braman, Slovic, Gastil, & Cohen, 2009; Renn, Burns, Kasperson, Kasperson, & Slovic, 1992). In this study, we examine how audience predispositions interact with exposure to a particular type of communication, uncivil audience comments in a newspaper blog post, in the formation of risk perceptions about an emerging technology.

The Effects of Incivility

The definition of incivility has been debated by various scholars (see, Papacharissi, 2004), but for the purposes of this study it will be defined as a manner of offensive discussion that impedes the democratic ideal of deliberation (Papacharissi, 2004; Shils, 1992). In this sense, incivility online can range from unrelated, rude critiques and name-calling (Jamieson, 1997) to outrageous claims and incensed discussion, which is also known as flaming (Papacharissi, 2004). However, concerns over incivility extend beyond online communication.

Over the past 50 years, incivility has been on the rise in the American political arena as well as in its coverage in mass media (Mutz & Reeves, 2005). Not only has Congressional debate become increasingly uncivil (Uslaner, 1993), such incivility is made strikingly apparent to the American public via television and the Internet. When considering current popularity of political pundits and cable news-entertainment programming, it not surprising that past studies have found that debate coverage on television highlighting political conflict is on the rise (Funk, 2001; McGraw, Willey, & Anderson, 1999; Robinson & Appel, 1979). Even print media have followed television's example of showcasing political incivility in order to remain competitive (Sigelman & Bullock, 1991). Incivility and conflict in media is not limited to the U.S. Congress, however. Many science issues have been politicized and framed as controversies by mainstream media (Nisbet & Mooney, 2007; Nisbet & Scheufele, 2007). Incivility and a focus on political conflict may be promoting political polarization in the United States, since it has become a mainstay in mass media coverage (Prior, 2007; Wilson, 2006).

This oversaturation of incivility in media has several profound effects on the public. Television coverage of uncivil Congressional debate is significantly related to dissatisfaction with the Senate (Elving, 1994); journalist commentaries and narratives that emphasize political incivility are also associated with negative attitudes towards politicians (Cappella & Jamieson, 1997; Patterson, 1993). Mutz and Reeves (2005) found that although political incivility on television promotes interest, it lowers political trust. It has been suggested that these negative attitudes associated with incivility exist because media portrayals of uncivil conversation violate social norms that expect a certain level of polite behavior, and television exacerbates these negative feelings because depictions of real people and close-up shots mimic the intimacy of face-to-face interactions (Mutz, 2007). These studies highlight effects of incivility by political actors, but lay individuals can also instigate incivility in discussions on news websites and blogs.

Social reprimands such as nonverbal communication and isolation can curb incivility in face-to-face discussion, but the Internet may foster uncivil discussion because of its lack of offline, in person consequences (Dutton, 1996; Hill & Hughes, 1998; Papacharissi, 2002). While incivility on the Internet may produce robust and diverse viewpoints, the heated, volatile expression can also fall short of the democratic ideal of rational and reasoned deliberation.

Although online incivility has the potential to increase cognitive recall of oppositional opinions, empirical evidence has shown that individuals respond negatively to online incivility directed at them or their views (Phillips & Smith, 2004). Other research suggests that incivility is linked to negative affective responses, such as hatred or humiliation, in those who utilize online deliberation (King, 2001). Furthermore, research demonstrates individuals' judgments of a blogger's comments are influenced by the author's tone (Hwang, Borah, Namkoong, & Veenstra, 2008; Price, Nir, & Cappella, 2006), and uncivil expression decreases perceptions of source and message credibility (Ng & Detenber, 2005). Finally—and most provocatively—when incivility targets an individual's ideological beliefs, it may influence the formation of negative attitudes about the issue at hand (Hwang, et al., 2008).

These findings all suggest that incivility on the Internet can have negative influences on individuals. If reading online incivility can incite negative feelings of hatred, negative attitudes towards a topic, and a reduction of source credibility, it is likely that it may also incite negative risk perceptions on a topic of emerging technology. Therefore, we pose the following hypothesis:

> HI: Exposure to incivility in online comments of a newspaper blog post on the issue of nanotechnology will be positively related to risk perceptions of nanotechnology.

However, people draw upon various predispositions when they process media messages, and it is likely these are an important part of how uncivil audience comments influence risk perceptions.

The Effects of Predispositions

People rely on shortcuts in information processing to make social judgments about complex policy issues (Popkin, 1991). In the context of an unfamiliar emerging technology, such as the issue of interest in this study, people will rely on cognitive shortcuts, otherwise known as heuristics, in order to form judgments (Scheufele & Lewenstein, 2005). Mental shortcuts may be employed when encountering uncivil online discussion because hostile language may cause individuals to be less receptive to new information. In this study, we examine whether issue familiarity, issue support, and religiosity, three common heuristics that influence perceptions about nanotechnology, make a difference in how individuals form judgments in the context of uncivil audience comments. In other words, will incivility further accentuate differences among individuals that rely on different mental shortcuts when making judgments about debate in an online setting?

Issue familiarity

For the issue of nanotechnology, a positive association exists between self-assessed knowledge and lower perceptions of risk, but exposing low-informed individuals to information about the technology does not automatically elicit support (Kahan, et al., 2007; Peter D. Hart Associates, 2007). Past scholarship has used measurements of self-perceived familiarity with nanotechnology interchangeably with factual knowledge about nanotechnology (see, Kahan et al., 2009; Satterfield, Kandlikar, Beaudrie, Conti, & Harthorn, 2009), but recent research suggests these two operationalizations of knowledge do not measure the same construct (Ladwig, Dalrymple, Scheufele, Brossard, & Corley, 2012). Issue familiarity was used in this study because it acts a heuristic that may mirror levels of confidence with the issue. High factual knowledge, on the other hand, does not necessarily reflect confidence with the issue. Furthermore, individuals who report knowing a lot about nanotechnology may already hold positive views because of other heuristic factors such as an interest in technology and deference to scientists. Therefore, we assume that a perceived familiarity with nanotechnology will mitigate any negative effects of exposure to incivility. We pose the following hypothesis:

> H2: Compared to those with high levels of perceived familiarity of nanotechnology who are exposed to civil comments, those with high levels of perceived familiarity who are exposed to uncivil comments will have lower risk perceptions.

Issue support

Several studies have shown a negative relationship between support for nanotechnology and risk perceptions (Cacciatore, Scheufele, & Corley, 2011; Scheufele & Lewenstein, 2005). In the context of exposure to hostile communication in uncivil comments, preexisting support for the issue likely attenuates any negative effects of incivility. Therefore, we pose the following hypothesis:

> H3: Compared to those who are highly supportive of nanotechnology and exposed to civil comments, those who are highly supportive of nanotechnology and exposed to uncivil comments will have lower risk perceptions.

Religiosity

Past research indicates that religiosity influences beliefs about technologies (Brossard & Nisbet, 2007; Brossard, et al., 2009; Cacciatore et al., 2011; Nisbet & Nisbet, 2005). Highly religious individuals may have higher risk perceptions of nanotechnology if they perceive the science is "playing God" or is disturbing natural order (Sjöberg, 2004; Sjöberg & Winroth, 1986). Thus, uncivil language may encourage those who are highly religious to focus more on that relationship between religiosity and risk perceptions. We therefore pose the following hypothesis:

> H4: Compared to highly religious people exposed to civil comments, highly religious people exposed to uncivil comments will have higher risk perceptions.

METHODS

Study Context

Nanotechnology is an interdisciplinary field of science conducted at the nanoscale. To provide perspective of its scale, a nanometer is one billionth of a meter, and a single sheet of paper is about 100,000 nanometers thick (National Nanotechnology Initiative, 2011). Because of size-to-volume ratios, materials behave differently at the nanoscale, and nanotechnology exploits these properties in order to create new products. For example, nanotechnology can be applied to improve drug delivery systems or to create waterproof and antibacterial garments (National Nanotechnology Initiative, 2011). Materials behave in different ways at the nanoscale, which allows for new applications, but also introduces potential risks and benefits, many of which are yet unknown.

Participants

This study employed a nationally representative sample of the American population ($N = 2,338$) for an online survey with an embedded experiment conducted by Knowledge Networks with a completion rate of 54.2 percent.

Experimental Design

Participants were asked to complete a pretest survey that asked about media use habits, science knowledge and efficacy, and nanotechnology support, among other items. The experiment was a between-subjects design and consisted of a neutral blog post from a Canadian newspaper that detailed equivalent risk and benefit information about nanotechnology. Specifically, the nanotechnology blog post discussed nanosilver particles and compared risks (e.g. water contamination) with benefits (e.g. antibacterial properties). Participants were given one of eight manipulations that varied by "user" comments under the post. We chose to utilize blog comments as a space for deliberation because this is a standard and stable platform utilized on most blog and news websites. Thus, the concept of commenting in online sites is a familiar one to most people who are Internet users, while other discussion platforms, such as discussion forums or social media sites, are not as widely used or have only gained traction in recent years.

The manipulations of interest in this study were that of civil vs. uncivil comments. For example, an uncivil comment began with "If you don't see the benefits of using nanotechnology in these products, you're an idiot." Alternatively, civil comments made the same argument as their uncivil counterparts, but used polite language and acknowledgement of other users by names and not expletives. After reading the stimulus, respondents were asked to complete a posttest survey that asked about the blog and comments, risk and benefit perceptions, and demographic information, among other items. This study focuses on respondents who received the nanotechnology issue, which gave a final sample size of $n = 1,183$[1].

Condition variables

Civility was a dichotomous variable based on the manipulation that each participant received, where 0 = uncivil condition and 1 = civil condition. *Read comments* ascertained the level of attention paid to the blog post's comments by asking participants their rate of agreement on a 10-point scale with the statement, "I read all of the comments," where 1 = "Do not agree at all" and 10 = "Agree very much" ($M = 7.73$; $SD = 3.08$).

Measurement

Dependent variable

To assess polarization of an attitude due to online incivility, we employed *risk perception* as the dependent variable in this study. The item asked respondents, "On the issue of nanotechnology, do you think the benefits outweigh the risks, the risks outweigh the benefits, or the risks and benefits are about the same?" This was measured on a 5-point scale where 1 = "Benefits far outweigh the risks" and 5 = "Risks far outweigh the benefits" ($M = 3.22$; $SD = 1.12$).

Independent variables

All independent variables, with the exception of demographic and condition variables, were measured prior to the experimental manipulation.

Demographic variables

Age was measured on a 7-point scale, where 1 = "18–24" and 7 = "75+" (*Median* = 4; $SD = 1.67$). *Gender* was a dichotomous variable with 0 = male and 1 = female (49.9 percent female). Socioeconomic status (*SES*) was created by compiling an index of two variables: level of education and family income (scale ranged from 3 to 16.5; $M = 10.79$; $SD = 2.72$).

Value predispositions

Religiosity was measured by asking respondents, "How much guidance does religion provide in your everyday life?" with 1 = "No guidance at all" and 10 = "A great deal of guidance" ($M = 5.97$; $SD = 3.23$). *Ideology* was measured by asking respondents to rate how socially liberal or conservative they are on a 6-point scale, with 1 = "Very liberal" and 6 = "Very conservative" ($M = 3.61$; $SD = 1.36$).

Media use

Newspaper use was assessed by asking respondents, "How much attention do you pay to news stories about the following topics when you read the newspaper, either in print or online?" Responses were measured on a 5-point scale, where 1 = "None" and 5 = "A lot." An index was created of three items: (1) "Stories related to science or technology," (2) "Stories about scientific studies in new areas of research, such as nanotechnology," and (3) "Stories about social or ethical implications of emerging technologies" ($M = 2.60$; $SD = .99$; *Cronbach's alpha* = .91). *Television use* was assessed by asking respondents the question, "How much attention do you pay to news stories about the following topics when you watch television news, either on a traditional television or in online sources (such as Hulu or websites of television networks, such as ABC, CBS, NBC, or Fox)?" Again, an index was created from three items worded identically to the items that made up the newspaper variable ($M = 2.68$; $SD = .99$; *Cronbach's alpha* = .92). *Internet use* was assessed by asking respondents the question, "How much attention do you pay to news about the following topics when you go online for news and information? Please exclude online versions of print newspapers or television shows and answer this question based on your usage of blogs, websites, and online-only newspapers." An index was created using the same topics that were examined in the newspaper and television items ($M = 2.17$; $SD = 1.06$; *Cronbach's alpha* = .95).

Nanotechnology familiarity, efficacy, and attitude

Familiarity was assessed by asking participants the question, "How much have you heard, read, or seen about nanotechnology?" This was measured on a 10-point scale with 1 = "Nothing at all" and 10 = "Very much" ($M = 2.81$; $SD = 2.19$). Familiarity is often used instead of factual knowledge questions because it allows respondents to judge their levels of knowledge according to their own terms rather than through what experts believe are the facts people must know in order to be scientifically literate (see Brossard & Shanahan, 2006). *Support* was assessed by indexing two 10-point items (1) "Overall, I support the use of nanotechnology," and (2) "Overall, I support federal funding of nanotechnology," where 1 = "Do not agree at all" and 10 = "Agree very much" ($M = 5.26$; $SD = 2.39$; *Pearson's R* = .78). *Efficacy* was created by indexing two 10-point items: (1) "Nanotechnology seems so complicated that a person like me can't really understand it," and (2) "I would need more information about nanotechnology before I could make any decisions about it." These items were recoded so that 1 = low efficacy and 10 = high efficacy ($M = 5.87$; $SD = 2.42$; *Pearson's R* = .68).

Finally, three interaction terms were created by separately multiplying the standardized value of *civility* by the standardized values of *support, familiarity,* and *religiosity.*

Analysis

This study employed an ordinary least squares hierarchical linear regression model with *risk perception* as the dependent variable. The independent variables were entered into the model in six different blocks based on their assumed causality. Block 1 contained variables related to the experimental manipulation, exposure to civility or incivility and read blog comments. Read blog comments was used as a control variable. Blocks 2 and 3 contained demographics and value predispositions, respectively, and both represent stable characteristics. Blocks 4 and 5 contained specific characteristics related to individuals' experiences with science, with general science-related variables coming first and nanotechnology-specific variables coming second. Block 4 contained science media use, and Block 5 contained specific nanotechnology familiarity, support, and efficacy. Finally, Block 6 tested interactions between civility and predispositions.

RESULTS

Overall, the regression model explained 17.0 percent of the variation of *risk perception* (see Table 9.1).

The condition and demographic blocks contributed to 2.0 and 4.5 percent of the explained variance, respectively. Our findings did not demonstrate a significant direct relationship between exposure to incivility and risk perceptions. Thus, our first hypothesis was not supported. *Age* was positively related to nanotechnology risk perception, and this demographic remained significant after adding the nanotechnology *familiarity*, *support*, and *efficacy* variables to the model ($\beta = .07$; $p < .05$). Women showed stronger perceptions of risk related to nanotechnology, although this relationship became nonsignificant after adding the *familiarity*, *support*, and *efficacy* variables. Neither *religiosity* nor *ideology* had a direct significant relationship with nanotechnology risk perception, and this block only contributed 0.2 percent to the regression's explained variation.

Newspaper use was positively related to risk perception ($\beta = .12$; $p < .01$), but *television use* showed no relationship. *Internet use* was significantly and negatively related to risk perception of nanotechnology ($\beta = -.15$; $p < .001$). The media use block had an incremental R^2 of 3.5 percent.

Nanotechnology *familiarity* ($\beta = -.12$; $p < .01$) and nanotechnology *support* ($\beta = -.23$; $p < .001$) were both significantly and negatively related to risk perception of nanotechnology. Nanotechnology *efficacy* was positively related to risk perception ($\beta = .10$; $p < .01$), and this block contributed 7.1 percent to the explained variation of this model.

The interaction block (incremental $R^2 = 1.0$ percent) showed that online incivility does indeed have a polarizing effect on attitudes when considering certain predispositions of support and religiosity. However, the interaction between familiarity with nanotechnology and incivility was not significant. Thus, our second hypothesis was not supported. We did find a significant interaction between support for nanotechnology and incivility on risk perceptions ($\beta = .09$; $p < .01$). When exposed to uncivil comments, those who have higher levels of support for nanotechnology were more likely to report lower levels of risk perception and those with low levels of support were more likely to report higher levels of risk perception (see Figure 9.1). This supports our third hypothesis. Our findings also reveal a significant interaction between religiosity and incivility on risk perception ($\beta = -.07$; $p < .05$). Among those exposed to uncivil comments, those

TABLE 9.1

Predictors of Nanotechnology Risk Perception (benefits < risk)

	Model 1 β	Model 2 β	Model 3 β	Model 4 β	Model 5 β	Model 6 β
Condition (N = 1,183)						
Online Civility (Civility = 1)	−.03	−.03	−.03	−.04	−.04	−.04
Read Blog Comments	.10***	.09**	.09**	.10**	.13***	.14***
Incremental R² (%)	2.0					
Demographics						
Age		.16***	.15***	.13***	.07*	.07*
Sex (Female = 1)		.10***	.10***	.08**	.04	.03
SES		−.05	−.05	−.02	.00	.01
Incremental R² (%)		4.5				
Value Predispositions						
Religiosity			.00	.01	.00	.01
Ideology (Lib < Cons)			.05	.05	.01	.02
Incremental R² (%)			0.2			
Media Use						
Newspaper				.10*	.13***	.12**
Television				−.04	.05	.06
Internet				−.21***	−.16***	.15***
Incremental R² (%)				3.5		
Nanotechnology						
Nano Familiarity					−.13**	−.12**
Nano Support					−.22***	.23***
Nano Efficacy					.09**	.10***
Incremental R² (%)					7.1	
Interactions						
Support*Civility						.09**
Familiarity*Civility						.03
Religiosity*Civility						−.07*
Incremental R² (%)						1.0
Total R² (%)						17.0

Cell entries are final standardized regression coefficients for Blocks 1 through 5 and before-entry standardized regression coefficients for Block 6. *p < .05, **p < .01, ***p < .001.

with high levels of religiosity were more likely to report higher levels of risk perception and those with low levels of religiosity were more likely to report lower levels of risk perception (see Figure 9.2). This finding supports our fourth hypothesis.

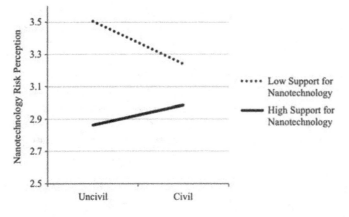

FIGURE 9.1

Interaction Effect of Online Civility Condition and Support for Nanotechnology on Risk Perception of Nanotechnology

Note: Nanotechnology Risk Perception is measured from 1–5 (benefit < risk).

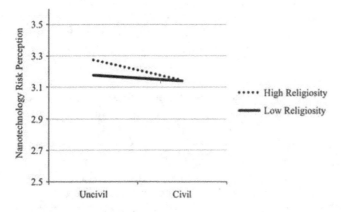

FIGURE 9.2

Interaction Effect of Online Civility Condition and Religiosity on Risk Perception of Nanotechnology

Note: Nanotechnology Risk Perception is measured from 1–5 (benefit < risk).

DISCUSSION

The purpose of this study was to explore online incivility's role in polarizing attitudes when reading deliberation in a blog setting. We employed a topic with low familiarity among the general public, nanotechnology, and assessed formation of the perception of its risk in order to shed light on online incivility's impact. The data reveal several important predictors of risk perception of nanotechnology as well as two significant interactions between civil or uncivil blog comments and value predispositions that individuals employ when processing information and making judgments about new technologies. Most importantly, this study found that uncivil blog comments contribute to polarization of risk perception of an issue depending on an individual's level of religiosity and support of that entity. Specifically, among individuals who do not support nanotechnology, those who are exposed to uncivil deliberation in blog comments are more likely to perceive the technology as risky than those who are exposed to civil comments. Similarly, highly religious individuals are more likely to perceive nanotechnology as risky when exposed to uncivil comments compared to less religious individuals exposed to uncivil comments.

These findings support past research that suggests people use certain heuristics as interpretational lenses of media. Because one's expectations about a message's validity are already established when employing value predispositions as heuristics (Eagly & Chaiken, 1993), these shortcuts influence the evaluation of arguments surrounding unfamiliar issues such as nanotechnology. Individuals may be focusing on congruent messages about the topic at hand and discrediting incongruent messages, thereby strengthening their preexisting beliefs about the technology. And it appears that online incivility may drive this polarization.

It is possible that when people encounter incensed comments in online discussions, they would employ their knowledge of the issue to process the information from the blog. According to this perspective, people with low knowledge would not have a cognitive store from which to draw in order to counteract the effects of incivility and therefore be more affected by it. Nevertheless, our study did not demonstrate enough evidence that people with low levels of knowledge respond differently than people with high levels of knowledge to uncivil comments.

The most striking—and perhaps most unsettling—aspect of our study is that the actual blog post about the topic of nanotechnology was neutral, with equal amounts of risk and benefit information across conditions. The incivility instigated by lay (albeit fictional) online users induced an increase in polarization of risk perception about nanotechnology. This study's findings suggest perceptions towards science are shaped in the online blog setting not only by "top-down information," but by others' civil or uncivil viewpoints, as well. While the Internet opens new doors for public deliberation of emerging technologies, it also gives new voice to nonexpert, and sometimes rude, individuals.

It is important to note limitations of this study before discussing the findings further. Concerning measurements, this study employed self-assessment items instead of factual nanotechnology knowledge. This is not too concerning, considering that this study assumed that previous nanotechnology familiarity might act as a heuristic when judging new information (e.g., the toxicity of silver nanoparticles). Future research may focus on breaking down the nanotechnology familiarity variable, perhaps by looking at an individual's deference to scientists, general interest in nanotechnology, or trust in science media. Another limitation of this study relates to the total amount of explained variance by our model, which was 17.0% of the total variance of our dependent variable. While this may be quite low for a model with six blocks of predictors, we were mainly interested in the effects of the stimulus. However, the stimulus we used was fairly weak with the main manipulation appearing at the end, and the exposure only occurred once. Our results are robust considering these limitations.

While we did not formally test the effects of all manipulations in our experimental design, it is possible that the other elements tested in the experiment played a role in our results. The other two elements included agreement vs. disagreement and emotion vs. reason. For instance, an emotional claim (e.g., on having hope about the benefits of a new technology) could be interpreted differently by people with high vs. low levels of familiarity. It is possible that someone with low familiarity would be more influenced by an emotional claim, although it is likely the effects of incivility would override that. Similarly, it is possible that a claim of disagreement made in conjunction with an uncivil statement has a greater chance of influencing risk perceptions than does a statement of incivility couched among commenters who agree with each other. We also controlled for these manipulations in the first block of our model.

Keeping these limitations in mind, this study offers several insights on how the online environment may shape and polarize perceptions about topics, including new technologies such as nanotechnology. Contrary to past research concerning our case study, our analyses found that the value predispositions of religiosity and ideology had no direct relationship with perceived risks of nanotechnology. Considering the cultural and sociological perspectives of risk communication, risk perceptions of certain issues may change for social groups based on certain events or changing cultural patterns in society (Dietz, Frey, & Rosa, 2002; Krimsky & Golding, 1992). For example, most conservative Americans long denied the existence of global warming, but recently a growing number of conservative evangelical groups have been advocating for climate change regulation based on the belief that Christians are "stewards of the Earth" (Janofsky, 2005; Michaud, 2008). While this study cannot provide evidence of changing attitudes about nanotechnology among different subsets of society, increasing coverage about the issue in the online environment may influence and drive polarization of perceptions about the technology for these groups in the future.

CONCLUSION

Online communication and discussion of new topics such as emerging technologies has the potential to enrich public deliberation. Nevertheless, this study's findings show that online incivility may impede this democratic goal. Much in the same way that watching uncivil politicians argue on television causes polarization among individuals, impolite and incensed blog comments can polarize online users based on value predispositions utilized as heuristics when processing the blog's information. The effects of online, user-to-user incivility on perceptions towards emerging technologies may prove especially trouble-some for science experts and communicators that rely on public acceptance of their information. The effects of online incivility maybe even stronger for more well-known and contentious science issues such as the evolution vs. intelligent design debate or climate change. Future research may explore these issues to gain a better understanding of the formation of risk perceptions for controversial political or science topics in the context of user-generated online comments.

NOTES

1. The experiment originally consisted of blog posts about nanotechnology and nuclear energy and the comments varied by civil vs. uncivil language, agreement vs. disagreement of opinions, and reasoned vs. emotional appeals ($N = 2,338$). This study focuses solely on participants who received the nanotechnology blog post ($n = 1,183$) and looks only at the effects of incivility (the other manipulations are controlled for in our analysis). This subset of the sample is representative of the population from which the entire sample draws because individuals were randomized across experimental conditions.

REFERENCES

Brossard, D., & Nisbet, M. C. (2007). Deference to scientific authority among a low information public: Understanding US opinion on agricultural biotechnology. *International Journal of Public Opinion Research*, 19(1), 24–52.

Brossard, D., Scheufele, D. A., Kim, E., & Lewenstein, B. V. (2009). Religiosity as a perceptual filter: Examining processes of opinion formation about nanotechnology. *Public Understanding of Science*, 18(5), 546–558.

Brossard, D. & Shanahan, J. (2006) Do they know what they read? Building a scientific literacy measurement instrument based on science media coverage. *Science Communication*, 28(1), 47–63.

Cacciatore, M. A., Scheufele, D. A., & Corley, E. A. (2011). From enabling technology to applications: The evolution of risk perceptions about nanotechnology. *Public Understanding of Science*, 20(3), 385–404.

Cappella, J., & Jamieson, K. (1997). *Spiral of cynicism: The press and the public good.* New York: Oxford University Press, USA.

Dietz, T., Frey, R., & Rosa, E. (2002). Risk, technology and society. In R. Dunlap & W. Michelson (Eds.), *Handbook of environmental sociology* (pp. 562–629). Westport, CT: Greenwood Publishing Group, Inc.

Dutton, W. (1996). Network rules of order: Regulating speech in public electronic fora. *Media, Culture & Society*, 18(2), 269.

Eagly, A., & Chaiken, S. (1993). *The psychology of attitudes.* Forth Worth, TX: Harcourt Brace Jovanovich College Publishers.

Elving, R. (1994). *Brighter lights, wider windows: Presenting Congress in the 1990s.* Washington D.C: American Enterprise Institute and The Brookings Institution.

Funk, C. L. (2001). Process performance: Public reaction to legislative policy debate. In J. R. Hibbing & E. Theiss-Morse (Eds.), *What is it about government that Americans dislike?* (pp. 193–204). New York: Cambridge University Press.

Hill, K., & Hughes, J. (1998). *Cyberpolitics: Citizen activism in the age of the Internet*. New York: Rowman & Littlefield Publishers, Inc.

Hwang, H., Borah, P., Namkoong, K., & Veenstra, A. (2008, May). *Does civility matter in the blogosphere? Examining the interaction effects of incivility and disagreement on citizen attitudes*. Paper presented at the 58th Annual Conference of the International Communication Association, Montreal, QC, Canada.

Jamieson, K. (1997). Civility in the House of Representatives. APPC report 10. Retrieved March 28, 2011, from http://democrats.rules.house.gov/archives/hear01.html.

Janofsky, M. (2005). When cleaner air is a biblical obligation. *New York Times*. Retrieved from http://www.nytimes.com/2005/11/07/politics/07air.html.

Kahan, D. M., Braman, D., Slovic, P., Gastil, J., & Cohen, G. (2009). Cultural cognition of the risks and benefits of nanotechnology. *Nature Nanotechnology*, 4(2), 87–90.

Kahan, D. M., Slovic, P., Braman, D., Gastil, J., & Cohen, G. (2007). *Nanotechnology risk perceptions: The influence of affect and values*. New Haven, CT: Yale Law School.

Kasperson, R. E., Renn, O., Slovic, P., Brown, H. S., Emel, J., Goble, R., et al. (1988). The social amplification of risk: A conceptual framework. *Risk Analysis*, 8(2), 177–187.

King, A. (2001). Affective dimensions of Internet culture. *Social Science Computer Review*, 19(4), 414.

Krimsky, S., & Golding, D. (1992). *Social theories of risk*. Westport, CT: Praeger.

Ladwig, P., Dalrymple, K. E., Brossard, D., Scheufele, D. A., & Corley, E. A. (2012). Perceived or factual knowledge? Comparing operationalizations of scientific understanding. *Science and Public Policy*. Advance online publication. doi: 10.1093/scipol/scs048.

Lee, C. J., & Scheufele, D. A. (2006). The influence of knowledge and deference toward scientific authority: A media effects model for public attitudes toward nanotechnology. *Journalism & Mass Communication Quarterly*, 83(4), 819–834.

McGraw, K., Willey, E., & Anderson, W. (1999, April). *It's the process stupid!? Procedural considerations in evaluations of congress*. Paper presented at the Annual Meeting of the Midwest Political Science Association, Chicago, IL.

Michaud, K. (2008). *The good steward: The impact of religion on climate change attitudes*. Paper presented at the APSA 2008 Annual Meeting.

Mutz, D. C. (2007). Effects of in-your-face television discourse on perceptions of a legitimate opposition. *American Political Science Review*, 101(4), 621–635.

Mutz, D. C., & Reeves, B. (2005). The new videomalaise: Effects of televised incivility on political trust. *American Political Science Review*, 99(1), 1–15.

National Nanotechnology Initiative. (2011). What is nanotechnology? Retrieved March 28, 2011, from http://www.nano.gov/html/facts/whatIsNano.html.

Ng, E., & Detenber, B. (2005). The impact of synchronicity and civility in online political discussions on perceptions and intentions to participate. *Journal of Computer-Mediated Communication* 10(3).

Nisbet, M. C., & Mooney, C. (2007). Science and society: Framing science. *Science*, 316(5821), 56.

Nisbet, M. C., & Nisbet, E. C. (2005). Evolution and intelligent design: Understanding public opinion. *Geotimes*, 50, 28–33.

Nisbet, M. C., & Scheufele, D. A. (2007). The future of public engagement. *Scientist*, 21(10), 38-44.

NRC. (1983). Risk assessment in the federal government: Managing the process: National Academy Press, Washington, DC.

Papacharissi, Z. (2002). The virtual sphere: The Internet as a public sphere. *New Media & Society*, 4(1), 9–27.

Papacharissi, Z. (2004). Democracy online: civility, politeness, and the democratic potential of online political discussion groups. *New Media & Society*, 6(2), 259–283.

Patterson, T. (1993). *Out of order*. New York: Alfred A. Knopf.

Peter D. Hart Associates. (2007). *Awareness of and attitudes toward nanotechnology and federal regulatory agencies*. Washington D.C.: Peter D. Hart Research Associates, Inc.

Phillips, T., & Smith, P. (2004). Emotional and behavioural responses to everyday incivility: Challenging the fear/avoidance paradigm. *Journal of Sociology*, 40(4), 378.

Popkin, S. L. (1991). *The reasoning voter: Communication and persuasion in presidential campaigns*. Chicago: University of Chicago Press.

Price, V., Nir, L., & Cappella, J. (2006). Normative and informational influences in online political discussions. *Communication Theory*, 16(1), 47.

Prior, M. (2007). *Post-broadcast democracy: How media choice increases inequality in political involvement and polarizes elections*. Cambridge, MA: Cambridge University Press.

Project on Emerging Nanotechnologies. (2011). An inventory of nanotechnology-based consumer products currently on the market. Retrieved March 28, 2011, from http://www.nanotechproject.org/inventories/consumer/.

Renn, O., Burns, W. J., Kasperson, J. X., Kasperson, R. E., & Slovic, P. (1992). The social amplification of risk: Theoretical foundations and empirical applications. *Journal of Social Issues*, 48(4), 137–160.

Robinson, M., & Appel, K. (1979). Network news coverage of Congress. *Political Science Quarterly*, 94(3), 407–418.

Satterfield, T., Kandlikar, M., Beaudrie, C. E. H., Conti, J., & Harthorn, B. H. (2009). Anticipating the perceived risk of nanotechnologies. *Nature Nanotechnology* 4(11), 752–758.

Scheufele, D. A., & Lewenstein, B. V. (2005). The public and nanotechnology: How citizens make sense of emerging technologies. *Journal of Nanoparticle Research*, 7(6), 659–667.

Shils, E. (1992). *Civility and civil society*. New York: Paragon House Publishers.

Sigelman, L., & Bullock, D. (1991). Candidates, issues, horse races, and hoopla: Presidential campaign coverage, 1888–1988. *American Politics Research*, 19(1), 5–32.

Sjöberg, L. (2004). Principles of risk perception applied to gene technology. *EMBO reports*, 5(Suppl 1), S47–S51.

Sjöberg, L., & Winroth, E. (1986). Risk, moral value of actions, and mood. *Scandinavian Journal of Psychology*, 27(1), 191–208.

Smith, G., John, P., Sturgis, P., & Nomura, H. (2009, September). *Deliberation and Internet engagement: Initial findings from a randomised controlled trial evaluating the impact of facilitated internet forums*. Paper presented at the European Consortium of Political Research General Conference, Potsdam.

Uslaner, E. (1993). *The decline of comity in Congress*. Ann Arbor: University of Michigan Press.

Wilson, J. (2006). How divided are we? *Commentary* 121(2), 15.

ABOUT THE AUTHORS

Ashley A. Anderson (e-mail: aander24@gmu.edu), Ph.D., is a Postdoctoral Research Fellow in the Center for Climate Change Communication at George Mason University. She conducts research on the intersection of communication technology, public opinion and deliberation, and issues of science and emerging technology.

Address: Mail Stop 6A8, Research 1, 4400 University Dr., Fairfax, VA 22030.

Dominique Brossard (e-mail: dbrossard@wisc.edu), Ph.D., is a Professor in the Department of Life Sciences Communication at the University of Wisconsin-Madison. Her current research focuses on the public opinion dynamics related to controversial scientific topics in the online environment.

Address: 324 Hiram Smith Hall, 1545 Observatory Drive, Madison, WI 53706.

Dietram A. Scheufele (e-mail: scheufele@gmail.com) is the John E. Ross Chair in Science Communication at the University of Wisconsin-Madison and Co-PI of the Center for Nanotechnology in Society at Arizona State University. His research deals with public opinion on emerging technologies and the political effects of emerging forms of communication.

Address: 1545 Observatory Drive, Madison, WI 53706.

Michael A. Xenos (e-mail: xenos@wisc.edu) is an Associate Professor in the Department of Communication Arts and Director of the Center for Communication Research at the University of Wisconsin-Madison. He has research interests in political communication, science communication, democratic deliberation, public opinion, and civic engagement.

Address: 6117 Vilas Hall, 821 University Ave., Madison, WI 53706.

Peter Ladwig (e-mail: peter.ladwig@gmail.com) is a former Master's student in the Department of Life Sciences Communication at the University of Wisconsin-Madison. His recent research has explored the role that blogs and comment postings play in shaping attitudes about emerging technologies.

I NDEX

A

Abimbola, Rotimi M., 29
Abortion, 45, 52, 140, 141, 143, 155–162
Activism, 50–51
Advertising, visual communication
    and, 90
Alignment
  backbone, 113
  with edges of page, 113
  visual unity and, 112, 113
Analogies, visual, 121
"Anchors, " 120
Anno Domini, 35
Aphthonius, 43
  chreia and, 60
Argument, 21
  from character (*See* Ethical proof)
  kairos and, 52–57, 59
  waiting to be used (*See* Extrinsic
    proof)
  intrinsic and extrinsic proofs,
    27–28
  written. *see* Written arguments
At-a-glance emphasis typefaces, 104
Atechnoi, 27
Audience
  visible, 86
  for visual text, 131

B

Backbone alignment, 113
Barthes, Roland, 120
BC/AD dating system, 35
Begala, Paul, 18
Black letter typeface, 105

Boldface, 116
Booth, Wayne *(The Rhetoric of Rhetoric)*, 37
Breast cancer awareness, 50–51, 53
Breitenstein, Dave, 148
Brightness, of color, 97
Brochure, testing and evaluating, 131
Bullet points, oral presentation slides
    and, 135

C

Canons, 39
Canons of rhetoric, 62
Carlson, Tucker, 18
Categories of type, 102
  type arrangement and, 113
Cause to effect, 28–29
Chabris, Christopher, 84
Change, *kairos* and, 48–59
Character
  arguments from (*See* Ethical proof)
  Chronos, 46, 49
Charts, 85
Cicero
  achieving status by asking questions
    and, 139, 143–144, 147, 149, 152
  rhetoric and, 17, 24
Clark-Fory, Tracy, 50–51, 53
Color
  analyzing rhetorical effects of, 97
  brightness, 97
  emotion and, 85
  hue, 96
  for oral presentation slides, 134
  pathos and, 96–99
  saturation, 97
  of typefaces, 117

Color (*Continued*)
  visual hierarchy and, 110
  visual unity and, 112
Comics, testing and evaluating,
    131–133
Commonplaces, 24, 34–36, 40, 51
Common topics, 51
Communication, 37
  oral (*See* Oral modes of
    communication)
  visual (*See* Visual modes of
    communication)
Community, 37
Comparative questions of quality,
    152–154, 160–162
Conjecture, 24
  stases of, 146–151
Constitutio, 139
Context of communication
  visible, 87
Contexts, 37–38
Contextual analysis, 62, 65, 71
Contrast
  building with typeface, 113–117
  visual hierarchy and, 109, 110
Copia, 39, 140–141
Crossfire (political show), 18–19
Cultural knowledge
  symbols and, 123

D

David, Laurie, 33
Debate shows, 18–19
Declamation, 36, 39
Decorum (appropriateness), 63
Definition
  stases of, 146–148, 151–152
Deliberative policy questions,
    154–155, 161
Demokratia, 22–23

Description, 40
Design plan
  for photo essay, 126–128
Design/Writing/Research (Lupton &
    Miller), 137
Desmet, Christy, 43
Difference, questions of, 153–154
Dispostio (arrangement), 62
Documentary photography. *See also*
    Photographs
  testing and evaluating, 132
Documentary photography book, 132
"Do Guns and College Mix?" (Kumeh),
    56–57
Doxa, 31
Dynamics, *kairos* and, 57–59

E

The Economist, 53–56, 57
Ehrenreich, Barbara, 53
Eide. See Special topics
Elocutio (style), 62
Emotion. *See also* Pathos
  type evocation of, 100
  visual argument and, 123
Enthymeme, 24, 28, 29
Essays
  photographic (*See* Photographic
    essays)
Ethos, 28, 65–66
  in photographs, 91
  professional, 92–95
  in visual communication, 90,
    91–95
Evaluation, of visual texts,
    131–133
Examples, 24, 27, 28
Extended reading typefaces, 103
Extrinsic proof, 24–30
  Aristotle on, 27–28

F

Fables, 40
Fact, 150
Factoids, 25
Farone, Mackenzie, 29
Feinstein, Dianne, 58
Feller, Ben.
Flag, U.S., 122
Flyers, 87
Forensic policy questions, 154–155,
    161–162

G

Generality, levels of, 144–146,
    156, 157
Gore, 33
Gorgias, 24, 36–37, 47
Graphs, 85
Greenwashing, 50
Gregory, Danny, 93
Grunge typeface, 105
Gun control, 53–59

H

Handwritten documents, 85
Hegemoon, 37
Hermagoras of Temnos, 28, 30
Hermogenes of Tarsus, 30, 43
  chreia and, 60
Heuriskein, 28
Heuristics, 51
  in invention, 51
  in stases, 140–141, 151,
    155–156
"How Green Is the College? Time the
    Showers" (Rimer), 31–33
Hue, 96
Hypothesis, 144

I

Illustrations
    combined with words, 119–121
    purposes of, 85
Institutes (Quintilian), 43
Interest, 150
    kairos and, 52–57
Interested reason, 21
Intrinsic proof, 24–30
    Aristotle on, 27–28
Invenire, 28
Inventio (invention), 62
Invention, 21, 24, 27–28
    definition of, Aristotle's, 21
    heuristic in, 51
    kairos and, 51–52
    in stases, 140–141
Inventor, 28
Isegoria, 23
Isocrates, 37, 48
Issues, 21, 28, 36
    definition of, 139
    kairos and, 52, 59
    as modern equivalent for stases, 139

J

Jordan, Barbara, "Statement on the
    Articles of Impeachment, " 74–76
Jordan, Chris, 124

K

Kairos
    ancient depiction of, 46–48
    arguments and, 52–57, 59
    change and, 48–59
    dynamics and, 57–59
    interests and, 52–57
    invention and, 51–52

Kairos (*Continued*)
   issues and, 52, 147
   moments in, 46–48, 49, 51, 56
   rhetorical situation and, 45–60
Kennedy, George, 60
Kumeh, Titania ("Do Guns and
      College Mix?"), 56–57

L

Lettershapes, describing, 100
Level of abstraction
   visual hierarchy and, 110
   visual unity and, 112
Levels of generality, 144–146, 156
Levels of specificity, 145
Liars, 30–31
Light typeface, 116
Logos, 64
   of type arrangement, 113–118
   using words and pictures together
      and, 119–121
   in visual communication, 90, 106
Lord, Rich, 29
Lupton, Ellen, 137
Lysippos, 46

M

Mailer, Norman, 25
Marrou, H. I., 17
Maxims, 24–28
McKibben, Bill, 33
Memoria, 62
Miller, J. Abbott, 137
Milton, John, 43
Modern typeface, 103
Mother Jones, 56–57

N

Network of interpretation, 26–27
New York Times, 126

Nicolaus, 43
   chreia, 60
Notion of space and/or time, 46
Novelty typeface, 104

O

Obama, Barack
   illegal immigration reform and,
      19–20
Olbrechts-Tyteca, Lucia, 18
Oldstyle typeface, 103
Opinion, 30–34
Opportunitas, 46, 52
Oral modes of communication
   designing slides to support,
      134–136
Orenstein, Peggy ("Think Before You
      Pink"), 53
Orthodoxy, 31

P

Panegyric. *See* Encomium
Paradeigma. See Examples
Paradox, 31
Partition, 152
Passionate appeals. *See* Pathetic proof
Pathos, 28, 64–65
   color and, 96–99
   in photos, 95
   of type, 100–106
   in visual communication, 90,
      95–106
Perelman, Chaim, 18
Photographic essays
   design plan for, 126–128
   sample student, 129–130
   statement of purpose for, 89
Photographs. *See also* Documentary
      photography; Visual modes of
      communication
   choices made in using, 83

combined with words, 119–121
ethos in, 91
for oral presentation slides, 135
pathos in, 95
purposes of, 85
Pictures, typeface, 104
Pinkwashing, 49–50, 52–53
Pinochet, Augusto, 126
Places. *See* Commonplaces
Pleasures, of visual communication,
83–84
Policy
stases of, 146–148, 154–155
Position
creating contrast using, 116
visual hierarchy and, 110
visual unity and, 112
Posters, 87
analyzing, 121, 123
testing and evaluating, 132
Pozner, Jennifer L., 118
Practical questions, 143–146,
156–157
Printed documents, 85
Probabilities, 28
Pro-choice arguments, 141
Professional ethos for visual texts,
92–95
Progymnasmata, 36, 40, 43
chreia, 60, 139
overview of, 43
Pro-life arguments, 141, 162
Pronuntiatio, 62
Prooemium. See Introduction
Proof, 28
extrinsic, 24–30
intrinsic, 24–30
Proponere, 28
Proposition, 28
Protest letter, 118
Purpose of communication
visible, 85
for visual text, 131

Q

Quality
stases of, 146–148, 152–154
"The question of fact, 150
Questions, to evaluate visual text,
131–133
Quintilian
achieving status by asking questions
and, 146, 147

R

Referees, 25–26
Refutation, 28, 155
"Relay, " 120
Repetition
visual hierarchy and, 110
visual unity and, 109, 111–113
Rhetoric, 62
ancient, 17–43
beginnings, 22–23
vs. contemporary rhetoric,
23–34
definition of, Aristotle's, 17
ideology and the commonplaces,
34–36
kairos-based, 46–48
language as action, 36–39
training and performance, 39–41
Rhetorica ad Alexandrum. See Rhetoric to
Alexander
Rhetorical analysis
building, 62
definition, 62
of essays (*See* Essays)
sample, student, 77–80
steps to writing, 71–73
writing, 71
Rhetorical effects of color, 97
Rhetorical engagement, 19–20, 39
Rhetorical reasoning, 24. *See also*
Logical proof

Rhetorical situation, 24, 67
  kairos and, 45–60
Rhetorical type arrangement, 118
Rhetoricians, 17, 23
The Rhetoric of Rhetoric (Booth), 37
Rhetors, 22, 23
Rimer, Sara ("How Green Is the
    College? Time the Showers"),
    31–33
Roe v. Wade, 141, 143, 157, 158, 161
Roman type, 116

S

St. Augustine, 43
Sans serif type, 101, 102, 103, 105
  contrasting with serif, 114
Saturation, color, 97
Scare quotes, 38
Scott, Robert, 46
Script typeface, 105
Self-test
  for visual texts, 131
Serif type, 101, 102, 103, 105
  contrast with sans serif, 114
  slab, 103
Shakespeare, William, 43
Shape
  of typeface, 100, 115
  visual hierarchy and, 110
  visual unity and, 112
Signs, 87
Silko, Leslie Marmon, "The Border
    Patrol State, " 64–69
Similarity, questions of, 153–154
Simons, Daniel, 84
Six-of-one typeface, 104
Size
  creating contrast using type, 115
  visual hierarchy and, 110
  visual unity and, 112
Slab serif typeface, 103

Slacktivism, 52
Slides, for oral presentation,
    134–136
Specificity, level of, 145, 157
"Spoof Ads, " 137
Stasis, 24, 51
  of conjecture, 146–151
  of definition, 146–148, 151–152
  example, 148–149
  expanding the questions, 149–152
  heuristic in, 140–141, 151, 155–156
  importance of achieving, 141–143
  invention in, 140–141
  issue as modern equivalent for, 144
  of policy, 146–148, 154–155
  of quality, 146–148, 152–154
  questions asked to achieve, 139–162
  theoretical *vs.* practical questions,
    143–146
  values in, 146, 147, 149, 152, 159–160
Stasis theory, 28
Statement of purpose
  for photo essay, 89, 126
"Statement on the Articles of
    Impeachment" (Jordan), 74–76
Stewart, Jon, 18–20, 39
Stochasmos, 150
Symbols
  typeface, 104
  visual, 122

T

Technical illustrations, 85
Testing
  photographs and drawings, 86
  visual texts, 131–133
Textual analysis, 62
"The Border Patrol State" (Silko), 64–69
Theon, Aelius, 40, 43, 144
Theoretical questions, 143–146, 156
Thesis, 43

"Think Before You Pink" (Orenstein), 53
Timeline, visual, 137
Titles
    for oral presentation slides, 134
Topics. *See* Common topic
Transitions
    slide, 136
Type arrangement
    logos of, 113–118
    rhetorical, 118
Typeface
    for at-a-glance emphasis, 104
    categories of, 102, 114
    emotion and, 85
    for extended reading, 103
    for oral presentation slides, 135
    pathos of, 100–106
    styles of, 101

U

Ultra typeface, 116

V

Value
    in stases, 146, 147, 149, 152,
        159–160
Video public service announcements,
    testing and evaluating, 133
Virginia Tech University shootings,
    53–59
Visual accumulation, 124
Visual analogies, 121
Visual arguments, analyzing, 121–126
Visual elements
    logos of arranging, 106–113
    number to include, 106, 107

Visual essays. *See* Photographic essays
Visual hierarchy, 106, 109
    contrast and repetition for, 110
Visual modes of communication,
        82–138
    analyzing visual arguments,
        121–126
    audiences for, 86
    contexts for, 87
    designing slides to support oral
        presentations, 134–136
    design plan for, 126–128
    ethos and, 90, 91–95
    logos and, 90, 106–121
    pathos and, 90, 95–106
    photo essay, 89, 126–130
    pleasures of, 83–84
    professional quality of, 92–95
    statement of purpose for, 89
    testing and evaluating, 92, 131–133
    visible purposes, 85
Visual symbols, 122
Visual timeline, 137
Visual unity, 107, 109
    creating through repetition,
        111–113

W

Webb, Ruth, 40
Weights of typeface, creating contrast
        using, 116
Whitewashing, 50
Wilson, Joe, 19–20, 30
Woods, Marjorie Curry, 43
Word-picture relations, 119–121
Written arguments, 61–81
Written discourse, 37